# NAVAL
# MISCELLANY

# NAVAL MISCELLANY

ANGUS KONSTAM

METRO BOOKS
NEW YORK

# METRO BOOKS
New York

An Imprint of Sterling Publishing
387 Park Avenue South
New York, NY 10016

This 2011 edition published by Metro Books, by arrangement with Osprey Publishing Ltd.

Osprey Publishing Ltd.
Midland House, West Way, Botley, Oxford OX2 0PH, United Kingdom.
44-02 23rd Street, Suite 219, Long Island City, NY 11101, USA.
Email: info@ospreypublishing.com

Page layout by Myriam Bell Design, France
Typeset in Adroit
Originated by PDQ Media, Bungay, UK
Front cover: istockphoto.com

ISBN: 978-1-4351-3265-8

For information about custom editions, special sales, and premium and corporate
purchases, please contact Sterling Special Sales at 800-805-5489 or
specialsales@sterlingpublishing.com.

Manufactured in China through Worldprint Ltd.

10 9 8 7 6 5 4 3 2 1

www.sterlingpublishing.com

**Editor's Note:** Throughout this title we have predominantly used nautical miles instead of
land miles, unless it especially concerns a land-based story. We have also used UK tons as
opposed to metric tonnes.

# CONTENTS

# INTRODUCTION

One of the best things about a miscellany is that readers can always find something new and interesting to stimulate them. The same attraction is there for the writer, who has the joy of being able to pick and choose all the juiciest historical extracts, and to present these as a single book. The idea behind a miscellany is that it presents the reader with a varied collection of articles, stories or facts, a diverse collection of pieces, all brought together under one cover. This means that a miscellany presents the reader and writer alike with the opportunity to explore new areas, and to look at some more familiar topics in a new light.

Of course, there are different kinds of miscellany. Some of them, most notably *Schott's Miscellany*, are a potpourri of trivia, presenting readers with information as diverse as the odds of rolling '7' on two dice, or the various levels of freemasonry. Some are specialist miscellanies, such as *Essential Militaria* or *A Military Miscellany*. They adopt a similar format, presenting the reader with short snippets of military facts – the armour worn by a Roman legionary, or the only serving US President to take part in a battle (apparently it was President James Madison at the battle of Stoney Creek in 1813, when he was almost captured by the British).

Our miscellany is a little different. For a start, it's the *Naval Miscellany*, which pretty much defines the ground it covers. Despite being a widely published historian, nobody has ever asked me to compile a miscellany before, so I looked upon it as a fresh challenge. Pretty early on I decided to avoid the easy route of simply compiling lists of naval facts, or subjective 'top tens'. I wanted to draw the reader – presumably a naval enthusiast – into an altogether more engaging arena. This meant adopting the style of a literary or detailed specialist miscellany, but to select subjects that I hoped would intrigue a nautical-minded audience. This allowed me to explore certain areas in a little more detail than the short list-like miscellanies, but also to offer a wide selection of historical information. That way even the most learned naval enthusiast would find something new and interesting.

It also struck me that this was a wonderful opportunity. I was able to select the little snippets of naval history that might interest the reader, working on the basis that they interested me, so therefore they should appeal to other naval enthusiasts. However, this has allowed me to recount facts, to describe events and to present information that I've found almost as fascinating to research as I have to recount. These entries include pieces as diverse as the Shinto and Buddhist-inspired warship names of the Japanese Navy, the careers of some of the less well-known admirals who shaped naval history, and even the way minesweepers carry out their dangerous job. I really hope that my enthusiasm for the subject is passed on. If any of them fall short of the mark then I'm the one to blame.

Angus Konstam
Edinburgh, 2009
*www.anguskonstam.com*

# RUM, SODOMY AND THE LASH

It has long been claimed that during a meeting of the War Cabinet, Sir Winston Churchill was pushed too far by an admiral who frequently talked about naval tradition. Churchill retorted with the memorable quip: 'Don't talk to me about naval tradition. The only traditions of the Royal Navy are rum, sodomy and the lash!' In fact, Churchill's Private Secretary Anthony Montague Browne said that although Churchill never uttered the words, when he was told of the quote, he said that he wished he had.

In 1985 the phrase 'Rum, Sodomy and the Lash' was used as the title of an album by the Irish folk-rock band The Pogues. According to the band's lead singer Shane McGowan, the idea for the album title came from fellow band member Andrew Ranken, who thought the alleged Churchill quote had a great ring to it. To add to the nautical theme, the cover of the album featured a retouched version of Théodore Gericault's painting *The Raft of the Medusa*.

In 1871 flogging was abolished in the peacetime Royal Navy, but it was still reserved as a punishment in time of war. It was abandoned entirely eight years later, by which time the most serious punishment which could be inflicted by a Royal Naval captain was '10A Punishment' – the stoppage of leave and a sailor's rum ration, his daily 'tot' of ⅛ pint (7cl). Officers stopped receiving a rum ration in 1881, and the daily issue of a rum tot finally ended in January 1970. Many sailors wore black armbands in protest, questions were raised in the House of Commons, and there was even fear of a possible mutiny. However, the Ministry of Defence were adamant. For them, operating complex missile systems was not helped by giving the operators large measures of rum every day. As for sodomy, there are some who might argue that it has never gone out of favour in naval service.

# AMERICA'S FIRST NAVAL HERO

John Paul Jones (1747–92) was a Scot who first went to sea when he was a young teenager. By 1770 he had become Captain Paul, but three years later he killed one of his crew during a brawl, and fled to America. To cover his tracks he adopted the new surname of 'Jones'. In 1775, when the American colonies rebelled, Jones offered his services to the fledgling US Navy, and he was duly appointed the second-in-command of the USS *Alfred*, a makeshift warship based in Philadelphia. Then, in June 1777, he was given his own command – the 18-gun brig USS *Ranger*.

Captain Jones sailed from Portsmouth, New Hampshire in November 1777, and arrived in France less than a month later, having captured two British merchant ships along the way. It was there, in Quiberon Bay, that the *Ranger* was saluted by the French fleet – the first official salute ever given to the new American flag. By April he was ready to begin his cruise, and so he headed north into the Irish Sea. He captured two prizes, then led a raid on the small coastal town of Whitehaven, in north-west England. He spiked the guns of a shore battery, burned the small vessels in the harbour, and sailed away, leaving mayhem in his wake.

His next raid was even more audacious. He landed on the Scottish coast near Kirkcudbright – his home county – and seized the house of leading landowner the Earl of Selkirk. The earl was away when Jones arrived, denying him a lucrative kidnap victim. Instead his sailors ransacked the house, and even stole the family silver. Jones returned to sea, and on 24 April the USS *Ranger* came upon the brig HMS *Drake* off Carrickfergus, in Northern

Ireland. Jones captured her after a brutal, hour-long fight, then sailed back, arriving in France in triumph, accompanied by his prize.

In early 1779, Jones was given the command of a new warship – a former French merchantman which he renamed the USS *Bonhomme Richard*. He set sail in August, accompanied by a small flotilla of French warships and privateers. This squadron captured three prizes in the Irish Sea before Jones steered north around Scotland, to enter the fresh hunting ground of the North Sea. On 23 September he was off Flamborough Head on the Yorkshire coast when lookouts spotted a British convoy returning from the Baltic, escorted by two warships. Jones gave chase, and steered his ship towards the 50-gun warship HMS *Serapis*.

Jones knew that the gunnery of the British ship would be superior to his own, so he decided to board the British ship. However, the boarding attempt failed, and so the two ships lay alongside each other, exchanging broadsides at point-blank range. At one point the American colours were shot away. Captain Pearson of the *Serapis* hailed the American, asking him, 'Has your ship struck?' Jones replied 'I have not yet begun to fight', and the bloodletting continued. Finally, a hand grenade detonated in *Serapis*' magazine, crippling the British ship. Captain Pearson had no choice but to surrender. By that time both ships were shattered, and the *Bonhomme Richard* foundered soon afterwards. Jones limped back to France in the captured *Serapis*. In the process he sailed into the history books as America's first naval hero.

When the war ended in 1783 Jones spent another five years in France on half pay, before taking employment in the Russian Navy. He served in Russia for two years, but eventually he returned to France, where he died in 1792. In 1905 his body was exhumed, and the 'father of the US Navy' was returned to America, to be buried in the chapel of the US Naval Academy in Annapolis.

# THE FIRST SUBMARINE

An ancient chronicler claimed that in 333 BC Alexander the Great climbed into a glass-bottomed barrel, and was lowered beneath the clear waters of the Mediterranean Sea, to see the undersea world for himself. However, it would be another two millennia before the idea of a powered submersible machine would become a reality. Leonardo da Vinci designed a submarine in 1515, although there is no evidence it was ever built. In 1620 the Dutch inventor Cornelius Drebbel built a small oar-powered submarine, coated in leather, which was tested in the River Thames. Its 12 oar ports were sealed by leather gaskets, and it submerged by adjusting its buoyancy through contracting the hull using hand-turned screws. Air was supplied by means of an air tube fixed to a float – a simple form of snorkel – and the machine could reputedly submerge to a depth of 12–15ft (3.6–4.6m).

Drebbel found a patron in the Duke of Buckingham, a favourite of King James I of England and VI of Scotland, and the head of the Admiralty. The duke commissioned a prototype, followed by two improved versions of this first submarine. The king even inspected one of the later versions of Drebbel's strange machine, and may even have dived in her. Despite the king's enthusiasm the longed-for commission never followed, and Drebbel was commissioned to design fireships instead.

In fact, Drebbel's submarine was actually the brainchild of William Bourne (c.1535–82), a scientist and gunnery expert, who first published sketches of the submarine in his book *Inventions and Devises* (1578). Although these were crude and unfinished, they were the first ever blueprints of a submarine to appear in print. However, Bourne died before he could put his ideas into practice, and it was left to Cornelius Drebbel to build the machine, and to see whether it worked. Incidentally, Bourne also published *Regiment for the Sea*, the first navigation manual written in English, as well as *The Art of Shooting in Great Ordnance* (1572) – the definitive Elizabethan treatise on gunnery, on land or sea.

For his part, Drebbel went on to invent a thermometer, a chicken incubator, a vivid red dye for cloth, and a microscope. Better still, Drebbel and his submarine appeared in a scene in *The Four Musketeers* (1974), where he demonstrated its merits to the Duke of Buckingham.


# 'HEARTS OF OAK'

This triumphant, rousing patriotic song was first composed by Dr William Boyce (1711–79), who held the post of Master of the King's Music from 1755 until his death. Actually, he only composed the march – the lyrics were added by the actor and playwright David Garrick (1717–79). The 'wonderful year' it mentions was 1759 – the Year of Victory – when the Royal Navy inflicted two decisive victories over the French, at the battle of Lagos in August and at the battle of Quiberon Bay in November. That same year General Wolfe captured Quebec, a victory which effectively secured the North American continent for Britain. It was first performed in 1760.

> Come, cheer up, my lads, 'tis to glory we steer,
> To add something more to this wonderful year;
> To honour we call you, as freemen not slaves,
> For who are so free as the sons of the waves?
>
> [Chorus]
> Heart of oak are our ships, jolly tars are our men,
> We always are ready; Steady, boys, steady!
> We'll fight and we'll conquer again and again.
>
> We never see the French but we wish them to stay,
> They always see us and they wish us away;

If they run, we will follow, we will drive them ashore,
And if they won't fight, we can do no more.

(Chorus)
They swear they'll invade us, these terrible foes,
They frighten our women, our children and beaus,
But should their flat bottoms in darkness get o'er,
Still Britons they'll find to receive them on shore.

(Chorus)
Britannia triumphant, her ships sweep the sea,
Her standard is Justice – her watchword, 'be free'.
Then cheer up, my lads, with one heart let us sing,
Our soldiers, our sailors, our statesmen, and king.
(Chorus, sung twice)

The song has changed very little over the past three centuries, and while references to French flat-bottomed invasion barges, beaus and even a powerful British Navy are all a little dated, the song still has a wonderful, stirring resonance. These days however, the fourth and final verse is usually sung with these slightly more nostalgic lyrics:

We'll still make them fear and we'll still make them flee,
And drub them ashore as we've drubbed them at sea,
Then cheer up, my lads, with our hearts let us sing,
Our soldiers, our sailors, our airmen, our Queen.

Today, 'Hearts of Oak' is the official quick march of the Royal Navy, as well as the Royal Canadian Navy, which – bizarrely enough – also sings it in French. It is, too, a firm favourite at military tattoos, and it is a cold-hearted landlubber indeed who can hear it being belted out by a Royal Marine band and not admit to a stirring of pride in Britain's naval heritage.

# PROFILE OF A WARSHIP:
# THE FIRST WARSHIPS

For evidence of the first warships in history, we need to look to Ancient Egypt. In fact, the Egyptians even gave us the first ever depiction of a ship – a small sailing craft built from bundles of papyrus reeds, portrayed onto a decorative vase, and painted over 5,000 years ago. This was purely a river craft, designed for use on the River Nile, but within five centuries far more complex vessels were being produced. The wooden 'Cheops' boat discovered in the Great Pyramid of Cheops dates from 2600 BC, but it was a state barge, not a warship. It would take another thousand years for dedicated warships to emerge, although enigmatic Minoan illustrations from 2800 BC may depict vessels fitted with a ram, which would make them the earliest pictures of warships in history.

Bas-reliefs in the burial chamber of Queen Hatshepsut at Deir-el-Bahari dating from 1500 BC depict the first proper seagoing vessels, with keels, frames and crossbeams, making them far more sturdy than the Cheops boat or other craft from the Nile River depicted in earlier carvings. Hawsers stretched from stem to stern provided extra strength to these vessels. The ships were propelled by both oars and sails, as they are shown both under sail and being rowed with their sails furled on the bas-reliefs, but, as no armed soldiers are visible, they are all clearly merchant ships, not warships. This was clearly a time of peace and prosperity, and contrasts with the maritime bas-reliefs of three centuries later, when the Sea Peoples invaded Egypt.

Around 1200 BC the enigmatic sea-borne nomads called the 'Sea Peoples' threatened to invade Egypt, and for the first time we see the representation of warships in bas-relief carvings. The invaders came from the northern Mediterranean, and probably included Cretans and Philistines, with their own tradition of boat construction. When the Pharaoh Ramses III defeated the Sea

Peoples, to celebrate the great victory he ordered the construction of a temple, and it was decorated with scenes depicting the naval battles which had saved the New Kingdom. His Egyptian fleet consisted of what appear to have been specially constructed ships, noticeably different from those seen in the Deir-el-Bahari reliefs and in other earlier depictions. Clearly they represent the first purpose-built warships in recorded history.

Outwardly these warships resembled earlier Egyptian craft, but they were much slimmer, and fitted with both rams and fighting positions. A single mast with a square sail carried a wicker fighting platform, allowing infantrymen to throw down rocks or javelins on the enemy decks. Unlike some earlier Egyptian ships, these vessels carried a single yard, without the additional lower yard seen on depictions of near-contemporary merchant vessels, emphasizing the fact that sail was less important to the performance of the ship. This was because between seven and eleven oars per side, arrayed in a single bank, were used to propel these craft, while the vessels used by the Sea Peoples were similar, but appear to have lacked oars. This would have placed the invaders at a grave disadvantage in the coastal waters of the Nile Delta where it seems these battles took place. Further, on the Egyptian craft a series of decorated panels or washboards protected the rowers from missile fire.

Evidence suggests that by the 13th or 12th century BC both Egypt and Babylon had powerful navies, charged with protecting shipping from pirate attacks, and protecting the coast in time of war. The main naval weapon used on these warships was the bow, supplied by ship-borne archers. This suggests that missile fire and ramming were favoured by the Egyptians over hand-to-hand clashes. In this respect they were simply taking advantage of their great resources: highly trained royal archers, equipped with large, heavy bows. This gave them another advantage over the raiding Sea Peoples, or any other invaders who threatened the Egyptian kingdom or its trade.

The single bank of oars on Egyptian warships of this period limited the effectiveness of these warships, as within reason more oars equated to a greater speed through the water, allowing a more effective use of the bronze ram fitted to the front of the vessels. In later centuries naval designers sought to increase propulsive power by adding further banks of oarsmen. In time, two or more tiers of oarsmen were carried, and warships came to be classified by the number of oar banks they carried. The Greek, Phoenician and Assyrian war galleys of the 10th to the 8th centuries BC were significantly more powerful than the craft available to Ramses III, mainly due to this second line of oars, which turned the warships into a vessel type known as a 'bireme', named after its two banks of oars. This, though, takes us into better known territory, as we move from the Bronze Age into better charted historical waters.

# THE LARGEST NAVAL BATTLES IN ANCIENT HISTORY

In the course of more than 2,500 years of naval warfare, several major fleet actions stand out, all of which – at the time – earned themselves the title of the greatest naval battle ever fought. Naval battles from ancient history are, however, notoriously difficult to quantify – ancient chroniclers frequently exaggerated the numbers involved in a battle, usually to make the victory they recorded all the more glorious. Of the four battles that follow, Salamis and Actium were the most decisive, while Ecnomus probably involved the greatest number of participants.

### The battle of Salamis (480 BC)

Approximately 350 Greek triremes commanded by Eurybiades of Sparta fought and defeated a Persian fleet of around 600 galleys. The battle was fought in the Strait of Salamis – within sight of the walls of Athens – and watched by the Persian King Xerxes. Their greater numbers hindered the Persians, who were unable to manoeuvre freely, allowing the better-trained Greeks to make the most of their tactical edge. By the end of the day the bulk of the larger Persian fleet was either sunk, captured or forced to flee.

### The battle of Arginusae (406 BC)

The greatest naval battle of the Peloponnesian War, fought between Athens and Sparta, took place amid a group of islands in the Aegean Sea. Some 150 Athenian triremes commanded by eight admirals fought and defeated a slightly smaller fleet of 120 Spartan warships, commanded by Callicratidas. The battle ended with the death of the Spartan admiral, and the sinking or capture of more than half of his fleet. Despite the scale of the Athenian victory the battle proved indecisive, and the following year the victorious Athenian fleet was destroyed at Aegospotami by a resurgent Spartan fleet, commanded by Admiral Lysander.

### The battle of Ecnomus (256 BC)

A fleet of 330 Roman quinquiremes (large war galleys) defeated a similarly sized fleet of Carthaginian galleys off the southern coast of Sicily. The Roman fleet was commanded by the consuls Marcus Attilius Regulus and Lucius Manlius Vulso Longus, whose joint achievement secured Rome's place as a naval power, and set the Roman Republic on the road to victory over Carthage in the First Punic War.

### The battle of Actium (31 BC)

Fought to decide the fate of the Roman Republic, this great battle took place off the port of Actium, on the Adriatic coast of Greece. It pitted the joint fleet of Mark Antony and his lover Cleopatra – around 500 galleys, most of which were Egyptian – against the slightly smaller fleet of Octavian, later to become the Roman Emperor Augustus. In fact, Octavian's fleet was actually handled by his trusted lieutenant Agrippa. When the battle appeared lost, Antony and Cleopatra abandoned their doomed fleet, and fled to Egypt.

# LANDLOCKED NAVIES

Some of the world's navies are destined never to put to sea – at least not in the way a blue-water navy can. Instead, they operate on lakes and rivers, patrolling these waters if they form part of a national border, or – if their country lacks decent roads – they allow the government to make its presence felt in places that more conventional armed forces might not be able to reach. Other states, most notably Switzerland, Hungary and the African states of Burundi and Malawi, also have small naval forces, but technically these aren't navies, as the vessels are operated by their national armies. Most of these navies are small, and usually consist of little more than a handful of patrol boats or armed launches. However, there is at least one surprising exception.

**Azerbaijan:** The Republic maintains a small squadron of patrol boats on the Caspian Sea, although the exact number and type of its fleet is unknown.

**Bolivia:** With 173 operational vessels, the Bolivians have the largest navy of any land-locked country, most of which are based in the one place. Their navy patrols the waters of Lake Titicaca, 12,500ft (over 3,800m) above sea level. The Bolivians also maintain a small naval station in the Argentinian riverside town of Rosario, from where – in theory – it could reach the open sea over 400 miles (611km) downstream. For the Bolivians, this is an important political statement, as it means they might one day try to reclaim access to the sea, which they lost in 1883.

**Central African Republic:** A small naval force is maintained on the Ubangi River, a tributary of the Congo. The river forms the Republic's border with the Democratic Republic of the Congo.

**Kazakhstan:** Like Azerbaijan, this former Soviet republic maintains a small navy, which operates in the Caspian Sea.

**Laos:** The Laos People's Navy patrols the Mekong River, which for much of its length forms the Laotian border with Thailand. These small patrol boats are mainly used to counter drug trafficking.

**Paraguay:** About a dozen armed launches patrol the Paraguay and Paraná rivers, but the land-locked country has no access to the sea, except downriver through Argentina to the Atlantic Ocean, some 1,500 miles (2,400km) away.

**Rwanda:** The Rwandan Navy patrols Lake Kivu, which forms the border with the Democratic Republic of Congo. It recently saw action during the Second Congo War.

**Serbia:** Following the breakup of Yugoslavia the Serbs inherited a small flotilla of river patrol craft, which now operate on the River Danube.

**Turkmenistan:** Like its neighbour Kazakhstan, the Republic of Turkmenistan operates a small flotilla of patrol boats on the Caspian Sea.

**Uganda:** The tiny Ugandan Navy patrols the waters of Lake Victoria.

# TEN WARSHIPS THAT SANK WITHOUT THE HELP OF THE ENEMY

**The *Mary Rose* (1545):** King Henry VIII of England's magnificent but ageing warship heeled over and sank as she sailed out of Portsmouth to do battle with the French. The ship had recently been overhauled, and extra heavy guns had been added to her, which made her ride low in the water. Her gunports were open, ready for battle, and the wind made her heel over so much that the water flooded in through them, and the ship sank within minutes, taking most of her crew down with her. Henry VIII watched the disaster from the shore.

**The *Vasa* (1628):** This Swedish warship was built in Stockholm, on the orders of King Gustavus Adolphus. She carried 64 guns, and according to critics she was both overloaded and unstable. Sure enough, she capsized on her maiden voyage in Stockholm Harbour – and like the *Mary Rose* she sank when she heeled over, and water poured in through her open gunports. The remains of the ship are now on display in Stockholm's Vasamuseet.

**The *Kronan* (1676):** Another Swedish warship, the *Kronan* (Crown) was the flagship of Admiral Creutz during the battle of Öland, fought against a joint Danish and Dutch fleet. At the time of her sinking, she was probably the largest and best-armed warship in the world. She was lost in exactly the same way as the *Mary Rose* and the *Vasa*, almost half a century before – when water poured in through her open gunports.

**HMS *Association* (1707):** Admiral Sir Cloudesley Shovell was returning home from the Mediterranean, when his squadron was wrecked on the Isles of Scilly. According to legend, shortly before the disaster a sailor warned the admiral that the islands lay in the path of the ships. Shovell threatened to hang the man for his impudence, and hours later the flagship *Association* hit a rock, and sank with all hands. Two other warships – the *Eagle* and the *Romney* – were also lost in the disaster. As a result the Admiralty offered a reward for anyone who could successfully determine longitude at sea – a competition which led to the invention of John Harrison's marine chronometer.

**USS *Monitor* (1862):** Famous thanks to her ground-breaking duel with the Confederate ironclad CSS *Virginia* (formerly the *Merrimack*, see p.236), the Union ironclad *Monitor* was an ungainly vessel, designed for her combat value rather than her seaworthiness. In late December 1862 it was decided to tow her down to Charleston, where she could reinforce the squadron blockading the port. However, she encountered a storm off Cape Hatteras, while under tow from the steam gunboat USS *Rhode Island*. High waves doused her boilers, and she foundered in the heavy seas; 16 of her crew perished.

**HMS *Victoria* (1893):** While conducting fleet exercises off Tripoli, Admiral Sir George Tryon ordered his fleet to sail in two parallel columns, and then to follow the lead ships in a turn towards each other. The plan was to form onto two close but parallel courses, heading the other way. Unfortunately the turning circles of the battleships were not tight enough, and HMS *Camperdown* rammed the flagship, HMS *Victoria*, which sank within minutes. Even though disaster was looming, the admiral refused to admit his mistake and order an alteration of course. He went down with his ship, as did half of the *Victoria*'s 700-man crew.

**HMS *Vanguard* (1917):** The powerful dreadnought HMS *Vanguard* had survived the battle of Jutland without suffering a single casualty. However, just over a year later she was destroyed in an accidental explosion while she lay at anchor in Scapa Flow. The cause was later thought to have been an accidental fire, in a compartment adjacent to a main cordite magazine. The heat ignited the explosive charges, and the 20,000-ton battleship was blown to pieces. Only two of her 843-man crew survived the explosion.

**HMS *Trinidad* (1942):** In March 1942 this British light cruiser formed part of the escort of the Arctic Convoy PQ-13. The convoy was attacked by a group of German destroyers, and during the action *Trinidad* fired a spread of six torpedoes at an enemy ship. They all missed their intended target, but one of them had a faulty gyro system, and consequently the torpedo went in a circle, and hit the cruiser in the stern, flooding her engine room, and killing 32 of her crew. Eventually the decision was made to rescue the rest of her crew, and the stricken cruiser was finished off by torpedoes fired by her own escorting destroyers.

**USS *Thresher* (1963):** The American nuclear submarine *Thresher* was conducting diving trials off Cape Cod, Massachusetts when something went wrong, and her reactor went off-line, possibly due to a failure in her water cooling system. The submarine descended rapidly, and sonar operators on board her support vessel USS *Skylark* heard her hull implode. The submarine had a 'crush depth' of around 1,300ft (400m), and soon after sinking deeper her hull was crushed by the pressure of the water. There were no survivors.

**The *Kursk* (2000):** The Russian nuclear submarine *Kursk* (K-141) was on exercise in the Barents Sea when a fault in her reactor system led to a leakage of rocket propellant – probably hydrogen peroxide, which caused a chemical reaction, which in turn triggered the explosion of a torpedo warhead. This triggered a second explosion, which ripped the hull open. The submarine sank in 328ft (100m) of water. While most of her crew were killed in the explosion, others remained trapped inside her hull, until they ran out of air. An international rescue effort was staged, but it came too late to save her crew.

# PRIVATEER OR PIRATE?

In history books, in films and even on the news, the word pirate is used to describe those who infringe copyright, illegally copy music or films, and hack into computers. However, according to the dictionary, piracy is a crime which can only take place on the high seas.

Just to confuse things, other terms are bandied about instead of pirate — names like privateer, corsair, buccaneer, freebooter or swashbuckler. Technically, most of these aren't real pirates.

A 'privateer' was a captain who was given permission to attack enemy shipping in time of war. He was given a 'letter of marque' — a privateering contract — which allowed him legally to capture enemy ships, as long as his country remained at war. Once peace was declared, the contract became invalid. In effect a privateer was a licensed pirate. The French often called privateers 'corsairs', although the term later became associated with Mediterranean 'pirates' rather than just 'privateers', just to confuse the issue further!

Another bewildering term is 'buccaneer'. It was given to the men who fought the Spanish in the Caribbean during the late 17th century. The word has its roots in *boucan*, the smoked meat produced by the backwoodsmen of Hispaniola — now Haiti and the Dominican Republic. Eventually it came to refer to all the English, French and Dutch raiders who preyed on the Spanish in the New World. The French used the term 'flibustier' or 'filibuster' for buccaneer, a word that was later anglicized into 'freebooter'. Another confusing term is 'swashbuckler', which was a 16th-century word meaning an armed brigand or outlaw. By the following century it meant 'swordsman', and in the 20th century it was adopted by pirate novelists and then by Hollywood to refer to dashing pirates.

Sometimes the line between 'privateer' and 'pirate' became a little blurred. Captain William Kidd was a 'privateer' who later turned to 'piracy'. Today, Sir Francis Drake is regarded as a national hero, but while he claimed he was a law-abiding 'privateer', he was actually a pirate, as for most of the time he fought the Spanish, England and Spain weren't at war with each other. For their part, the Spanish never saw him as anything other than a bloodthirsty pirate. Similarly, Sir Henry Morgan was an English privateer, who attacked the Spanish in the Caribbean, regardless of whether the two countries were at war or not. He ended up being Deputy Governor of Jamaica, which proves that just sometimes crime pays, and that the definition of pirate or privateer meant little, as long as you were successful.

# US NAVY ACRONYMS

Most navies rely heavily on acronyms, to avoid the repetitive use of technical jargon. As a result, it seems that naval personnel speak a language all of their own. The following are some of the most common acronyms in use in the US Navy today. Thanks to the involvement of the US Navy in NATO, and in joint peacekeeping operations with other navies, American acronyms have been adopted to some degree by most other major navies. Naturally, the Royal Navy has its own unique collection of acronyms. The following are US Navy acronyms, which are widely recognized by most of the world's naval personnel.

| | |
|---|---|
| **AAW** | Anti-Air War |
| **ASAU** | Air Search and Attack Unit |
| **ASUW** | Anti-Surface Warfare |
| **ASW** | Anti-Submarine Warfare |
| **AWOL** | Absent without Official Leave |
| **CAG** | Carrier Air Group |
| **CAP** | Combat Air Patrol |
| **CIC** | Command Information Center |
| **CICO** | Combat Information Centre Officer ('Sikko') |
| **CIWS** | Close-In Weapons System ('Sea Whiz') |
| **DESRON** | Destroyer Squadron |
| **DOD** | Department of Defense |
| **DON** | Department of the Navy |
| **ECM** | Electronic Counter-Measures |
| **FOD** | Foreign Object Damage |
| **JTF** | Joint Task Force |
| **NEX** | Naval Exchange |
| **NSWG** | Naval Special Warfare Group |
| **OOD** | Officer on Deck |
| **OPSO** | Operations Officer |
| **POD** | Plan of the Day |
| **RT** | Radio Telephone |
| **SAG** | Surface Action Group |
| **SAM** | Surface-to-Air Missile |
| **SEAL** | Sea Air Land |
| **SOPA** | Senior Officer Present (Afloat) |
| **SUBRON** | Submarine Squadron |
| **SWO** | Submarine Warfare Officer |
| **TE** | Task Element |
| **TF** | Task Force |
| **TG** | Task Group |
| **TU** | Task Unit |
| **UDT** | Underwater Demolition Team |
| **UNREP** | Underway Replenishment |

| USNA | United States Naval Academy |
|------|---------------------------|
| VERTREP | Vertical Replenishment |
| WSO | Weapons System Operator ('Wizzo') |
| XO | Executive Officer |

# THE WATCH SYSTEM

From the first days of sail, the crew of a warship were organized into 'watches' or shifts. After all, most ships sailed through the night, and so some system of regulating the activities of the crew was vital in order to ensure enough people were on duty at any one time, and that the sailors also managed to have time to eat, sleep and relax.

Traditionally, the Royal Navy organized its watch system by dividing the crew into two divisions, labelled Port and Starboard. The personnel of the two divisions then stood alternate watches. In other words they were on duty for one watch, then off for the next, then back on duty for the one after that, and so on. Historically, the naval day began at noon – the time when the sun was at its highest, when navigational position fixes were often taken. More recently the watch-keeping day has tended to start with the First Watch. The watch system makes sure that the ship is manned and operated around the clock, even though half the crew is off duty at any one time. The watches are as follows:

| The First Watch | (2000 to 0000hrs) |
|-----------------|-------------------|
| The Middle Watch | (0000 to 0400hrs) |
| The Morning Watch | (0400 to 0800hrs) |
| The Forenoon Watch | (0800 to 1200hrs) |
| The Afternoon Watch | (1200 to 1600hrs) |
| The First Dog Watch | (1600 to 1800hrs) |
| The Last Dog Watch | (1800 to 2000hrs) |

The division of the later afternoon into two 'dog watches' is important. This was traditionally a time of recreation for the crew, and not only did it make sure that both watches had at least two hours of free time, but it also divided the list into an uneven number of watches. This meant that no division would stand the same watch two days in a row. The 'dog watches' also fell around dinner time, which made the scheduled feeding of the crew a little easier.

Other watch systems exist. A three-watch system (where the three divisions are labelled Foremast, Mainmast and Mizzen, or Red, White and Blue) is similar to the traditional two-watch system, but it gives the crew more free time, as they stand fewer watches. There's also a 'Swedish System', which encompasses several different watch-keeping permutations, using different periods of watch time. On merchant ships the watch system is different, and usually runs on a more regular four-hour watch cycle. That means that the same people tend to stand the same watches each day.

Of course, on board a warship being off-watch doesn't necessarily guarantee a period of rest. Unless a seaman has been standing a Middle Watch the previous night, his naval day begins with the Forenoon Watch, and continues until the end of the dog watches. That means he has a day job, but is also expected to stand watches during the night. It is little wonder that sailors look forward to a spell in port.

# NAVAL GUN SALUTES

The firing of salutes in honour of royalty, representatives of another country or an important person, or to celebrate special events is a custom which can be traced back to the mid-16th century. In most naval gun salutes an odd number of guns are fired, as traditionally an even number of guns was reserved as a sign of mourning.

A salute is referred to by the number of guns being fired – for instance 'a 21 gun salute'. In the days of the sailing navy, this usually involved 21 different guns. These days the firing is normally done by three or four guns, and even then they tend to be special saluting guns, rather than full-sized pieces of naval ordnance. This means that each gun will fire several rounds.

It used to be the custom that, when at sea, the saluting ship would turn her bow towards the ship being saluted. This stemmed from the days of the sailing ship of war, when guns were mounted to fire in broadsides. The salutes were usually made with actual shot in the barrels of the guns. By turning her broadsides away from the enemy, the saluting ship demonstrated that she meant no harm, and her live rounds should – in theory – land in open water, well away from other shipping. These days such niceties have been abandoned, and salutes are fired using blank charges.

The Royal Navy also has a tradition involving the firing of salutes in the River Thames. In the 16th century, the Admiralty banned the firing of salutes above Gravesend, a few miles downstream from London. It was said that on one occasion an Elizabethan galleon was approaching Greenwich, and fired a salute to honour Queen Elizabeth. She was in residence in Greenwich Palace, and the live saluting rounds came dangerously close to her windows. Whether there is any truth in the story is open to question – more likely the Admiralty simply didn't want these salutes to alarm the population of the capital.

These days, both the Royal Navy and the US Navy fire 21 gun salutes – the British as a royal salute, and the Americans as a presidential one. For other heads of state, and important dignitaries, 19 guns are reserved. Back in 1775, John Paul Jones fired a 13 gun salute when his warship the USS *Ranger* arrived in France – one for each State.

According to both the British *Admiralty Manual of Seamanship* and the American *Bluejacket's Handbook*, the interval between successive rounds is five seconds. In the Royal Navy, before the invention of digital stopwatches, the interval was timed by the gunner repeating the couplet: 'If I wasn't a gunner I wouldn't be here – number ** gun fire!' This, spoken deliberately, takes about five seconds!

# PIPING THE SIDE

In naval terms, the pipe is the shrill-sounding metal whistle, or boatswain's call, which was once used to relay orders. Now it is more often used as a signal, made over a ship's broadcast system, to indicate the start or the end of a certain activity. In effect, the pipe represents the smooth, orderly flow of shipboard routines, from the 'Special call' (a wake-up call, preceding another pipe by the bosun's mate as a call of the hands and finally a verbal call) to 'Pipe down' – the naval equivalent of lights out. Other common calls include 'Still' (calling the hands to attention), 'Carry on' (resume what you were doing), or the 'Hail' (to attract someone's attention).

The boatswain's pipe or call was in use in medieval times, as one was recorded in a 13th-century inventory of stores on board a royal warship. It later became a badge of rank, and during the 16th century it was a symbol of an admiral. However, by the mid-17th century it was used as a device for transmitting orders, and was carried by a master, a quartermaster, a boatswain or a coxswain.

Piping the side is a mark of naval respect. In the Royal Navy it is reserved for the sovereign, a uniformed member of the royal family above the rank of captain, members of the Admiralty Board, officers of Flag Rank, commodores, commanding officers of commissioned HM warships, and other naval officers when carrying out certain special duties. It is also given to foreign naval officers in uniform, and when a corpse is brought aboard or sent out of a ship.

This mark of respect owes its origins to the days when captains used to visit other ships when at sea. On these occasions the visiting captain was often hoisted aboard from his longboat, using a chair suspended from a rope running from the lower yardarm.

The business of hauling him aboard was accompanied by the pipe of the boatswain, relaying orders to the men hauling on the rope. These men were called the 'side party', and over time this business evolved into 'piping the side'.

For the record, the 'Pipe the side' call lasts 12 seconds, starting off with a low note, then going high for four seconds, before sliding down and finishing off with another low note.

# NAMES OF IMPERIAL JAPANESE NAVY WARSHIPS IN THE SECOND WORLD WAR

While the British tended to give their warships names like *Invincible* or *Victory*, and the Americans opted for the names of States or people (sailors, statesmen and the like), the Imperial Japanese Navy adopted a far more poetical approach. While some were named after places, others were altogether more lyrical. Here is a small selection of Japanese warship names and their meanings, divided by ship type. All these warships saw service during the Second World War.

## Aircraft Carriers

*Akagi* (Red Castle)
*Chitose* (Long Life)
*Hiryu* (Dragon Flying in Heaven)
*Hosho* (The way a phoenix dives – a symbol of power)
*Juno* (Wandering Falcon)
*Kaga* (Increased Joy)
*Ryujo* (Sacred Dragon)
*Shokaku* (Happy Crane, or Crane Flying in Heaven)
*Soryu* (Blue-Grey Dragon)
*Zuiho* (Lucky Phoenix)
*Zuikaku* (Lucky Crane)

## Battleships

*Fuso* (The Land of the Divine Mulberry Trees – an old name for Japan)

*Hiei* (The Cold – also a Japanese mountain-top monastery)

*Kirishima* (Misty Island – also the name of a Japanese volcano)

*Kongo* (Stability – it also means the invincibility of Buddha)

*Yamato* (An ancient name for Japan, and a Japanese province)

## Cruisers

*Aoba* (Green Leaf – also the name of a Japanese mountain)

*Furutaka* (Old Falcon – also the name of a Japanese mountain)

*Isuzu* (Clear Water – also the name of a Japanese river)

*Jintsu* (Wonderful Godly Works – also the name of a Japanese river)

*Kinugasa* (Silk Parasol – also the name of a Japanese mountain)

*Mikuma* (Three Corners – also the name of a Japanese river)

*Oi* (Great Fountain – also the name of a Japanese river)

*Sendai* (Natural Lake – also the name of a Japanese river)

*Takao* (High Hero – also the name of a Japanese mountain)

*Tenyru* (Heaven's Dragon – also the name of a Japanese river)

*Tone* (Land Possessor – also the name of a Japanese river)

## Destroyers

*Akatsuki* (Dawn)

*Akitzuki* (Autumn Moon)

*Arashio* (Strong Tide, or Rough Sea Flood)

*Asagiri* (Morning Mist)

*Asagumo* (Morning Clouds)

*Asanagi* (Morning Calm)

*Asashio* (Morning High Tide)
*Fubuki* (Snowstorm)
*Harukaze* (Spring Wind)
*Harusame* (Spring Rain)
*Hatsutsuki* (New Moon)
*Ikazuchi* (Thunder)
*Kagero* (Glimmering Spring Air)
*Kamikaze* (Divine Wind)
*Makinami* (Rolling Waves)
*Natsuzuki* (Summer Moon)
*Oyashio* (Cold Current)
*Samidare* (Early Summer Rain)
*Sazanami* (Curling Waves)
*Shigure* (Autumn Shower)
*Shimakaze* (Island Wind)
*Shiratsuyu* (Shimmering Dew)
*Shirayuki* (White Snow)
*Suzukaze* (Cool Breeze in Summer)
*Suzutsuki* (Colder Moon)
*Tanikaze* (Wind from the Mountain to the Valley)
*Teruzuki* (Pale Moon)
*Umikaze* (Sea Breeze)
*Uranami* (Waves in a Bay)
*Usugumo* (Thin Misty Clouds)
*Yagumo* (Evening Clouds)
*Yunagi* (Evening Calm)

# RATING THE FLEET

During the age of fighting sail, an international system of rating warships was used, based on the number of guns they carried. The system first appeared during the early 17th century, and it remained in use until the introduction of steam-powered warships in the mid-19th century.

Actually, in its original form, the rating system involved the size and type of ship, rather than the number of guns it carried. These original categories divided the largest men-of-war into Royal ships, Great ships, Middling ships and Small ships. Below these were the unrated vessels – the small craft which brought supplies and mail to the fleet, carried messages between ships, or scouted for the enemy. By the mid-17th century these groups had become graded by rank, with Royal ships becoming warships of the First Rank, and Small ships classed as Fourth Rank vessels. By the 1670s, the word 'Rank' had been replaced by 'Rate', and in 1677 the diarist Samuel Pepys, who was Secretary to the Admiralty, laid down the classification which would remain in use for almost two centuries.

The rating of warships was an important administrative tool. It allowed men like Pepys to regulate the manning of the fleet, and to allocate supplies and ordnance more efficiently. The rating system was revised regularly, and usually this meant an increase in the number of guns for each category. For instance, in Pepys' day, a First Rate carried 90–100 guns, but by the time of Nelson it carried 100 guns or more. Ships smaller than Sixth Rates were 'unrated', which meant – in essence – that they could be commanded by junior officers, below the rank of captain. Of course, the number of guns a ship carried didn't always correspond to its rating. For instance, carronades were introduced in the 1770s – short weapons with a short range, but a lot of destructive power. These were never included in the rating – in effect they were extra weapons, which weren't included in the rating system until after the end of the Napoleonic Wars.

Over the years, certain rates of ships proved their worth, particularly the Third Rate – the 74-gun ship-of-the-line, which became the workhorse of the world's major navies during the Napoleonic Wars. Similarly Sixth Rate frigates were rendered obsolete by the carronade, and by a new breed of large 40-gun heavy frigates. Consequently while frigates as a whole proved popular, these smaller Sixth Rates declined in numbers during the Napoleonic era.

| Rate | Number (approx.) | Gun Decks | Tonnage of Guns | Number in Service |
|---|---|---|---|---|
| 1st Rate | 100–120 | 3 | 2,500 tons | 5 (7) |
| 2nd Rate | 90–98 | 3 | 2,200 tons | 9 (5) |
| 3rd Rate | 64–80 (usually 74) | 2 | 1,750 tons | 71 (87) |
| 4th Rate | 48–60 | 2 | 1,000 tons | 8 (8) |
| 5th Rate (Frigate) | 32–44 | 1 | 800 tons | 78 (123) |
| 6th Rate (Frigate) | 20–28 | 1 | 500 tons | 32 (25) |

Note: Two numbers are given for the number of ships of each rate in Royal Naval service. The first gives the number in commission at the start of the French Revolutionary Wars (1793), the second number in parenthesis represents the number at the end of the Napoleonic War (1814). Many of these ships were subsequently 'mothballed', and weren't available for service in 1815.

# THE TWO OCEAN NAVY

In July 1940, while the United States of America remained neutral, Europe was being torn apart by war. A month before, the German Army had marched into Paris, knocking France out of the war. Norway, Denmark, Holland, Belgium, Yugoslavia, Czechoslovakia and Poland were already occupied by the Germans. The British

Army had been forced to retreat from Dunkirk, and the country was bracing itself for invasion. Only Britain remained in the fight, a last bulwark against fascism.

President Franklin D. Roosevelt (1882–1945) was a staunch supporter of Britain, and was determined that America should help her leading ally. Public opinion was swaying away from the isolationism that had been a cornerstone of American policy, and it was also clear that American military spending was woefully inadequate. If America were to be dragged into a war with either Nazi Germany or a dangerously expansionist Imperial Japan, then it needed to be better prepared.

In July, FDR appointed two anti-isolationist Republicans to key positions – Henry L. Stimson became Secretary of War, while Frank Knox was appointed as Secretary of the Navy. This helped ensure cross-party support for military expansion. US strategists had been advocating an expansion of the US Navy, so that it could fight a simultaneous war in both the Atlantic and the Pacific Oceans. It was estimated that to build up naval strength to fulfil this need, the US Navy would have to be expanded by about two-thirds – an immense commitment for a country which had only just climbed out of a major recession. Still, FDR was determined. Chief of Naval Operations Harold Stark drew up the proposal, which involved the building of an extra 257 ships, with a total displacement of more than 1.3 million tons.

The result was the Vinson-Walsh Act of 19 July 1941, named after Democratic Senators Carl Vinson of Georgia, and Irvine I. Walsh of Massachusetts who laid the bill before Congress. This – the largest naval procurement bill in American history – authorized a 70 per cent expansion of the fleet – more than enough to fulfil the requirements of the naval strategists. Inevitably, the press dubbed it the Two Ocean Navy Act. The act would cost the US taxpayers almost $4 billion, but it was a price FDR was more than willing to pay in order to protect the nation.

Harold Stark's plan was put into effect immediately, and orders were placed for no fewer than 13 new battleships and battlecruisers, 18 aircraft carriers, 27 cruisers, 115 destroyers, 43 submarines and 15,000 naval aircraft. A vital by-product was that it allowed Roosevelt to 'lend' the Royal Navy 50 old destroyers – vessels which Britain desperately needed to keep her sea lanes open, and to counter the U-Boat threat.

The creation of a 'Two Ocean Navy' meant that the US Navy became a force worthy of a superpower, and when the Vinson-Walsh Act came to fruition she duly eclipsed the Royal Navy as the largest naval force in the world. The US Navy has remained a force with global reach ever since. It is therefore fitting that some of its fleet's most powerful warships include the super carriers USS *Franklin D. Roosevelt* and USS *Carl Vinson* and the nuclear submarine USS *Henry L. Stimson*.

# PROFILE OF A WARSHIP: *SOVEREIGN OF THE SEAS*

When she was launched in 1637, the *Sovereign of the Seas* was the largest and most powerful warship in the world. She was also the most expensive – almost £7,000 was spent on carvings and paintwork alone – the equivalent of £11 million today. Still, King Charles I (reign 1625–49) thought she was worth it. She was a showpiece, designed to demonstrate the power and the majesty of his joint Anglo-Scottish kingdoms. The great 1,500-ton ship was designed by Phineas Pett and built in Woolwich, on the River Thames. She carried 100 guns, on three full gun decks, making her the first true First Rate in history.

The man who designed all her magnificent carvings wrote that he hoped the ship 'should be a great spur and encouragement to all his [the king's] faithful and loving subjects to be liberal and willing contributories towards the Ship-Money'. It wasn't to be.

A few years later, public outrage over the Ship Money tax (a royal tax levied across England to fund the navy) led directly to the outbreak of the English Civil War. Most of the Navy sided with Parliament, and so the *Sovereign of the Seas* spent the war serving against the king who commissioned her. Just over a decade after the *Sovereign of the Seas* was built, King Charles I was executed by his own people.

By that time her name had been abbreviated to *Sovereign*, but despite plans to re-name her *Commonwealth*, she retained her royal-sounding name throughout the years of Oliver Cromwell and the English Republic. She played a minor part in the First Dutch War (1652–54), but she spent much of the conflict in the dockyard. After the restoration of the monarchy in 1660 she was renamed *Royal Sovereign*, becoming the centrepiece of Charles II's Navy. She took part in the Second Dutch War (1665–67), engaging in the battles of St James' Day and Sole Bay. During the Third Dutch War (1672–74) this veteran warship was Prince Rupert's flagship, a floating symbol of Royal Naval power.

She was rebuilt in the 1680s, and in 1690 she took part in the battle of Beachy Head, followed by the battle of Barfleur two years later. Unfortunately, this magnificent old ship was then sent to Chatham for another refit, and it was there in January 1696 that a fire broke out as she lay at anchor. She was burned to the waterline, a sad end to one of the most powerful sailing ships in history. For nearly six decades she had served her country well, and also served as a forerunner of a whole new breed of powerful First Rate ships-of-the-line.

# ANCHORS – THE BOTTOM LINE

The basic idea of an anchor is quite simple – an object used to temporarily attach a ship to the seabed. In the Ancient World anchors were made from stone, but over the centuries they became more specialized, as mariners tried to improve the ability of their anchors to grip the seabed, yet to lift away from it when they wanted. The result of this was that anchors changed their appearance, although the basic concept behind them remained the same. Strictly speaking, permanent anchors exist, but they are almost always called 'moorings'.

Anchors work by resisting movement, either through sheer weight, or by hooking themselves onto the seabed. Moorings tend to rely on weight, and anchors on their ability to snag into the seabed, or bury themselves in the seabed. That explains the flukes – the hook – on an anchor. The first anchors were little more than rocks tied to the end of ropes. Slightly more sophisticated versions involved holding the rock in a wooden frame, which could snag on the seabed – a combination of weight and hooking ability. Around the 5th century BC, the metal fluked anchor came into being, a device which would remain in use until the end of the era of sailing ships, in the early 19th century. These anchors

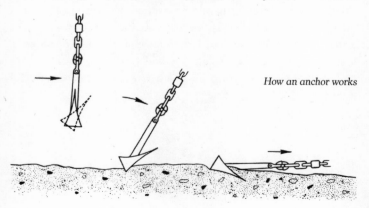

*How an anchor works*

might have increased in size, but their basic design remained the same. They had a metal crown and shank, but the crosspiece was usually made from wood. By the age of fighting sail, what really changed was the hawser – the rope which connected the anchor to the ship. These became thicker, more resilient and heavier.

Then, when iron or steel hulls and steam engines came into being, steel anchors became the norm, with steel hawser cables. Obviously these were much stronger than previous designs, and heavier. Fortunately, this was also the period of steam-powered capstans and winches, so the business of raising the anchor was actually easier than it had been before. Various designs were tried – the first resembling the old anchors, only made entirely from metal, then some designed along new scientific principles. Nowadays, the majority of anchors have thick but quite short shanks – the stem of the anchor – while the main part – the crown – is actually flat-bottomed, ending in two flukes. The crown is hinged so that when it hits the seabed it can unfold slightly, to provide a better grip on the seabed.

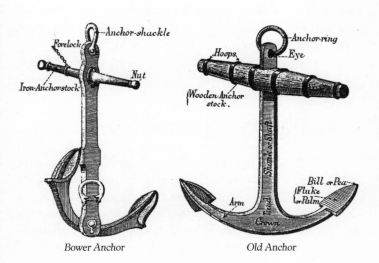

Bower Anchor          Old Anchor

*Modern anchor*

When an anchor is let go the flukes are usually pointing towards the surface. When it hits the seabed these fold out, and the pull of the ship on the other end of the anchor cable makes the anchor drag along the seabed. This ends when the flukes dig themselves in, and the anchor embeds itself completely. The cable ends up almost horizontal when it emerges from the seabed, after the anchor has dug itself in. The length of the cable depends on the depth and the type of sea bottom – in effect a long anchor cable is more efficient than a short one.

Back on the surface, the ship swings around on its anchor cable, depending on wind and tide. This is known as the 'anchor berth' or 'swinging circle' – the diameter of the ship and its length of cable. Weighing anchor is relatively straightforward – the anchor is 'aweigh' when it finally breaks free from the seabed, and is hauled in until the anchor is completely stowed.

# PRESERVING ADMIRAL NELSON

After the death of Lord Nelson at the battle of Trafalgar on 21 October 1805, Captain Hardy, who commanded Nelson's flagship HMS *Victory*, was left with a problem. One of Nelson's dying wishes was that he should not be buried at sea, as was the custom, but that he should be transported back to Britain. Hardy and his superior, Admiral Collingwood, both agreed that it was important that the body of Britain's great naval hero be sent home, where Nelson could be given a state funeral. The problem was how exactly this could be done.

For a start, HMS *Victory* was in no fit state to make the voyage, as she had been badly damaged during the battle. First she would have to put in to Gibraltar for repairs. In the meantime, something had to be done with Nelson's body. It was decided to place the body in a leaguer – a large cask, about 5ft (1.5m) high. It held 184 gallons (836 litres) of liquid, and was the largest watertight container available on board the ship. Rather than water, though, the body was preserved in spirits.

The body had been shaved of hair, then stripped and folded into the barrel, so that Nelson's head and feet were at the bottom. Popular myth has it that rum was used, but brandy was considered to have medicinal properties, and was carried on board as a drink for officers. The cask was guarded round-the-clock by a Royal Marine sentry, more out of respect for Nelson than to prevent the crew from helping themselves to the spirits. The following account by the surgeon Sir William Beatty describes what happened next:

> In the evening after this melancholy task was accomplished, the gale came up with violence, and continued that night and the succeeding day without any abatement. During this boisterous weather Lord Nelson's body remained under the charge of a sentinel on the middle deck. The cask was placed on its end, having a closed aperture at its top, and another below; the object of which was, that as the frequent renewal of the spirit was thought necessary, the old could be drawn off below, and a fresh quantity introduced above, without moving the cask or occasioning the least agitation of the body.

The gale was a terrible ordeal, and many of the ships of both sides which had survived the battle foundered during the storm.

HMS *Victory* was one of the lucky ones, and she was eventually towed safely into port. Beatty picks up the story:

> On the 24th there was a disengagement of air from the body, to such a degree that the sentinel became alarmed on seeing the head of the cask raised. The spirit was drawn off at once, and the cask filled again, before the arrival of the *Victory* at Gibraltar on October 28th, where spirit of wine was procured; and the cask, showing a deficit produced by the body's absorbing a considerable quantity of the brandy, was then filled up with it.

On 4 November HMS *Victory* sailed from Gibraltar, bound for Portsmouth. The voyage home took just over a month, during which time the spirits in the leaguer were changed twice. Finally, around 14 December, Beatty removed the body, and took out Nelson's bowels, which would have decayed faster than the rest of the body. The remains were wrapped in cotton, and then swathed in bandages. Finally the body was placed in a lead-lined coffin, filled with brandy mixed with camphor and myrrh. Nelson's body was taken to Greenwich, where it lay in state. On 9 January 1806, Nelson was interred in St Paul's Cathedral, after his coffin had been transported by royal barge up the River Thames, watched by thousands of mourners.

# THE SEVEN SEA BATTLES FOR GUADALCANAL

By the summer of 1942, in the midst of the Second World War, the Japanese had overrun all of the Dutch East Indies, and were poised to occupy both New Guinea and the Solomon Islands. On the island of Guadalcanal, Japanese engineers began work on an airfield, which – when completed and in operation – would have covered the Coral Sea and the eastern approaches to Australia.

Then on 7 August US Marines landed on Guadalcanal and seized the airfield. This was the first move in a land, sea and air campaign that would decide the fate of the South Pacific. In the months that followed no fewer than seven full-scale naval battles were fought for control of the waters around Guadalcanal. Of these, two were carrier actions, while the remainder involved surface ships. So many warships were lost off the northern coast of the island that these waters were renamed 'Ironbottom Sound'.

### The battle of Savo Island (9 August 1942)

Vice-Admiral Mikawa launched a surprise night attack against the Allied warships protecting the landing beaches. Fought off Savo Island, this resulted in the loss of one Australian and three American heavy cruisers, all victims of Japanese torpedoes.

### The battle of the Eastern Solomons (24 August 1942)

A Japanese attempt to reinforce Guadalcanal was thwarted when a US carrier force located and attacked a covering force of Japanese carriers. Both sides launched air strikes against the enemy carriers, resulting in the loss of the Japanese light carrier *Ryujo*, and the crippling of the American carrier *Enterprise*. The Japanese transports were recalled when the covering carrier force withdrew.

### The battle of Cape Esperance (11 October 1942)

On 11 October the Japanese made another attempt to reinforce Guadalcanal, the convoy covered by a surface force which was ordered to bombard the airfield (now known as Henderson Field). Instead, Rear Admiral Goto's force ran into Rear Admiral Scott's task group of American cruisers and destroyers off the north-west tip of the island. In the confused night action that followed the Japanese heavy cruiser *Furutaka* and the destroyer *Fubuki* were both sunk, while the Americans lost only one warship – the destroyer *Duncan*.

### The battle of Santa Cruz (26 October 1942)

In late October the Japanese launched a major attack on Guadalcanal, and a force of four carriers was ordered to support the offensive. This led to another clash with the outnumbered US carrier force, which consisted of the newly repaired *Enterprise* and the *Hornet*. Both sides launched air strikes during the day, which resulted in the sinking of the *Hornet* and the crippling of the *Enterprise*. The Japanese carriers *Zuiho* and *Shokaku* were both badly damaged. Although the battle ended with a Japanese tactical victory, they lost many veteran pilots in the battle, which severely curtailed their ability to fight another carrier battle.

### The first battle of Guadalcanal (13 November 1942)

In November another batch of Japanese reinforcements was transported to Guadalcanal, protected by Vice-Admiral Abe's covering force, which included two battleships. Rear Admiral Callaghan's task group encountered the Japanese in 'Ironbottom Sound', and in the close-range night action that followed two American cruisers and four destroyers were sunk, for the loss of two Japanese destroyers. However, the battleship *Hiei* was badly damaged, and the following day she was sunk by American torpedo planes before she could limp to safety. Callaghan was killed when the bridge of his flagship *San Francisco* was hit.

### The second battle of Guadalcanal (14–15 November 1942)

The Japanese returned the next evening, led by Vice-Admiral Kondo. This time the Americans were ready for them, having reinforced their task group with the battleships *South Dakota* and *Washington*. Rear Admiral Lee's battleships made short work of the Japanese battleship *Kirishima*, using radar to direct their fire. In addition to the Japanese battleship, one Japanese and three American destroyers were sunk during the battle.

**The battle of Tassafaronga (30 November 1942)**

By late November the 'Tokyo Express' (the Japanese operation to ferry supplies and reinforcements to Guadalcanal using fast destroyers) was proving highly successful, and so an American surface group of cruisers and destroyers commanded by Rear Admiral Wright was ordered to intercept the nightly operation. Rear Admiral Tanaka's force of eight destroyers used their superior torpedoes to keep the Americans at bay, sinking the heavy cruiser *Northampton* and crippling three other cruisers in the process, all for the loss of one Japanese destroyer.

# HMS *CROMWELL*

Winston Churchill was an admirer of Oliver Cromwell, England's Lord Protector and the man responsible for the execution of King Charles I and the establishment of a republic. In 1911 Churchill became First Lord of the Admiralty, the civilian politician and cabinet member who oversaw the activities of the Royal Navy. He took office at the height of a naval arms race, and one of his first tasks was to commission the 1912 programme of battleship construction. Unlike previous dreadnought battleships, these ships would carry 15in guns, making them some of the most powerful warships in existence.

The first of five ships of the new class was laid down in October 1912. With the ships underway, Churchill was left with the problem of naming them. He proposed several names, one of which was HMS *Cromwell*. As Churchill put it: 'Oliver Cromwell was one of the founders of the Navy and scarcely any man did so much for it. It seems right that we should give to a battleship a name that never failed to make the enemies of England tremble.' He was right – under Cromwell's leadership the English Commonwealth became a naval power to be reckoned with. On the restoration of the monarch in 1660, this powerful force became the Royal Navy. During his time as Lord Protector Oliver Cromwell named ships after his military victories (e.g. *Naseby*, *Marston Moor* or *Langport*), but never after himself.

Unfortunately King George V was able to veto the names of warships he didn't like. The king had no intention of naming a battleship after the man responsible for executing a king and replacing the monarchy with a republic. Churchill was 'asked' to consider alternative names, and the vessel was eventually renamed, becoming one of the Queen Elizabeth Class (*Queen Elizabeth*, *Warspite*, *Barham*, *Valiant* and *Malaya*). Churchill had a low opinion of the king, whom he saw as a dim-witted reactionary, who spoke 'cheap and silly drivel'. The dislike was mutual. However, the king's son was more tolerant, or probably less inclined to be contrary, as the destroyer HMS *Cromwell* was commissioned in 1946, just after the end of the Second World War. Incidentally, in the previous year the cruiser HMS *Blake* had been launched, named after Cromwell's most successful admiral, and arguably the founder of the modern British Navy. After a decade in mothballs she finally entered service in 1961, four years before Churchill's death. The destroyer HMS *Cromwell* was sold to the Norwegian Navy in 1946, and since then no politician has had the audacity to suggest that the name be used again.

# SEA BATTLE: THE BATTLE OF CAPE ST VINCENT, 1797

Even before 1797, Commodore Horatio Nelson was seen as a naval commander of great ability. After the battle of Cape St Vincent, he was regarded both as a reckless genius and as a man who could win battles. In effect, the battle established his reputation.

In 1796, after four years of constant warfare, the French had survived, fighting off all attempts to crush the Revolution.

In 1795, the Spanish had been forced to make peace with the Revolutionaries. Even worse for the allies, the following year the Spanish crown signed the Treaty of San Ildefonso with the French, and the two nations became allies. The two most important maritime powers on the mainland of Europe had now joined forces, and threatened to sweep the British from the seas. The Royal Navy was stretched to the limit, and its ships were unable to maintain a tight blockade of both the French and the Spanish ports. In December 1796 a French invasion fleet slipped out of Brest, heading for Ireland. The only reason the amphibious landing did not occur was because of bad weather, not the British fleet. Although gales and snowstorms prevented an invasion, the French planned a second attempt, this time with the help of the Spanish fleet. Word of the enterprise leaked out, and the warning was passed to the British Admiralty. The British Mediterranean fleet was duly moved into position off Cadiz, stopping any Spanish or French move from the Mediterranean into the Atlantic.

Admiral Don José de Cordova was ordered to sail from Cartagena with his full fleet of 27 Spanish ships-of-the-line and 12 frigates in February 1797. The plan was for the Spanish fleet to sail to Cadiz, then on to Brest, where it would link up with the French fleet. Together the force would form an unstoppable armada, which would then sail to either Ireland or England, whichever seemed the more feasible in the circumstances. The Spanish admiral flew his flag in the *Santissima Trinidad*, the largest First Rate ever to put to sea, and a triumph of Spanish shipbuilding. The Spanish were spotted by a British frigate as they passed through the Straits of Gibraltar, and the sighting was duly reported to Vice-Admiral John Jervis, commanding the British fleet off Cadiz. His flagship was none other than HMS *Victory* (100 guns). With just 15 ships-of-the-line, the British were heavily outnumbered, but Jervis did not hesitate. He gave the order to prepare for battle.

The two fleets sighted each other off Cape St Vincent at 0830hrs on 14 February. The Spanish fleet was to the south, and its ships lay in two groups. Jervis formed his fleet into line-of-battle, and the two sides slowly closed with each other, looking for an advantage over their opponent. Shortly after noon the British line passed between the two Spanish groups and opened fire. In an equally daring move, one portion of the Spanish fleet changed course, shaving close to the British line, but managing to rejoin the rest of the fleet. The British reversed course, trying to intercept the Spanish fleet which was now sailing away from it towards the east. What had begun as a race to isolate a part of the Spanish fleet now became a race to catch it at all. Turning a battle-line was a slow, cumbersome business, and it soon became apparent that the Spanish were likely to get away, or at least to buy time to bring their overwhelming force to bear on a portion of the British line. Nelson in HMS *Captain* (74 guns) was third from the end of the British line, and far closer to the enemy than his commander. He duly decided to use his initiative, and broke away from the line-of-battle, spinning his ship round to port in an effort to overhaul the Spanish. By 1330hrs, *Captain* had caught up with the *Santissima Trinidad*, and the two exchanged broadsides. Soon other British ships reached the scene, but Nelson headed for the *San Nicolas* (80 guns), which collided with the *San José* (112 guns). Nelson boarded the *San Nicolas*, his crew overpowering the Spanish defenders within minutes.

He continued to attack, ordering his men to board the even larger Spanish First Rate beyond. Both Spanish warships struck their colours, dumbfounded by the stratagem which was duly nicknamed 'Nelson's patent boarding bridge': attacking a Second Rate warship with a Third Rate, then using the larger ship to attack a First Rate on her far side! By this time Jervis and the rest of the fleet had arrived, and although most of the Spanish managed to escape, the ships embroiled in the battle around Nelson's *Captain* were unable to flee.

Even the *Santissima Trinidad* had to surrender, but she was spirited to safety in a daring rescue by part of the Spanish rearguard. By 1700hrs the guns had fallen silent, leaving the British the clear victors. Four powerful Spanish warships had been captured, and the Spanish had been forced to flee into Cadiz, where they were blockaded. The initiative shown by Nelson, and the boldness displayed by Jervis, ensured that there would be no Spanish fleet available for the invasion, and the risk to Britain was greatly reduced. Nelson's daring had paid off, and his actions were acclaimed as those of a brilliant commander. Nelson was on the ascendancy, and the short road to Trafalgar had begun.

# LOUIS XIV'S WEAPONS OF MASS DESTRUCTION

In 1682, French shipping in the Western Mediterranean was plagued by the Barbary Pirates, and pirate galleys belonging to the Bey of Algiers attacked the French ships. By way of retaliation, the French Mediterranean fleet sailed to Algiers, and used five bomb vessels to bombard the city.

Bomb vessels (known as 'bomb ketches', or *galiots à bombes* in French) were a relatively new invention, and each of the French ships carried two large mortars, mounted on their centreline. The vessels were anchored, and fired along a pre-determined bearing. Powder-filled mortar bombs (shells) caused damage when they exploded, and their iron casings burst, sending shrapnel – bits of casing – flying in all directions. They killed, they destroyed buildings, and they started fires, which could swiftly gut an enemy town.

The bombs were, however, indiscriminate – while they could be aimed with a reasonable degree of accuracy, most of the time the gunners simply fired towards the centre of an enemy town. Their other limitation was that the range of these late 17th-century mortars was less than the range of most shore batteries. The ships were therefore usually anchored under cover of darkness, and then moved back to safety before dawn.

The first bombardment on Djidelli wasn't particularly successful, as the bomb vessels were anchored too far out to sea. The attack was repeated twice more, in August and September, and considerable damage was done to the North African port, including the destruction of the city's Grand Mosque. According to eyewitnesses, hundreds of civilians had taken shelter there, and were buried in the rubble.

As the Bey of Algiers continued his attacks, the French returned the following summer, this time with seven bomb vessels in their fleet. This time they concentrated on the shore batteries, and put them out of action. Then the French moved close inshore and bombarded the port by day and by night, leaving the city in ruins. Admiral Duquesne only withdrew when his ships finally ran out of ammunition. The port was left a smoking ruin, and the Bey sued for peace. The whole operation was a brutal demonstration of the efficiency of this new weapon. However, this was only a prelude for what was to come.

In 1685 the *galiots à bombes* bombarded Tripoli, firing more than 500 shells at the city, and killing more than 300 people. The Bey of Tripoli agreed to liberate all his Christian slaves, and pay a substantial financial tribute to the French king – anything to avoid a repeat of the destruction. While these events were followed with interest in Europe, the destruction made little impact, as the Barbary Pirates weren't Christians, and were – after all – a threat to trade. What had, however, caused outrage throughout the continent the previous year was the way the French used this deadly weapon against a Christian, European city.

In 1684, Spain and France were at war, and the Italian city-state of Genoa offered its support to the Spanish. Louis XIV ordered Admiral Duquesne to teach the Genoese a lesson. Therefore, in May 1684 the French fleet arrived off Genoa, and Admiral Duquesne was delighted to discover that the port's protective batteries were obsolete, and posed no threat to his ships. He anchored his *galiots à bombes* just outside the entrance to the harbour, and when the Genoese responded by firing on them, he unleashed a furious bombardment. First his bombs destroyed the obsolete batteries, and then they turned their fire onto the city itself. Within hours fires had broken out in the port, but still the bombs kept raining destruction on the city.

Between 17 and 28 May, the French fired more than 13,000 bombs at Genoa, and destroyed over two-thirds of the city. More than 10,000 people were reported to have been killed or injured. The destruction came to an end only when Admiral Duquesne was ordered to cease fire, by royal command. It turned out that the elderly Doge of Genoa and his leading senators had raced to Louis XIV's court, where they offered a grovelling apology for backing the Spanish. Only then did Louis call off the bombardment. To add insult to injury, before he left Versailles, the Genoese Doge was given a diamond-studded miniature portrait of the French king – a likeness of the man who had destroyed his city! Within a decade bomb vessels had become an integral part of every major fleet. However, they were never used to such destructive effect again.

# QUOTES BY NAVAL COMMANDERS

Occasionally a quotation by a naval captain or an admiral served as a rallying cry, either because it summed up the spirit of the moment, or because it sounded particularly patriotic. The following examples are among the most famous – and are often the most misquoted. This is what these naval commanders or leaders actually said:

🦇 *There seems to be something wrong with our bloody ships today.*

Spoken by Vice-Admiral David Beatty, Royal Navy, during the battle of Jutland (1916), just after the battlecruiser HMS *Queen Mary* exploded after being hit by a German shell. She was the sister ship of Beatty's own flagship, HMS *Lion*.

🦇 *Damn the torpedoes!*

During the battle of Mobile Bay (1864), aides to Flag Officer David Farragut, US Navy, expressed their concern about Confederate torpedoes (mines). Although different versions of his reply have been quoted, the likelihood is that he replied, *Damn the torpedoes! Four bells, Captain Drayton! Go ahead, Jouett, full speed!*

🦇 *No captain can do very wrong if he places his ship alongside that of the enemy.*

Vice-Admiral Nelson, Royal Navy, when describing his preferred tactics to his officers immediately before the battle of Trafalgar (1805). In fact, what he actually said was, *In case signals can neither be seen nor perfectly understood, no captain can do very wrong if he places his ship alongside that of the enemy.*

🦇 *You can fire when ready, Mr Gridley.*

The orders by Commodore George Dewey, US Navy, to his flag captain on board the USS *Olympia*, which led to the opening shots of the battle of Manila Bay (1898). In fact, he probably said, *You may fire when you are ready, Gridley.*

🦇 *It takes three years to build a ship – it takes three centuries to build a tradition.*

Admiral Andrew Cunningham, Royal Navy, when it was proposed that due to losses from German dive-bombers, he should withdraw his warships from the waters around Crete in 1941.

🔔 *I have not yet begun to fight.*

Captain John Paul Jones, US Navy, after his ensign was shot away during the sea battle between HMS *Serapis* and the USS *Bonhomme Richard* in September 1779. Captain Pearson of the *Serapis* had hailed Jones to see if he had surrendered, and that was his reply.

🔔 *There is plenty of time to win this game, and to thrash the Spaniards too.*

Attributed to Sir Francis Drake, of England's Navy Royal in 1588, when news reached him that the Spanish Armada had appeared off the English coast. Drake and his commander Lord Howard were in Plymouth at the time, playing a game of bowls. Unfortunately there is no evidence that Drake ever sad this.

🔔 *Don't give up the ship.*

The final order of the mortally wounded Captain James Lawrence, US Navy, as he was carried below during the battle between HMS *Shannon* and the USS *Chesapeake* off Boston harbour in 1813. Lawrence's plea was in vain – the *Chesapeake* was captured after a short, vicious boarding action.

🔔 *I have only one eye, I have a right to be blind sometimes ... I really do not see the signal!*

Vice-Admiral Nelson, Royal Navy, during the battle of Copenhagen (1801), when his superior, Admiral Hyde-Parker, ordered him to withdraw. Nelson continued to attack the Danish fleet, and went on to win a singular victory.

🔔 *Take her down!*

In February 1943, Commander Gilmore of the submarine USS *Growler* attacked a Japanese gunboat. He was badly wounded in the exchange of fire, and knocked overboard. Unable to climb back into his submarine, he gave this self-sacrificing order to his bridge crew.

# THE NUCLEAR FLEET

In 1946 Operation *Crossroads* – the testing of nuclear weapons – took place at Bikini Atoll, one of the Marshall Islands in the central Pacific Ocean. The US Navy was asked to provide obsolete warships as targets, and they produced a fleet of 90 vessels. Most of these redundant warships were American, but a few were warships captured from America's wartime enemies Germany and Japan. This fleet of nuclear targets included many once-proud veterans of the war in the Pacific – warships which had already earned a place in the history books before their ultimate sacrifice.

Two bombs were exploded amongst the anchored ships. The first on 1 July 1946 (Test Able) was dropped from a B-29 bomber, and sank five warships outright, while seriously damaging 14 more. The second on 25 July (Test Baker) was detonated underwater, directly underneath the battleship USS *Arkansas*. This time nine ships were sunk, while many of the rest were so badly damaged or irradiated that they were scuttled shortly afterwards.

The following ten veteran warships all met their end in the shallow waters of Bikini Atoll, or were scuttled afterwards:

1. **USS *Saratoga* (aircraft carrier):** During the battle of the Eastern Solomons her aircraft sank the Japanese carrier *Ryujo*. She also supported the landings on Tarawa and Iwo Jima.

2. **HIJMS *Nagato* (battleship):** Once rated the third most powerful battleship in the world, she served as Admiral Yamamoto's flagship during the attack on Pearl Harbor. She also fought in the battle of Leyte Gulf.

3. **USS *Arkansas* (battleship):** A warship of First World War vintage, in 1944 the *Arkansas* fired in support of the Normandy landings, then steamed to the Pacific, where her 12in guns bombarded Iwo Jima and Okinawa.

4. **KMS *Prinz Eugen* (heavy cruiser):** This sleek German warship accompanied the battleship *Bismarck* during her sortie into the North Atlantic in May 1941, and took part in the battle of the Denmark Straits, when the battlecruiser HMS *Hood* was blown up. In February 1942 she took part in the 'Channel Dash', before ending the war in the Baltic Sea. Although she survived the two Bikini Atoll explosions, she was badly damaged, so she was eventually scuttled off Kwajalein Atoll.

5. **USS *New York* (battleship):** After she served alongside the Royal Navy during the First World War, the guns of this veteran battleship fired in support of American landings in North Africa, and on the Pacific islands of Iwo Jima and Okinawa.

6. **USS *Nevada* (battleship):** This venerable battleship was badly damaged and forced to beach during the Japanese attack on Pearl Harbor. After being raised and repaired she fired her guns in support of the Normandy landings, and during Allied landings in southern France. In 1945 she returned to the Pacific, where she took part in the bombardment of Okinawa. She survived the two atom bomb explosions, so she was towed to Pearl Harbor, where she was used as a target for gunnery practice, and was finally sunk in July 1948.

7. **USS *Salt Lake City* (heavy cruiser):** During the Pacific War this cruiser took part in more engagements than any other warship in the US Navy, including the battles of the Coral Sea, Midway, Cape Esperance, the Komandorski Islands and the Philippine Sea, as well as the bombardment of Iwo Jima and Okinawa.

8. **USS *Pensacola* (heavy cruiser):** Another veteran of the battles around Guadalcanal, this cruiser took part in the battle of Tassafaronga, and helped protect US carriers during the battle of Santa Cruz. She also fired her guns in support of the landings on Saipan and Iwo Jima.

9. **HIJMS *Sakawa* (light cruiser):** Although this Japanese warship entered service too late to take part in the battles of the Pacific War, she was held in reserve, to launch a suicide attack in support of the Japanese homeland.

10. **USS *Anderson* (destroyer):** This battle-scarred American destroyer took part in most of the major battles of the Pacific War, including the Coral Sea, Midway, the Eastern Solomons, Santa Cruz, Kwajalein and Leyte Gulf.

# USS *NAUTILUS* – THE FIRST NUCLEAR SUBMARINE

In July 1951, Congress approved the building of the world's first operational nuclear-powered submarine. Following the development of the atomic bomb, other uses for nuclear power were explored, and in 1946 a nuclear-powered electrical generating plant was developed. The US Navy was quick to realize the potential of this new source of energy, and it sent Admiral Hyman G. Rickover to investigate. A convert to nuclear power, by 1949 Rickover had become the head of the Navy's fledgling nuclear programme. He was a determined man, and the Navy felt that he would push through development regardless of whatever opposition he might encounter. While this hard taskmaster might have been unpopular, he certainly got results.

His first achievement was the commissioning of a nuclear-powered submarine, even though the means to power it still had to be developed. In the summer of 1952 the keel of this revolutionary submarine – the USS *Nautilus* – was laid down in the General Dynamics' shipyard in Groton, Connecticut. She was launched by the First Lady, Mamie Eisenhower, less than two years later. This was followed by the business of fitting her with her untried propulsion system. The US Navy built its first test reactor called

S1W in early 1953, on the campus of the Idaho National Laboratory. By March this pressurized water reactor was on-line, and Admiral Rickover and his staff began working on the myriad of technical problems which needed to be ironed out before the reactor could be fitted into the new submarine.

That summer the reactor was used for a test run, simulating a transatlantic voyage. It was a resounding success, and demonstrated the immense potential of this new form of propulsion. Before this, submarines were powered by conventional diesel engines on the surface, and electric batteries when submerged. Submerged speeds were slow, and a submarine needed to surface or use its snorkel repeatedly to replenish stocks of air, and to recharge the batteries by using the diesel engines. Nuclear power meant that a submarine now had the potential to make the entire voyage underwater, which of course greatly reduced its chances of being detected. Better still, the tests showed that a nuclear-powered submarine could make the underwater voyage at an average speed of 25–30 knots (46.3–55.6km/h) – more than double the speed of a submerged conventional submarine. A new era in naval propulsion was about to begin.

By the time the *Nautilus* was launched in January 1954, Rickover and his team were completing work on a modified version of the test reactor. Dubbed S2W, this new nuclear reactor was designed for use in the new submarine. It was shipped from Idaho to Connecticut, and fitted into the *Nautilus* during the last months of 1954. Rickover supervised everything, so he could completely guarantee the safety of the reactor. As he put it: 'I have a son. I love my son. I want everything that I do to be so safe that I would be happy to have my son operating it. That's my fundamental rule.' Everything was tested, improved, then tested again until the admiral was satisfied.

Commander Eugene P. Wilkinson was named the submarine's first commander, and he and his crew were trained in the new technology as the engines were fitted around them. Finally, in

January 1955 everything was ready. On 17 January 1955, the USS *Nautilus* put to sea for the first time, to test her new engines, and the reactor that powered them. Shortly after 1100hrs, Commander Wilkinson sent the signal everyone was waiting for – 'Underway on Nuclear Power!'

The *Nautilus* (SSN-571) began extensive sea trials in May, making the 1,200-mile (2,200km) voyage from the US Navy's submarine base in New London, Connecticut to Roosevelt Roads, Puerto Rico in just under 90 hours. She stayed submerged for the entire trip – making it the longest underwater voyage in history. Rickover's nuclear-powered vision had become a reality. For the next three years the *Nautilus* was tested thoroughly, and she demonstrated just how potent this new type of warship actually was. For a start, all existing forms of anti-submarine warfare were rendered obsolete. By staying submerged for longer than was previously possible, she was safe from radar and search aircraft, while her engines meant she could dive deep, and escape from a threat whenever she needed to.

Then, in April 1958, the USS *Nautilus* began her most ambitious voyage yet. Despite the success of his nuclear programme, and the commissioning of new nuclear-powered submarines, Admiral Rickover needed to underline the importance of this new invention. The result was Operation *Sunshine* – a publicity exercise which caught the imagination of the world. Her new skipper, Commander William R. Anderson, sailed her into the Pacific, putting in to San Diego, San Francisco, Seattle and Pearl Harbor, in order to drum up publicity for what would come next. He announced that the *Nautilus* was about to embark on a historical voyage – the first ever underwater transit of the Polar icecap – passing directly underneath the North Pole. He sailed from Hawaii on 23 July, and submerged on 1 August. Two days later, at 2315hrs on 3 August, she became the first marine vessel to reach the North Pole, passing 200ft (60m) below its surface. She finally surfaced off the coast of Greenland, after an epic 1,600-mile (3,000km) voyage beneath the Polar ice.

The voyage wasn't without its problems. For a start, conventional magnetic compasses were useless, so Commander Anderson had to rely on an untested new gyrocompass. It worked. In case of an accident, or a navigational failure, Anderson had planned to use his torpedoes to blow a hole in the ice, and force his way to the surface. In the end everything went smoothly, and the *Nautilus* ended her voyage in Portland, the Royal Navy base in the English Channel.

The *Nautilus* remained in service until 1980, by which time improvements in submarine technology had rendered her obsolete. For a start, new nuclear boats were much stealthier, and carried a far more powerful suite of weaponry and safer and more efficient reactors. She then became a historic ship and 'national historic landmark', the centrepiece of the US Navy Submarine Force Museum in New London, Connecticut. This pioneering old lady remains a powerful reminder of the trailblazing days of nuclear power, and the drive of Hyman G. Rickover (1900–86) – 'the father of the nuclear navy'.


# 'ANCHORS AWEIGH'

The unofficial song of the US Navy was first composed in 1906 by Lieutenant Charles A. Zimmerman USN, who based the tune around the lyrics of Alfred Hart Miles, a midshipman at the United States Naval Academy in Annapolis, Maryland. Zimmerman had been the bandmaster at the Academy, and composed the piece as a football song, to be played at Academy sporting events. Its first airing was just before the Army–Navy football game in December 1906 – a game the Navy won 10–0.

The song was gradually adopted by the US Navy as a whole, although the lyrics were changed by George D. Lottman, to make it less an Academy anthem than a naval one. The melody was also rewritten by Domenico Savino – a composer for the music industry, who gave the tune more energy. Despite all these changes the lyrics still reflected the college football origins of the song. Therefore other changes followed, until what we have is a version with no references at all to college, sport or beating the army.

## Original version

Stand Navy down the field, Sails set to the sky.
We'll never change our course, So Army you steer shy-y-y-y.
Roll up the score, Navy, Anchors aweigh.
Sail Navy down the field and sink the Army, sink the Army Grey.
Get underway, Navy, Decks cleared for the fray,
We'll hoist true Navy Blue, So Army down your Grey-y-y-y.
Full speed ahead, Navy; Army heave to,
Furl Black and Grey and Gold and hoist the Navy, hoist the
    Navy Blue.

## Modern version

Stand, Navy, out to sea, Fight our battle cry;
We'll never change our course, So vicious foe steer shy-y-y-y.
Roll out the TNT, Anchors Aweigh. Sail on to victory
And sink their bones to Davy Jones, hooray!

[Bridge]
Yo ho there shipmate
Take the fighting to the far off seas
Yo ho there messmate
Hear the wailing of the wild banshees
All hands, fire brands
Let's Blast them as we go. So
Anchors Aweigh, my boys, Anchors Aweigh.
Farewell to college joys, We sail at break of day, of day.
Through our last night on shore, Drink to the foam,
Until we meet once more. Here's wishing you a happy voyage home!

# SEA BATTLE: THE BATTLE OF
# THE NILE, 1798

In 1798 General Napoleon Bonaparte proposed a bizarre scheme to invade Egypt, as a means of threatening British control over India. Surprisingly the Revolutionary Directory in Paris approved the idea, possibly as a means of ridding themselves of the pushy young general. Consequently some 40,000 French troops were sent to Toulon, where the French fleet waited to escort them to Egypt. Bonaparte was lucky. A storm drove the British blockading fleet from the coast, allowing Admiral Brueys to sail from Toulon without being detected. The fleet sailed to Malta, where Bonaparte paused to capture the island before ordering Brueys to continue on towards Egypt. When he learned that the expedition had sailed, Lord St Vincent, commanding the British Mediterranean fleet, sent the newly promoted Rear Admiral Nelson in pursuit, at the head of a squadron of 14 ships-of-the-line.

Thanks to the secrecy surrounding the departure the British had no real idea where the French were heading, but Nelson eventually picked up the trail, and followed them eastwards. In early July the French landed near Alexandria, then captured the city. Admiral Brueys decided not to anchor in the port, which was poorly defended, but moved his fleet 13 miles (24km) to the east, and anchored in Aboukir Bay, under the guns of a captured Turkish fortress. His 13 ships-of-the-line were anchored in a line parallel to the shore. Brueys' four frigates and other smaller warships anchored between the main line and the beach. This meant that all of Brueys' ships-of-the-line had their guns trained on the wide entrance to the bay. The French flagship *L'Orient* was anchored in the centre of the French line.

Nelson had searched in vain for the French fleet for almost four months. Then, on 1 August, a British frigate spotted the French transports in Alexandria harbour. Later that day another frigate looked into Aboukir Bay, and sighted the main French fleet. Nelson set a course for the anchorage, and arrived off the entrance to the bay a little after 1600hrs. Although Admiral Brueys had had weeks to prepare for the encounter he was taken by surprise, and over 3,000 French sailors were on shore, refilling water casks, when the British appeared. The French admiral ordered his ships to prepare for battle, but as he didn't expect the British to attack until the following morning, his ships remained where they were.

However, Nelson was no ordinary commander, and he had no intention of delaying the coming battle. He decided to launch an immediate attack. His plan was to concentrate his fleet against the front of the French line, then to work his way down its length, overpowering each anchored ship in turn. As the sun was setting around 1830hrs, the British rounded the shoal waters protecting the western edge of the bay and closed with the enemy. HMS *Culloden* (74 guns) ran aground, but the rest continued on, ignoring the fire from the French ships and the fort. Captain Foley in the leading ship HMS *Goliath* (74 guns) passed the bow of the French Third Rate *Guerrier*, followed by four more Third Rates, each of which raked the hapless *Guerrier* as they passed.

Nelson in the *Vanguard* led the rest of his squadron towards the *Spartiate* – the third ship in the French line – before turning to sail parallel to the French battle line. This meant that British ships were now passing the leading French ships on two sides. The French crews fought with incredible bravery, but the odds were against them. Under fire from both sides, the *Guerrier*, *Conquérant* and *Spartiate* were all battered into submission one after the other, and they hauled down their colours. HMS *Bellerophon* took on *L'Orient*, but Brueys' flagship pummelled the British 74-gun warship, dismasting her, and forcing her to pull back from the fight. Still, this was an isolated success. By 2100hrs, the French vanguard had been overrun, even though the rest of the line were still holding their own. The *Peuple Souverain* cut her anchor cables and drifted out of the line, and the 50-gun HMS *Leander* moved into the vacant space, anchoring and firing broadsides into the *Aquelon* and *Franklin* – the two French ships to either side of her.

The fighting raged on. By that time *L'Orient* was on fire, having been engaged by HMS *Alexander* and HMS *Swiftsure*. Then shortly after 2200hrs the French flagship blew up – a colossal explosion that sent masts, guns and crewmen hundreds of feet in the air. Barely a hundred of her 1,000-man crew survived the catastrophe, and the already mortally wounded Admiral Brueys was lost along with his flagship – and his fleet. By that stage the battle was all but over. Of the 13 French ships-of-the-line only two – the *Guillaume Tell* and the *Généreux* – managed to escape, accompanied by two frigates. *L'Orient* and two other ships-of-the-line were beached and burned to the waterline, and the rest of the French fleet was captured.

This was a spectacular victory, and one that made Nelson a national hero. For a mere 218 British dead, he had captured a fleet in a dangerous and somewhat reckless night action, fought at point-blank range. As Nelson himself put it, 'Victory is not a name strong enough for such a scene.' Without his fleet, General Bonaparte's army was stranded in Egypt. Without setting foot ashore Nelson had decided the fate of the French expedition to the Orient, and given the young Napoleon Bonaparte a spectacular lesson in naval seapower.

# THE EVACUATION OF DUNKIRK – A MIRACLE OF PLANNING

In May 1940 the German Army unleashed its Blitzkrieg on France and the Low Countries. German tanks poured through Northern France and Belgium, throwing the French, Belgian and British allies into disarray. Within a week the Netherlands had fallen, Belgium had been all but overrun, and the French and British were in full retreat. The bulk of the British Expeditionary Force

(BEF) headed towards the ports of the English Channel – mainly Calais, Dunkirk and Boulogne. The army was in disarray, discipline was in danger of crumbling, and a military disaster was looming.

On 20 May, Admiral Bertram Ramsay held a meeting in his headquarters beneath Dover Castle. As the commander of Royal Navy forces in the English Channel, it was his responsibility to keep the sea lanes open, either to supply the army with what it needed, or, in the event of a disaster, to spirit the soldiers to safety in Britain. He asked his staff to make plans for a possible troop evacuation. It was felt that given the available resources, the Royal Navy could evacuate 10,000 men a day from each of the three ports. Unfortunately, the situation was deteriorating fast. The following day the spearhead of the German Panzers reached the English Channel near Abbéville, and the bulk of the BEF found itself cut off from the French, with its backs to the Channel.

Ramsay ordered his staff to make a list of civilian ships which could be pressed into service to ferry troops to safety. Then, on 22 May, the Germans entered Boulogne. Only a handful of soldiers had been picked up by destroyers before the port fell. Calais was besieged the same day, and surrendered four days later. That left Dunkirk. By 26 May, almost a third of a million Allied troops were inside the shrinking Dunkirk perimeter, while the Germans seemed to be massing their forces for a last great push. Meanwhile 40 miles (70km) away in Dover, Ramsay ordered his staff to scour the south coast of England, rounding up anything that could float. It was clear that the evacuation would take every last resource Ramsay and the British government could muster. The evacuation was to be codenamed 'Operation *Dynamo*', after the former engine room built into the cliffs beneath Dover Castle, where the admiral had his headquarters.

Until then, only non-essential personnel were evacuated, but on the 26th the embarkation began in earnest. Still, only 7,000 soldiers were rescued. It was all taking too long. Ramsay fully expected the

Germans to capture the port in a day or two. In the end he was granted a reprieve. Although the Germans shelled the beaches, and the evacuation craft were subject to near-constant air attacks, the long-awaited attack never materialized. Instead, Ramsay had ten vital days to work a miracle.

First, he pressed into service every warship he could, from fleet destroyers to minesweepers and tugs. Then there were his 'little ships' – the civilian craft he gathered and sent over to help the evacuation. They included liners, freighters, tramp steamers, cross-Channel ferries, fishing boats and private pleasure craft. This flotilla of little ships played a vital role in the evacuation, as many of these smaller vessels could lift troops straight off the beaches, rather than use the battered and crowded harbour at Dunkirk.

On 27 May almost 8,000 men were evacuated, and the following day the total climbed by almost 10,000. On 29 May the little ships began arriving, and that day's total was an impressive 47,000. Another 120,000 men were rescued over the next two days, by which time most of the BEF had been extracted. That left the French rearguard, and almost 120,000 more troops – mostly French – were evacuated over the next four days. That meant that between 26 May and 4 June, Ramsay's ships managed to evacuate 338,226 soldiers – of whom almost 200,000 were British, and the rest French.

The cost, though, was high. Dozens of ships were sunk by German aircraft, including nine Allied destroyers. Over 200 other craft were sunk, ranking from liners to small motor boats. However, the army was saved – and was able to re-equip itself, and prepare to meet an invasion which never came. Sir Winston Churchill dubbed Operation *Dynamo* a miracle, and the press referred to Dunkirk more as a triumph than as a defeat. However, Admiral Cunningham gave a far more balanced assessment. He said that if there was a miracle of Dunkirk, it was one created by Admiral Ramsay and his staff – a miracle of improvisation, planning and hard work.

# THE WORLD'S GREATEST NAVAL BASES

Over the centuries the fortunes of nations and their navies ebbed and flowed, as did the nature of naval warfare. A place that served as a major naval base in one war was not necessarily so important in another later conflict. However, the following ten naval bases were all of great strategic importance at a particular stage in history, and many of them are still in use today. They are offered here in a chronological sequence rather than according to geographical importance.

**Carthage (Tunisia):** At the start of the Punic Wars in the 4th century BC the Carthaginians maintained a powerful fleet, based in a special naval harbour close to the city. The remains of these remarkable shipyards and covered docks can still be seen today.

**Athens (Greece):** During the 3rd and 2nd centuries BC the Athenian Navy was the most powerful fleet in the Ancient World. Its main shipyards were actually at Piraeus, which was linked to the city of Athens by long, high defensive walls.

**Venice (Italy):** As the naval superpower of the Mediterranean Sea during the Medieval and early Renaissance periods, the Venetians built and maintained a powerful fleet of galleys. These were built, housed and repaired in a sprawling shipyard on the eastern side of the island city.

**Portsmouth (Great Britain):** This great naval port served as the principal base of the Royal Navy throughout the age of fighting sail, from the 17th century until the 19th century. Together with the fleet anchorage of Spithead, Portsmouth served as the base of the Channel Fleet during Britain's many wars with France in the 18th and early 19th centuries. It still remains in use today, serving both as a repository of historic warships and as a working dockyard.

**Toulon (France):** Like Brest and Cherbourg on the French coast of the English Channel and Atlantic Ocean, Toulon was a major naval base – the home of the French Mediterranean fleet. However, of the three, Toulon was the largest and most important, and it was from here that the French fleet sailed out to do battle with its foes during the age of fighting sail. It remained an important French naval base during the 19th and 20th centuries, and it is still in use today.

**Scapa Flow (Great Britain):** This great natural harbour in the Orkney Islands served as the Royal Navy's principal naval base in Home Waters during both the First and the Second World War. It was from Scapa that the Grand Fleet sailed out to do battle with the Germans at Jutland (1916), and to hunt down the *Bismarck* (1941) and *Scharnhorst* (1943). After each war the base was decommissioned, and the anchorage was abandoned.

**Pearl Harbor (Hawaii, USA):** During the Second World War the main base of the US Pacific Fleet was here, on the island of Oahu in Hawaii. Although the base was first established shortly after the annexation of the islands in 1893, it only really developed into a major naval port during the 1930s. It was here that the US Pacific Fleet was attacked by the Japanese as it lay at anchor on 7 December 1941, an unprovoked assault that plunged the United States into the Second World War. Pearl Harbor still remains a major naval base, and home of the US Pacific Fleet.

**Truk (Pacific Ocean):** During the Second World War, Truk Lagoon served as the principal forward base for the Imperial Japanese Navy. The lagoon provided the Japanese with a relatively safe anchorage, and it was from here that the fleet waged its war against the US Navy in the South and Central Pacific. However, in February 1944 Truk was attacked by American aircraft, and the Japanese withdrew their exposed warships. Today the lagoon is a paradise for divers, as it remains littered with the wrecks of Japanese warships.

**Murmansk (Russia):** The Soviet naval base at Murmansk in northern Russia first came into prominence during the Second World War, where it served as the destination for many of the Arctic convoys. During the Cold War, Murmansk, or rather its satellite bases at Severomorsk, Sevmorput and Polyarni, became the home of the Soviet Northern Fleet, and the principal submarine base of the post-war Soviet Navy. In effect it was the very epicentre of the Cold War. Since the collapse of the former Soviet Union Murmansk has become a naval backwater, and home to an ageing fleet of mothballed nuclear submarines.

**Norfolk (USA):** The US Navy's principal Atlantic base, Norfolk, Virginia, has been an important naval base since before the American Civil War. In Confederate hands it was where the CSS *Virginia* was built – the warship that fought the USS *Monitor* in the duel between ironclad warships. Norfolk Naval Base reached its peak during the Second World War, both as a base and as a shipyard and a place where Allied warships could be repaired. Today it is the home of the US Fleet Forces Command, which supervises US Navy operations in the Atlantic, the Mediterranean, the Indian Ocean and the Persian Gulf.

# NAVAL DISASTER: THE SINKING OF THE *MARY ROSE*

The story of the sinking of the *Mary Rose* has all the hallmarks of a Shakespearean tragedy. In 1545 England and France were once again at war, and the Tudor kingdom was threatened with invasion. In mid-July a French fleet under the command of Admiral Claude d'Annebault appeared in the Solent and began preparations to land troops. The English fleet under Viscount Lisle was in Portsmouth harbour, and Henry VIII arrived to muster an army and watch the ensuing naval battle. On 19 July the Tudor fleet of around 100 ships sailed out to give battle.

They were outnumbered, but the fleet had confidence in their ships and their firepower. As befitted their rank as flagships, the first warships out of the narrow harbour entrance were the *Mary Rose* and the *Henri Grace à Dieu*. Early that morning the French admiral had sent a squadron of French galleys forward to probe the harbour entrance, and they began bombarding the fleet at long range. It has been suggested this goaded Viscount Lisle into making a sortie, but in truth the move had been planned the night before. However, nobody expected what happened next.

Without any warning the *Mary Rose* began to heel over and sink. The French gunners probably imagined they had scored some lucky hit, but the reason was far more prosaic. The great warship had heeled over in the wind as she emerged from the harbour entrance. This could have easily been corrected, but instead the heel to starboard increased – probably due to some small error in seamanship on the part of her helmsman as he concentrated on steering toward the enemy rather than compensating for the wind. There is archaeological evidence that the ballast in her hold shifted, which would have aggravated the problem.

The whole process might well have gone on for several minutes, as the crew fought to bring the ship under control. The largely inexperienced crew might well have panicked. The commander of a passing ship hailed Sir George Carew of the *Mary Rose*, and asked him what the problem was. Carew shouted back that he, 'had the sort of knaves whome he could not rule'. The ship continued to list further over, and eventually this brought her lower gunports in line with the water. Naturally the gunports were open because the ship was about to engage the French in battle. The sea began to pour in.

The crew didn't have a chance. Anti-boarding netting had been stretched over her waist to prevent the French from clambering on board. It now prevented the crew from escaping. The cold waters of the Solent flooded into her hull, and she sank within minutes, taking almost all of her crew of 700 men and boys down with her.

Henry VIII had watched the disaster from the safety of Southsea Castle, and together with the thousands of other onlookers he could do nothing but watch in horror as his great warship slipped beneath the waves. Soon only her masts remained, surrounded by a cluster of floating debris and a few lucky survivors. Although there were a few half-hearted attempts to salvage her in the months that followed, after her masts and sails were removed she was left in peace for the best part of three centuries.

# THE SMASHING CARRONADE

Until the late 18th century, all naval guns were fairly similar – the only difference were the size of the piece, and the fact that some were cast from bronze, and others made from cast-iron. A gun used on board a warship during the Seven Years War (1756–62) was virtually the same as one which had seen service on board an Elizabethan warship during the late 16th century. Then, in 1779, a revolutionary new type of naval gun began to enter service.

This new weapon was called the carronade, named after the Carron Company's ironworks in Falkirk, Scotland, where the guns were produced. These weapons were much shorter and lighter than conventional long guns, and due to their low muzzle velocity they were only effective at short range. However, they packed an incredible punch, and were nicknamed 'smashers' by the Royal Navy. They were first developed by Charles Gascoigne (1738–1806), the manager of the Falkirk ironworks. However, the idea behind them came from a retired Scottish soldier, Brigadier Robert Melville (1723–1809).

In 1771 Melville designed a prototype of the weapon, which he called a 'Melvillade'. He in turn based his new gun on short-barrelled weapons which had been designed for service on board merchant ships during the mid to late 18th century. These guns could be operated by a much smaller crew than a conventional piece of ordnance, which made them perfectly suited for the merchant service. However, the guns designed by Gascoigne were exclusively meant for the Royal Navy. He saw them as a battle-winning weapon which could give British warships a decisive advantage over their foes. Unfortunately the Navy didn't seem interested in them, so he modified his design, and sold them to private buyers, the first ones being sold in 1769. Part of the reason for the Navy's hesitancy was the Carron Company itself, which had developed a reputation for poor-quality guns. They ignored the fact that Gascoigne had greatly improved the quality of the guns his company produced. In fact, the reputation of the company was so bad that in 1773 the Admiralty cancelled all its contracts with the Carron Company, and removed its guns from their ships.

During the American War of Independence (1775–83) the mercantile short guns designed by Gascoigne proved their worth, helping to defend British merchant ships against attacks by American and French privateers. These early pieces were called 'Gascognades', but by 1780 the term 'carronade' was generally adopted. In 1779 the Admiralty reluctantly agreed to buy a few sample carronades to evaluate their performance. Gascoigne supplied them with his powerful naval guns – larger and more potent than their mercantile equivalents. The Navy were impressed, and an order was placed for more. The weapons were officially introduced into service later that year.

The guns were certainly revolutionary. They saved weight by having a very short barrel, and a large bore – thanks to the low velocity of the guns there wasn't the need to strengthen the barrels in the way conventional long guns were reinforced – which saved even more weight. Typically, a carronade was around a third of the weight of a long gun of the same calibre. Of course, they had their disadvantages. The most significant shortcoming was their range – less than a third of that of a conventional long gun. Another disadvantage was that it was considered more fragile than a conventional gun, and the carriage was more easily overturned by enemy shot when in action. However, this was more than compensated for by its power. As a low velocity 'smashing' weapon it had no equal, and at the short ranges at which the British preferred to fight their sea battles, its short range was less of a drawback than the advantage of its weight of shot.

Part of the carronades' secret lay in their mounting. The guns sat on a small carriage, which was attached to the side of the hull by a pivoting pin. The carriage was also fitted with rollers, which made it easy to traverse. Instead of conventional trunnions, the barrel was fixed to its carriage by a cast-on lug, which was bolted in place. The carronade was elevated using a screw, which made it simple to operate. They could be used to fire roundshot designed to smash open an enemy hull, or grapeshot, used to shred an enemy's crew. During the battle of Trafalgar (1805) HMS *Victory* loaded her two 68-pdr carronades with grapeshot, and fired them repeatedly through the stern windows of the French warship *Bucentaure*. As each grapeshot canister contained 500 musket balls, each shot was the equivalent of a full volley from a battalion of infantry. These two guns caused havoc on the gun decks of the French vessel.

The carronade was soon adopted as a quarterdeck and forecastle armament on board most British ships-of-the-line. During the decades that followed a range of different carronade types were used, corresponding to the main calibres of naval guns in British service (12, 18, 24 and 32-pdrs). During the French Revolutionary and Napoleonic wars, a 42-pdr carronade entered service, and production culminated in the devastatingly powerful 68-pdrs, which were carried on board First Rate ships-of-the-line such as HMS *Victory*.

The carronade remained in service until the 1850s. The trouble with carronades was that they were too successful. Although the first warships to employ them did so with great effect, the enemy soon learned to keep their distance. Worse, rival navies such as the French, the Spanish and the Americans all developed their own equivalents. Even Russia introduced carronades, when Gascoigne became a gunnery advisor to the Tsar. As everyone had carronades, then nobody had a battle-winning advantage. Still, a few carronades were used on board most British warships until the introduction of a reliable shell gun in the late 1840s, which effectively rendered them obsolete.

# THE FIRST DREADNOUGHT

During the late 19th century, considerable advances had been made in naval gunnery and warship design. Steam propulsion, armoured hulls, breech-loading guns and armour-piercing shells had all transformed the appearance of major warships, and by 1900 most battleships carried a powerful armament of four heavy guns, mounted in two twin turrets. A typical warship of this era was HMS *King Edward VII*, which was launched in 1903. She was armed with four 12in, four 9.2in and ten 6in guns. In theory, this made her one of the most powerful battleships afloat. Unfortunately, by the time she entered service in early 1905, she was about to be rendered obsolete.

By then, work had already begun on a battleship which was not only fast and well armoured, but also carried two and a half times her armament (instead of four guns she carried ten). More importantly, these guns were capable of being fired with much greater accuracy. This new and deadly efficient warship was the brainchild of Sir John 'Jackie' Fisher (1841–1920), who became the First Sea Lord in 1904, a post he held until he retired in 1911. Fisher was an advocate of the big gun – arming battleships with the largest and most effective ordnance available, and augmenting this firepower by accurate fire control. In other words he saw naval gunnery as a balance between range, accuracy, shell size and rate of fire, and he saw it as his mission to transform the Royal Navy, by building warships designed around these big guns. He was also a supporter of other technical innovations, including the steam turbine, the use of fuel oil rather than coal, and even the use of submarines and torpedoes, which had long been deemed too ungentlemanly for the Navy.

Fisher was lucky enough to have an ally who shared his enthusiasm for technological progress. In 1902, Sir Philip Watts (1846–1926) became the Director of Naval Construction, and like Fisher he believed that the future lay in battleships which were dramatically faster and better armed than current designs. Before 1904 his suggestions were rejected by a conservative Admiralty who had no desire to make their existing battlefleet redundant. However, once Fisher took over this changed, and the two men embarked on a project which would revolutionize naval warfare.

Fisher and Watts favoured a battleship that carried multiple turrets of big guns, with armour which was proof against other capital ships, and whose modern turbine-powered engines meant that she was faster than her rivals. The two men were spurred on by developments in America and Japan, where naval designers were already working on similarly ambitious projects such as plans for the South Carolina and Satsuma Class battleships. It was clear to Fisher that unless action was taken, then the Royal Navy could lose its numerical and technological edge over its naval rivals. Reluctantly the Admiralty agreed to commission a new battleship, designed by Watts. The result was HMS *Dreadnought* – a warship which was so revolutionary that her very name gave rise to a type of warship – the 'dreadnought'.

HMS *Dreadnought* was laid down in Portsmouth Dockyard in October 1905, and was completed in a record-breaking 14 months, a whole two years before her foreign rivals. This great 18,000-ton battleship wasn't much bigger than existing battleships. However, she was armed with ten 12in guns, mounted in five twin turrets. This gave her a firepower larger than two battleships of the King Edward VII Class, and that wasn't taking into account her more accurate gunnery direction system. As a result these earlier designs were rendered obsolete virtually overnight, and were soon given the collective and somewhat derisory name of 'pre-dreadnoughts'. The future of naval warfare clearly lay in the *Dreadnought*, and ships like her.

Her propulsion system was almost as revolutionary as her armament. She was powered by a combination of boilers and turbines, and although these were coal-fired, they represented a significant technological advance over previous warships. It also made her significantly faster. The *Dreadnought* had a top speed of 21 knots (38.9km/h) – 3 knots (5.6km/h) faster than the *King Edward VII*. While this mightn't seem like much, it made her the fastest battleship in the world.

Of course the emergence of HMS *Dreadnought* meant that all existing battlefleets became obsolete. Warships like the brand new HMS *King Edward VII* were rendered almost worthless. All of the world's navies faced the same problem, but it was Britain, with the largest battlefleet in the world, which had the most to lose from this overturning of the naval status quo. As a result, the government had little option but to pour vast sums of money into building up a new battlefleet, this time one consisting of dreadnought battleships. Other navies followed suit, and this led directly to a naval arms race between Britain and Germany – a race that became a contributing factor in the outbreak of the First World War.

# THE TEN MOST USEFUL NAVAL KNOTS

Even in this age of nuclear-powered aircraft carriers, ballistic-missile carrying submarines and computer-operated weapon systems, the sailors of the world still have a need to use ropes, and to tie knots. An essential part of seamanship, knot-tying remains an important element in naval training. According to the Royal Navy, the US Navy and the Royal Canadian Navy, the following ten knots are considered the most important. Any sailor worth his or her salt should be able to tie any of these in the dark.

**Reef knot:** The basic knot used to join together two ropes of similar thickness.
**Figure-of-eight knot:** This stops a rope from running through an eye or a block.

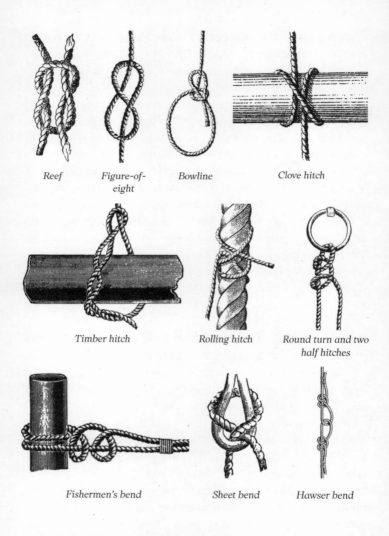

Reef     Figure-of-eight     Bowline     Clove hitch

Timber hitch     Rolling hitch     Round turn and two half hitches

Fishermen's bend     Sheet bend     Hawser bend

**Bowline:** This is used to make a temporary loop or eye in a rope, for instance when it is used as a lifeline. The knot doesn't slip. A variant is the running bowline, which is designed to slip and tighten if pulled.

**Clove hitch:** Used to secure a rope to a spar or rail. This knot has many other uses, but it will slip along a rail or spar if it is pulled from the side.

**Timber hitch:** This is used to secure the end of a rope to a spar, or a cargo such as a sack. Sometimes it can be used in conjunction with a half hitch, when the user wants to tow, hoist or lower a spar. A half hitch is simply a loop of rope passed around a spar.

**Rolling hitch:** used to secure a rope to a spar when the pull is expected to be from one side or the other.

**Round turn and two half hitches:** Used to secure a heavy load to a ring or shackle. It can also be released quickly.

**Fishermen's bend:** An alternative to a round turn and two half hitches, this is often used to secure a rope or a hawser to the ring of an anchor. It isn't easily undone, and becomes tighter if pulled.

**Sheet bend:** This is used to secure the end of a rope to a small eye or ring, such as the painter of a small boat to the end of a boat boom. A more complex version is the double sheet bend, which is also a more secure knot.

**Hawser bend:** the most common knot used to join two steel or rope hawsers together, this is in effect two interlinked bowlines. The ends of the ropes are usually seized or tied to the standing part of the rope.

# PROFILE OF A WARSHIP: THE *CONSTANT WARWICK*

In the mid-17th century, there was no type of warship that bridged the gap between the larger men-of-war and the smaller, lighter warships that acted as scouting vessels or message carriers. In the 1620s, the waters of the English Channel were plagued by pirates and privateers, so the Admiralty considered creating a new type of warship, which could counter the problem. Its first solution was to build ten patrol ships, but they proved too slow and cumbersome to do what was expected of them. The designers went back to the drawing board, and this time they came up with a ship which was more like a conventional small man-of-war, only a lot sleeker.

The typical sailing warship of the mid-17th century had a length to beam ratio of around 3 or 3½ to 1. In effect, they were little more than improved versions of the Elizabethan galleons which had performed so well during the Spanish Armada campaign of 1588. This new type of warship would be a lot sleeker, with a ratio of 4 to 1 or even greater. The first of them was the *Constant Warwick*, which entered service in 1646, during the dying months of the English Civil War. She was named after Richard, Earl of Warwick, who had commanded the English fleet, which had sided with the Parliamentarian cause during the conflict. She had a 90ft (27m) keel, a beam of 28ft (8.5m) and a draught of 12ft (3.7m). This revolutionary new vessel was the first of a whole new breed of warship – the frigate.

The *Constant Warwick* was much narrower than conventional warships, and had a shallower draught, which made her less stable as a gun platform, but much more speedy and agile. A second frigate – the *Adventure* – entered the service of Parliament later that same year. Unfortunately, the Admiralty seemed unable to avoid tampering with these highly successful new warships. Both were turned into two-deckers, and more guns were added. Consequently, after being the fastest large warship in the English fleet, the *Constant Warwick* found herself described by a contemporary as 'a slug'.

Fortunately, the sleekness of these first frigates provided an inspiration for more warships, and during the Cromwellian period (1649–59) several fast new frigates entered service with the Commonwealth Navy. By the early 18th century the frigate had become an essential part of all the major navies, characterized by being three masted and ship-rigged, with sleek, fast lines, and a powerful main armament carried on a single gundeck.

# ROUNDSHOT, CHAINSHOT AND GRAPESHOT

During the age of fighting sail, warships fired several different types of shot, each of which had its own deadly function. The most common type of projectile was the roundshot – a solid sphere of cast-iron – the type of shot known colloquially as a cannon ball. Technically, a cannon was a type of gun, so naval gunners preferred to describe the projectile by its appearance. During this period guns were classified by the weight of shot they could fire – a 12-pdr, an 18-pdr, a 32-pdr and so on.

These were essentially anti-ship rounds, designed to strike the hull of an enemy vessel, punch through its wooden sides and disable guns, smash their crews and damage other vital parts of the ship. Usually, only one such round was fired from a gun at any one time, although the double-shotting of guns was common for the first discharge of a battle, for extra punch. Sometimes heated shot was used by shore batteries in an effort to set enemy ships on fire. This was simply roundshot heated in a furnace, then placed down the barrel of the gun.

Grapeshot or canister rounds were used when a captain decided to target an enemy crew rather than the ship itself. Although the range of these projectiles was less than half that of roundshot, they could devastate a crew massing to board another ship if fired at point-blank range, scattering a hail of little musket balls or metal fragments into the enemy ranks. Like roundshot, these could be fired by conventional long guns, or by carronades. Grapeshot was often clustered together around a central wooden core, and placed in a canvas bag. The bag and the wooden core were destroyed when the round was fired, leaving the grapeshot to spread out slightly, and so cover a wide swathe of the enemy's deck. Canister shot was similar, except that the musket balls were held in a metal canister, which ripped open when the gun was fired. These projectiles could be extremely deadly, particularly if they were fired over the upper decks of an enemy warship. Whole boarding parties or gun crews would be swept away by this shower of small and lethal iron or lead balls.

A less commonly used type of projectile was chainshot. This was used when the rigging of an enemy ship was targetted rather than the hull. If an enemy sailing ship was immobilized, it was helpless, as the firing ship could manoeuvre so it could fire on the target, but remain out of the enemy's own arc of fire. Chainshot and barshot were specifically designed to damage rigging by scything through ropes, sails and even masts. A round of chain shot usually consisted of two half spheres – essentially half roundshot, joined together by a length of chain about a foot (30cm) long. Barshot worked on a similar principle, only instead of using chain, the two half spheres were joined together by an iron rod.

Captains or sometimes fleet commanders decided what ammunition to use in any particular circumstance. After that it was down to the skill of the gun crews. On board a typical British ship-of-the-line of the Napoleonic Wars, a well-trained crew could fire and reload their guns once every two minutes, a rate of fire which their French and Spanish counterparts were usually unable to match.

# PASSING THE PORT AND OTHER WARDROOM ETIQUETTE

In the Royal Navy, things are done a little differently from the Army, the Air Force or the other navies of the world. Centuries of tradition and circumstance have created a wardroom etiquette which is almost unique to the British Senior Service. Actually, the key word is 'almost', as many other navies – particularly those from Commonwealth countries – have adopted some if not all of these. Other navies such as the US Navy and the Canadian Navy have adopted their own forms of wardroom etiquette, but many of the same rules apply, whichever navy you might serve in. The wardroom is the place where officers eat their meals, relax and mingle at the end of their watch or working day. Given the fact that many of these officers have to share the same living quarters for extended periods, some form of wardroom etiquette is essential. Here are a few examples.

- Caps (covers in the US Navy) are never worn in a wardroom. Wearing one will usually lead to the culprit buying a round of drinks for his fellow officers. In the US Navy – a dry service – this round is bought at the ship's next port of call.

- Captains and flag officers dine alone, which leaves the first lieutenant (or executive officer – XO) as the senior member of the wardroom. He usually sits at the head of the table. The Royal Navy and the Canadian Navy remain fairly informal, but in the US Navy your place at the table is dictated by rank, with the more junior officers sitting at the far end of the table from the XO.

- Conversation is usually kept general and non-controversial. 'Talking shop' is usually frowned upon in the wardroom, as is the discussion of religion, sex or politics.

- On board Royal Navy or Canadian Navy warships, toasts – even a toast to the reigning monarch – are drunk sitting down. This comes from the days of the sailing navy, where there was often insufficient headroom to drink a toast standing up. The first lieutenant would propose the toast – 'Gentlemen, the Queen', and the officers would reply 'The Queen' before sipping their port. In the days of the sailing navy, toasts were a daily occurrence, with a different one for each day of the week. These usually went as follows:
Monday: 'Our ships at sea'
Tuesday: 'Our men'
Wednesday: 'Ourselves' (as nobody else cares)

Thursday: 'A bloody war or a sickly season' (to encourage
   promotion)
Friday: 'A willing foe and sea room'
Saturday: 'Sweethearts and wives' (may they never meet)
Sunday: 'Absent friends'

Port or wine is passed clockwise from the first lieutenant's place, after being placed in front of him by the wardroom steward. It should never be raised from the table unless the port is actually being poured into a glass. Passing it the wrong way leads to another round being bought by the miscreant.

In most navies, due to the watch system, lunch and often dinner is considered a running meal, with no formal starting and finishing times. There is no need to stand up if joined by a senior officer, or wait for a neighbour to finish their meal before leaving the table. Everything is designed to fit around the routine of the ship, not to enforce unnecessary regulations on the officers.

Dress is usually smart – the uniform of the day being acceptable if watchkeeping precludes the opportunity to dress for dinner.

Drinking is permitted in most navies apart from the US Navy, but it is generally discouraged when at sea. Drinks are never paid for, but signed for on bar chits, which are deducted from the officer's pay or paid by cheque at the end of the month. Guests to the wardroom are made welcome by everyone, and aren't allowed to buy their own drinks. Otherwise, buying drinks for others is discouraged – buying 'rounds' is frowned upon.

In more formal times, junior officers never spoke to more senior officers unless spoken to. While things have changed since these days, guests at the Captain's table are generally expected to let him lead the conversation, rather than initiate their own.

# FIGHTING ADMIRAL: MICHAEL DE RUYTER

On the waterfront of Flushing in Holland stands an imposing statue to a 17th-century admiral – Michael Anfrienzoon de Ruyter (1607–76). He glares across the North Sea towards the shores of England, as if he still wants to lead a fleet in action against his old enemy. After all, it was De Ruyter who humiliated the Royal Navy in its own waters, and who remains its most accomplished historical opponent. De Ruyter was born in Flushing, and went to sea as a teenager, serving as a merchant seaman. For much of this time Holland was at war with Spain, but a lengthy truce gave the Dutch breathing space, and they used the time well. They built up a formidable fleet, and many of their larger merchant ships – particularly the Dutch East Indiamen – were designed to double up as warships in time of war.

By 1641 De Ruyter had become a well-respected merchant captain, who had also demonstrated his abilities in action. It was then that he was given his first naval fleet command – a powerful Dutch squadron from Zeeland that fought alongside the Portuguese, who had rebelled against their Spanish overlords. He distinguished himself, but on his return he went back to his former life as a merchant captain.

He was called to serve his country again in 1652, at the start of the First Anglo-Dutch War (1652–54). De Ruyter's first mission was to escort a homeward bound East Indies convoy through the English Channel. He performed well, and in August he fought off an attacking English squadron during a running battle fought in the western approaches to the Channel. He then joined up with the main Dutch fleet, commanded by Admiral de With. He distinguished himself during the battle of Kentish Knock in October, when he defeated a larger English fleet in an evenly-matched engagement. In the following spring he went on to fight alongside Admiral Tromp during the bruising three-day battle of Portland. By now, De Ruyter was seen as a highly accomplished naval commander, and a possible contender for the job of fleet commander. Unfortunately for him, the Dutch lost the battle of Scheveningen, fought off the Dutch coast in August 1653, and his flagship *Law* was so badly battered she had to be towed back into port, her survivors manning the pumps to keep her afloat.

Although Cromwell's Navy won the war, the reasons the war was fought in the first place hadn't been resolved. The English remained the main economic rivals of the Dutch, and English ports were still barred to Dutch merchant ships. Despite a decade of peace, everyone realized that another war was all but inevitable. Meanwhile, De Ruyter continued to impress. He spent a year fighting the Barbary Pirates in the Mediterranean, and then he led a Dutch fleet into the Baltic to support the Dutch in a war against the Swedes. He returned to the Mediterranean in the early 1660s, and his squadrons ranged as far afield as the West African coast and the Caribbean, protecting Dutch trade and showing the flag.

He was in the West Indies when the Second Dutch War (1665–67) began. That meant that he was well placed to attack the poorly defended English colonies in the Americas. After a failed assault on Barbados, he concentrated on snapping up English ships. He caused mayhem in the Caribbean that spring, before returning home with dozens of prize ships following in his wake. He was just in time. The Dutch gave him command of the fleet, and sent him to seek revenge for Holland's defeat a decade before. His first fleet action was the epic Four Days Battle, fought off the Thames Estuary in June 1666. Despite inflicting heavy casualties on the English, his larger fleet failed to win a spectacular victory, and the battle ended in a stalemate. The English even claimed it as a moral victory. Less than two months later, in late July the two fleets met again, in the St James' Day Fight. This time it was the English who were the clear winners, largely because De Ruyter's subordinate failed to support the main fleet. As a result the Dutch were forced back into port, with the loss of 20 ships. De Ruyter, though, was bloodied, but unbowed. He spent the winter planning bloody revenge.

That winter, Charles II ordered the bulk of his fleet to be laid up in the River Medway, to help preserve his ships. Peace negotiations were underway, and the English felt the war was about to come to an end. De Ruyter had other plans, and that spring he secretly prepared the Dutch fleet for action – a carefully planned raid, designed to end the war at a stroke. Therefore the English fleet was still in the Medway in June, when De Ruyter led his Dutch fleet to sea. He arrived off the Thames Estuary on 19 June, and while he sent a diversionary force to threaten the River Thames and London, he landed troops on the Isle of Sheppey. He then captured the fort and town of Sheerness at the mouth of the River Medway. With Sheerness in Dutch hands there was nothing to stop De Ruyter attacking the defenceless English fleet, which lay further up the river at Chatham.

On 22 June he broke the flimsy boom which had been laid across the river and fell upon the defenceless fleet. The triumphant Dutch captured or destroyed 16 of England's most powerful warships, and to add insult to injury De Ruyter towed the 90-gun fleet flagship *Royal Charles* back to Holland with him. It was a deeply humiliating defeat for the English – the result of complacency and incompetence. The English sued for peace, and the following month the Treaty of Breda was signed, whereby England lifted its ban on Dutch merchantmen.

War broke out again in 1672, and the ageing Dutch admiral commanded his national fleet during the indecisive battle of Sole Bay that summer. The minor Dutch victory at the battle of the Texel the following year was the last engagement of the war, as a peace treaty was signed shortly afterwards. In 1676 the ageing De Ruyter led a small Dutch fleet into the Mediterranean, where he defeated the French in a sea battle fought beneath the volcanic island of Stromboli, off the north coast of Sicily. However, De Ruyter was mortally wounded in his hour of victory, and he died a week later.

His death marked the end of an era. For most of the 17th century the Dutch had been a naval force to be reckoned with, and a maritime trading power without peer. By his death it was clear that Dutch mastery of the seas was passing, and soon either the English or the French would become the world's new naval superpower. Still, in all the naval battles of the age of fighting sail, where the British and the French vied for naval supremacy, nobody else inflicted a defeat on the Royal Navy which was anywhere near as decisive or as humiliating as De Ruyter's raid on the Medway. There is good reason why the Dutch still regard him as one of their great national heroes.

# PROFILE OF A WARSHIP: HMS *VICTORY*

In 1758, when Sir Thomas Slade was ordered to produce plans for a new First Rate ship-of-the-line to counter vessels being built by the French, he already knew exactly how she should look. It took him just six months to design the new warship, drawing on the experience he acquired designing 74-gun, Third Rate ships-of-the-line for the Navy. His earlier ships were regarded as the best Third Rates afloat. His new First Rate would be even more impressive – a battle-winning design – the perfect balance between firepower, manoeuvrability and reliability. He also took note of the latest shipbuilding ideas used on the continent of Europe, as both the French and the Spanish had a reputation for designing excellent warships. Another major influence was the *Royal George*, a successful First Rate launched in 1756. Slade's new design was therefore an amalgam of what went before, and an improvement on all these earlier warships. She would be called HMS *Victory*.

The *Victory*'s oak and elm keel was laid in June 1759, when the Seven Years War was at its height. The work would continue for another six years. First, her heavy frames were fitted, rising up from her keel like skeletal ribs. Then came the hull – two thick layers of oak, with a combined thickness of over 2ft (60cm). This made her hull impervious to all but the most powerful close-range shot. Below the waterline her hull was skinned in copper sheathing, as protection against the timber-eating *toredo* worm. A pronounced tumble-home (an inwardly cambered hull side) meant that she was a stable ship, which of course made her a steady gun platform, as well as a safe and comfortable ship to sail in.

Her hull was divided into five decks; the lower orlop (or overlap) deck was the lowest one, closest to the keel, and was where the ship's stores were kept. Next came the orlop deck, which held the ship's magazines, and her sick bay. Above that were two gun decks, running almost the whole length of the ship. These were called the lower gundeck and the middle gundeck, and were where the heaviest, most powerful guns were mounted. The upper gundeck above them was in effect the upper deck, although for the most part it was covered over by the superstructure of both the forecastle and the quarterdeck. The exposed waist of the main deck was covered by a spar deck, a series of beams designed to support the ship's boats. Finally the quarterdeck and forecastle contained even more guns – the smallest on the ship, which were exposed to the elements. The quarterdeck was the command area of the ship, where the captain and the admiral stood when the *Victory* sailed into action. As a First Rate, the *Victory* was designed as a flagship, with cabins and a set of stern windows for both the captain and an officer of flag rank.

The quarterdeck was also the spot where Vice-Admiral Lord Nelson was felled by a French musket shot during the closing stages of the battle of Trafalgar. Behind the quarterdeck was the much smaller poop deck, an open area surrounding the mizzen mast which was devoid of any guns. It provided a secluded gathering place for the ship's officers when the *Victory* wasn't in action.

*Victory*'s three masts – fore, main and mizzen – tower above her upper decks, and rise respectively 182, 205 and 152ft

(55.5, 62.5 and 46m) above the waterline. To the modern observer these masts, and the 37 miles (60 km) of running and standing rigging they support, appear incredibly complex. However, to the late 18th-century mariner they represented a logical and efficient means of propelling the great ship, using her suite of canvas sails.

The *Victory* was launched in 1765, but she wasn't fitted out completely because the war with France had ended. Instead she was 'mothballed' – kept in readiness – until 1777, when Britain and France were once again at war with each other. She was finally commissioned in March 1778, during the American War of Independence. The conflict ended in 1783, and from then until 1795 she served with the Channel Fleet. Then, from 1801 to 1803 she went back to the dockyard for a refit, during which she was almost rebuilt, and her appearance was altered to suit an even heavier armament, including the latest 68-pdr carronades – the most powerful naval close-range weapons of their day.

Large sailing ships of this period were probably the biggest and most complex manmade structures in existence at the time – a floating testimony to British seapower. Despite her size, the *Victory* managed a simplicity of operation and a grace of performance which made her every bit as fast and manoeuvrable as far smaller sailing ships of war. That demonstrated the true genius of Sir Thomas Slade, Surveyor of the Navy. Unfortunately, Slade died in 1771, so he never saw his greatest creation under sail. He would have been delighted. First Rates of the time were notoriously hard to sail, and they usually performed sluggishly. The *Victory* was an exception – a magnificent sailing vessel which had a top speed of eight knots in good weather, under full sail.

Of course, as well as being an excellent vessel, she was also the perfect floating gun battery. She carried a devastatingly powerful battery of guns, crewed by some of the best-trained seamen of the period. In the hands of a naval genius like Horatio Nelson, Slade's great floating masterpiece became a truly battle-winning weapon – the arbiter of victory in the naval war against Napoleon. Even more remarkably, HMS *Victory* is still afloat – and at least on paper, she remains the flagship of the Flag Officer Portsmouth. She is now moored in a dry dock inside Portsmouth Historic Dockyard, so that we can do what her designer never did, and gaze up at her rigging and bristling gunports before stepping aboard her. As soon as you step off the gangplank, you are transported back into the lost age of fighting sail – the world of Lord Nelson and Sir Thomas Slade.

# SEA SHANTIES AND SHIPBOARD MUSIC

Traditionally, sea shanties were sung on board both warships and merchant ships to help lighten the work involved in sailing the ship. They are usually divided into two groups – 'capstan shanties', designed to accompany the hard effort involved in heaving on the bars of the ship's capstan, and 'halyard shanties', where either the rhythm or the words were designed to help the men pull together, for instance when raising a sail or raising up a new spar to the masthead.

Most shanties follow the same pattern, with short verses and boisterous but repetitive choruses. Sometimes the lyrics were either made up as the seamen went along, or else improvised or repeated, especially if the task proved longer than the shanty. The words were often less important than the rhythm of the song, although some shanties such as 'Shenandoah' or 'Blow the Man Down' have become famous as songs in their own right. The first known shanties date from the mid-16th century, recorded in the *Complaynt of Scotland* (1549), but their origins probably lie much further back than that – in the earliest days of sail.

It has been argued that sea shanties were much more commonplace on merchant vessels than on warships, as the latter were comparatively well manned, so the labour involved in sailing the ship was less arduous. This theory isn't borne out by what we know about life in the sailing navies of the world. While shanties might have been less commonly used as working songs, they were widely sung as a means of recreation. Music was important on board a sailing man-of-war, and instruments such as fiddles, fifes and flutes were often played when sailors were off-duty. There are reports of sailors singing on board until ordered to their hammocks at 'pipe down', and then continuing to sing in their darkened berth. Dancing was also popular, and many captains encouraged it, as a way of keeping spirits high and of providing exercise.

Popular songs in the Royal Navy during the Napoleonic Wars were 'Nancy Dawson', 'Spanish Ladies' and 'Drops of Brandy'. Some ships carried an official band, and during the approach of the British fleet to the enemy at the battle of Trafalgar (1805), many ships played 'Rule Britannia', 'Hearts of Oak' or 'Britons Strike Home'. Captains also sometimes paid a seaman to play the fiddle while the capstan was being turned, and the sailors would have sung along, singing the same sea shanties that would have been heard in contemporary merchant ships. Of course, some captains insisted on silence when working the capstan, so that orders could be heard and relayed. This was a case where regulations said one thing, and common sense another. The truth was, music such as sea shanties made the work appear easier, whether on board a merchant vessel or a sailing man-of-war.

Sea shanties went out of favour with the coming of steam. With no sails to raise, and with steam-powered capstans there was little need to sing sea shanties. By the later 19th century they had lost their original workmanlike purpose, and shanties became something that were sung for fun, rather than as a song of work.

# SEA LANES AND PREVAILING WIND

Over the centuries, war at sea often involved hunting down and destroying an enemy fleet, or patrolling the sea lanes in an attempt to disrupt the enemy's commerce. During the age of sail these sea lanes had to follow the course of the prevailing wind. In the North Atlantic the prevailing wind direction was westerly – the 'westerlies' blowing from America to Europe. The same was largely true in the Mediterranean.

South of a line running from Florida to Morocco the 'north-east trades' blew in a south-westerly direction. This made it necessary for a ship sailing to America to take a southerly route if possible, then to head northwards after reaching the Caribbean. It was the same for a ship bound for Europe – it was important to pick up the westerly winds somewhere north of Bermuda in order to ensure a fast passage. In a band between the two was an area of variable winds – here the wind direction and therefore progress were unpredictable.

The same was true in the South Atlantic. The 'south-east trades' blew from the southern African coast towards Brazil and the mid-Atlantic, but in between the north-east and south-east trades lay the 'doldrums' – an area where wind was often scant, and therefore progress was agonizingly slow. In the Bight of Africa a local weather phenomenon meant that the winds there were predominantly from the south or south-west. South of the Cape of Good Hope the colder waters of the far south enjoyed a steady westerly wind, which was constant around the globe – a reliable prevailing westerly wind, albeit one that often blew with ferocious strength.

The westerlies, south-east trades and north-east trades also formed global bands that were the same around the whole circumference of the earth. This meant that both the Indian Ocean and the Pacific Ocean were divided into bands of wind – westerlies to the north and south, with north-east trades and south-east trades lying above and below the equator respectively, with bands of variable winds in between. The Pacific also suffered from the doldrums. Another slight anomaly was in the northern Indian Ocean, which enjoyed south-easterly winds, even though it lay within the band bisected by the north-east trades. Finally both the waters of the northern Indian Ocean and the western Pacific Ocean were known for monsoons, where weather patterns varied depending on other weather conditions.

All this meant that ships sailing from Europe to the Far East would take a long, curving route into the Atlantic, almost touching the coast of Brazil before picking up the westerlies for the run past the Cape of Good Hope. Ships in the Indian Ocean tended to sail to the east of Madagascar on the voyage to India or the Far East, and returned on the western side, between the island and the African coast. In the Pacific sailing ships took a northerly route to the Americas, and a more southerly route through the north-east trades if sailing towards Asia.

The busiest shipping lanes were therefore along these routes, with obvious bottle-necks forming in the Western Approaches to Britain and Europe, near the Azores and Canary Islands, the Leeward Islands of the Caribbean, the waters off the Cape of Good Hope and Madagascar, and the waters off what is now Sumatra and Malaysia. Of course, the advent of steam meant that all these winds no longer mattered. Ships were free to sail by more direct routes, and commerce rather than meteorology dictated where the shipping lanes would be. That meant naval predators would have to learn a whole new set of rules.

# FIGHTING ADMIRAL: RICHARD KEMPENFELT

One of the more obscure naval heroes in the British pantheon is Richard Kempenfelt (1718–82), a man who died at the height of his success. More intriguingly, if he had lived a little longer, he might have prevented Britain from losing her American colonies.

Kempenfelt was born into a Swedish military family who had settled in Britain during the 1690s, and he first joined the Royal Navy as a teenage midshipman in 1731. He passed his examinations for lieutenant seven years later. It was then that he saw his first action, as Britain had just gone to war with Spain, and he distinguished himself at the capture of Porto Bello on the Spanish Main (1739). His capture of the Spanish fort there earned him the recognition of both Admiral Vernon and the Honourable Edward Boscawen, who led the landing party.

He was given his first command in 1741, and in 1755 he was given command of a ship-of-the-line, the 64-gun Third Rate HMS *Elizabeth*. However, it wasn't until the end of the Seven Years War (1756–63) that his star began to shine. At the start of the war he was sent to the Far East, serving as the flag captain of Admiral Cornish. This was a special expedition, which saw a small British force of warships and troop transports sail halfway around the world, in order to launch a surprise attack on Manila in the Philippines. It was a resounding success. Unfortunately, this also showed how good Kempenfelt was as a staff officer, and so he spent the next two decades serving as chief-of-staff to a succession of admirals, reorganizing the fleet rather than leading it into battle.

He was finally rewarded with promotion to flag rank in 1780, after almost half a century of service. During the American War of Independence (1775–83), Rear Admiral Kempenfelt flew his flag in HMS *Victory*, the great 100-gun First Rate that later became Lord Nelson's flagship. In 1781 he was given his chance. He was ordered to lead a squadron out into the Atlantic, to intercept a French convoy of 20 ships bound for America, escorted by a powerful squadron commanded by the highly respected Admiral de Guichen, one of France's finest naval commanders. Kempenfelt got the better of him, diverting the admiral and his squadron, while the rest of his ships seized the convoy. It was a triumph, but it was also his one and only independent fleet command.

On his return to Britain Rear Admiral Kempenfelt was ordered to prepare a squadron to help relieve Gibraltar, and he shifted his flag into the 100-gun First Rate HMS *Royal George*. She was undergoing temporary repairs at Spithead, the great naval anchorage off Portsmouth. This involved heeling the ship over by shifting all her guns to one side – a method known as giving the ship a 'Parliament keel'. The aim was to fit a new water-cock to her lower hull. On the evening of 29 August 1782 she was in this precarious position when for some unexplained reason she rolled over, and water poured in through her open gunports. She sank within minutes, taking Kempenfelt and most of her 900-man crew down with her, together with many sailors' wives, girlfriends and other female companions, who were spending the night on board.

The Royal Navy lost a fighting admiral who stood on the brink of greatness. It also lost one of its finest minds. As well as being a skilled commander, Kempenfelt was a gifted naval administrator. He overhauled the signalling methods used in the fleet, introducing his own system, which soon became the Navy's standard method of communication. He introduced the 'divisional system' which ensured the proper welfare of a ship's crew for the first time, and treated sailors as human beings rather than as a labour force. He also actively promoted other changes, including improvements in gunnery methods, ship hygiene and naval tactics – making him one of the great intellects of Britain's 18th-century navy – and one of her unsung heroes.

# NAVAL RANKS IN THE US, UK AND CANADA

While naval ranks in the US, UK and Canada appear similar at first glance, the US Navy has a far more complex ranking structure. They may argue that this reflects the complexities of the world's largest modern combat fleet. For their part, the British will argue that theirs was the original system, and – as with driving on the left – they see no reason to change. For the most part the Canadian Forces Maritime Command (formerly the Royal Canadian Navy) follow the British system.

To allow navies from different countries to compare ranks, a NATO rank code is sometimes used. It also allows the navies to determine seniority within a multi-national task force, and to

| Royal Navy | US Navy | Canadian Forces Maritime Command ('Canadian Navy') | Nato Rating |
|---|---|---|---|
| **Commissioned Ranks** | | | |
| Admiral of the Fleet | Fleet Admiral | - | OF-10 |
| Admiral | Admiral | Admiral | OF-9 |
| Vice-Admiral | Vice-Admiral | Vice-Admiral | OF-8 |
| Rear Admiral | Rear Admiral (Upper Half) | Rear Admiral | OF-7 |
| Commodore | Rear Admiral (Lower Half) | Commodore | OF-6 |
| Captain | Captain | Captain | OF-5 |
| Commander | Commander | Commander | OF-4 |
| Lieutenant-Commander | Lieutenant-Commander | Lieutenant-Commander | OF-3 |
| Lieutenant | Lieutenant | Lieutenant | OF-2 |
| Sub-Lieutenant/ Midshipman | Lieutenant Junior Grade | Sub-Lieutenant | OF-1 |
| | Ensign | Acting Sub-Lieutenant | |
| - | Midshipman | Naval Cadet | OF (D) |

| Non-Commissioned Ranks | | | |
|---|---|---|---|
| Warrant Officer Class 1 | Master Chief Petty Officer of the Navy | Chief Petty Officer First Class | OR-9 |
| | Fleet Master Chief Petty Officer | | |
| | Command Master Chief Petty Officer | | |
| | Master Chief Petty Officer | | |
| Warrant Officer Class 2 | Senior Chief Petty Officer | Chief Petty Officer Second Class | OR-8 |
| Chief Petty Officer | Chief Petty Officer | Petty Officer First Class | OR-7 |
| Petty Officer | Petty Officer First Class | Petty Officer Second Class | OR-6 |
| - | Petty Officer Second Class | Master Seaman | OR-5 |
| Leading Seaman | Petty Officer Third Class | Leading Seaman | OR-4 |
| Able Seaman | Seaman | Able Seaman | OR-3 |
| Ordinary Seaman | Seaman Apprentice | Ordinary Seaman | OR-2 |
| - | Seaman Recruit | Seaman | OR-1 |

provide a rough guide to equivalent naval ranks. Officer ranks go from OF-1 to OF-10, while an additional category – OF(D) – covers officers under training. Other ranks ('enlisted men' in the US Navy) are classified from OR-1 to OR-9. Warrant officers in the US Navy – specialists in their particular field – are a special case, as there is no NATO equivalent for them.

# NAVAL DISASTER: THE WRECKING OF THE SPANISH ARMADA

In August 1588, Elizabethan England faced invasion. The small English Army was no match for King Philip II of Spain's veteran Spanish soldiers, so it was vital to prevent these troops from gaining a foothold on English soil. During the first week in August the great Spanish fleet – the Spanish Armada – had sailed up the English Channel, to rendezvous with the veteran Spanish army of the Duke of Parma, which was waiting for it on the Flemish coast. However, on the night of 7/8 August the fleet was scattered by English fireships, and in the battle that followed it was damaged, and driven from the coast.

The prevailing wind made it almost impossible to return to the rendezvous, so instead the Duke of Medina Sidonia, who commanded the Spanish fleet, decided to return to Spain, to try again the following year. This meant circumnavigating the British Isles. The Armada was pursued by the English far into the North Sea, but eventually, on 12 August, Elizabeth's warships returned to port. This meant that the Spanish were left to sail home in peace. The fleet had been bloodied, but it was still a cohesive, intact fighting force.

That was when it all started to go badly wrong. The fleet was caught by unseasonably bad weather, and its progress up the North Sea was attended by 'constant storms, fogs and squalls'. Many of the already battered ships started to founder, but the majority passed between Orkney and Shetland, and into the Atlantic Ocean. One casualty was *El Gran Grifon*, a store-ship which was shipwrecked on Fair Isle, between the two northern Scottish archipelagos. The crew spent the winter on the island before being repatriated to Spain through Scotland.

By mid-September the Duke of Medina Sidonia was somewhere west of Ireland, but the rest of his fleet was scattered over hundreds of miles of ocean. The weather grew worse, and on 12 September the fleet was hit by a severe gale from the south-west, forcing many of the battered ships inshore towards the Irish coast. *La Trinidad Valencera* was beached in Kinnagoe Bay, in County Donegal, and her survivors were duly massacred by patrols, supported by the local Irish. A similar fate befell shipwrecked mariners from the three Levant Squadron ships *Lavia*, *Juliana* and *Santa María de Visión*, wrecked off Streedagh Strand, in County Sligo. Over 600 bodies were washed up on the beach, and the few sailors who survived were massacred.

A second gale in late September finished off many other Armada ships, including the *Santa Maria de la Rosa*, which foundered off County Kerry, and *El Gran Grin*, which was wrecked off County Connaught. Probably the worst of all these disasters was the wrecking of the galleass *Girona*, the flagship of the Spanish squadron commander Don Alonso de Leiva. The galleass was crammed with 1,300 men, many of whom were survivors from earlier shipwrecks. She tried to escape the storms by sailing east towards Scotland, but she was driven ashore onto Lacada Point, in Ulster. Only a handful of her crew survived.

Of the 138 ships and 24,000 men who set sail in the Armada, some 45 vessels were lost, along with over 10,000 sailors. This disaster was not the result of English naval prowess, but was brought about by a series of freak storms of hurricane-force proportions. This horrible end to Philip II's invasion became a cause of celebration in England, and Protestant propagandists claimed that the storms were evidence of God's displeasure with the Spanish, and His support for the Protestant faith. Even the devout Philip II went through a crisis in his previously unshakeable faith in God and the Catholic cause.

# KEELHAULING

Keelhauling was a draconian naval punishment which involved dropping a miscreant over the side of a ship, then passing him underneath it. It was said to have been invented by the Dutch in the Middle Ages, then introduced to other navies during the centuries that followed. The word itself derives from the Dutch word *kielhalen* (meaning 'to drag along the keel'). In France the punishment was given the more exotic name of *le supplice de la grande cale* ('the torture of the grand ducking'). However, the earliest illustration of a keelhauling can be found on a Greek vase dating from the 5th century BC, so the punishment has been around almost as long as man has involved himself with the sea.

The punishment involved passing a rope underneath the ship, from one end of a yardarm to another. The victim was tied to this rope, and often weights were added, to make sure he passed more easily beneath the ship, without snagging on some part of the hull. He was then dropped into the sea, then hauled under the ship, to emerge on its far side. From there he was hauled back to the far side of the yardarm where he began his punishment. Whether he survived his experience or not was often immaterial.

There were variations. According to Captain Boteler's *Discourse* (1634) a gun was fired when the victim was about to be dropped into the water, as a warning to others in the fleet to watch the punishment. Other examples cite that the victim was dropped overboard from a ship's boat, then hauled beneath the main ship, and recovered by another boat on its far side. Worse, if the Captain ordered it, the punishment could be repeated more than once. Obviously the victim would become progressively weaker and more battered each time, which reduced his chances of survival even more.

In Falconer's *Marine Dictionary* (1711) the dangers of this punishment were catalogued in all their gory detail. 'As this extraordinary sentence is executed with a serenity of temper peculiar to the Dutch, the culprit is allowed sufficient intervals to recover the sense of pain, of which indeed he is frequently deprived during the operation.' It added that in winter the victim could be cut by ice in the water, implying that he could alternatively freeze to death before he was hauled out. He could also be cut to pieces on the barnacles clinging to the underside of the ship, or knocked unconscious by striking the side of the ship. Then again, he might simply not have enough air in his lungs to survive the immersion.

If a sailor was pulled too quickly, he was more likely to be badly cut – too slowly and he could drown. In keelhauling timing was everything, and obviously the bigger the ship the longer and more traumatic was the punishment. In some waters another danger was sharks – particularly if the victim was cut by barnacles, and bled in the water. Keelhauling went out of favour soon after Falconer described it, and by the 1730s it was no longer listed as an acceptable form of punishment in the Royal Navy. Flogging and hanging from the yardarm were considered far more effective, if a lot less dramatic.

# NAVAL SIGNALLING

Before the mid-17th century, there was no established method of signalling between friendly warships. If an admiral wanted to tell one of his captains what to do, he would either sail alongside and shout his orders across, or else send the message by boat. It was General-at-Sea Robert Blake who introduced the world's first naval signalling system in the 1650s. This basic system gave the English Commonwealth Navy a distinct advantage over its rivals during the First Dutch War (1654–56). Still, it only consisted of five flags, which meant that the number of signals which could be conveyed was very limited.

During the last decades of the 17th century the Royal Navy introduced a system which involved over 20 flags, in either solid colours or a combination of two. In this respect they began to resemble the international flag signalling system which is used today. A combination of several flags was used to send a specific message, and this was deemed sufficient to cover most eventualities a fleet would encounter.

In the 1760s the British introduced a new and more flexible system. Flags could be used to send specific messages, but they could also be used to represent specific letters or numbers. A signal book was issued in 1799, in which a combination of three or four flags was used to express a particular word or phrase. This meant that, for the first time, naval commanders were not limited in the messages or orders they could transmit using signal flags. Before the battle of Trafalgar (1805), Vice-Admiral Nelson wanted to send the signal that England requires every man to do his duty. He was told that the word 'requires' would have to be spelled out, but a flag combination was already available to express the word 'expects'. Nelson agreed to change the wording, thereby saving the signalling staff extra time and effort.

Modern signal flags represent a letter, but they can also be used to send an internationally recognized message, such as 'require assistance', 'preparing to sail' or 'handling explosives'. Of course, flags are no longer the only means of sending naval signals. In darkness or fog, lanterns were used during the age of sail, and during the 18th and early 19th centuries the Royal Navy recognized signals involving a combination of four lanterns, hoisted in a combination of ways. By the time of the Napoleonic Wars, these were augmented by a crude light signalling system, using a lantern which could be opened or closed using a wooden shutter. It is fairly easy to see how these developed into the signalling lamps used to send Morse Code messages today. (See page 120)

By the mid-19th century, most of the major navies used a system of semaphore messaging, where a sailor used two hand-held flags to send messages, by holding them in a variety of ways. Each pose spelled out a letter. This was augmented by better-quality signalling lamps by the end of the century, and it was discovered that the long and short dashes of Morse Code were perfectly suited to signalling using lights. The advent of electricity meant that these signalling lamps became much more powerful, and therefore could be seen by ships which were several miles apart.

By the start of the 20th century, radio messages had become the most versatile method of signalling, although in most navies radio signals were sent using ciphers, to reduce the risk of the message being intercepted. Ciphers were no guarantee of security, and during the Second World War the Allies managed to crack the Japanese and German signal codes, which gave them a useful advantage in the naval war. The other problem was that when a warship transmits a radio message, its location can be detected by an enemy's direction-finding equipment. This meant that when secrecy was important, warship commanders preferred to return to earlier, simpler methods, and when they could they used lamps and signal flags, which couldn't be intercepted. Today, modern warships use a variety of signalling systems, including 'burst messages', where a complex series of messages can be sent during a single split-second burst. These are then decoded using computers. The aim is to reduce the risk of giving away the signalling ship's position. Other methods involve satellite links, underwater telephones which allow submarines and surface ships to communicate, and computer data transfer. However, as naval commanders discovered during the two world wars, the navies of the world still need the older methods of signalling by flag, light or simply yelling into a megaphone.

# PROFILE OF A WARSHIP FLEET: THE SPANISH NAVY DURING THE NAPOLEONIC WARS

In 1793, Spain entered the French Revolutionary War as a member of the anti-Revolutionary coalition. At that time her Navy was one of the finest in the world, and the third largest, after Britain and France. She maintained a fleet of 56 ships-of-the-line, with another 20 'in ordinary' (hulked, and in theory ready for refitting and re-use in the event of a major war). Another 105 smaller warships supported this battlefleet: frigates, brigs and xebecs, corvettes, cutters and gunboats.

The 'Armada Real' was an extremely powerful force, but it also had a job to match its size. The Spanish Empire covered Spain, southern Italy, Sicily, parts of North Africa and the Azores. Across the Atlantic the Spanish controlled a million square miles west of the Mississippi River, most of the Caribbean basin, Mexico, Central America, Peru and Chile. Their possessions even extended into the Pacific, with colonies in the Philippines and numerous smaller islands and archipelagos. Contrary to the popular opinion that Spain was in terminal decline during the 18th century, she continued to maintain her grip on her sprawling empire, and built a fleet capable of protecting Spanish interests at home and abroad.

These Spanish ships had a reputation for being well designed and superbly built. Of all the vessels in this magnificent fleet, it was the Spanish First Rates such as the *Salvador del Mundo*, later captured at St Vincent (1797) or the *Santissima Trinidad*, which was captured and sank at Trafalgar (1805), which were the pride of the nation, and the envy of the other maritime powers. In 1795 the Armada Real boasted a 130-gun ship-of-the-line, ten First Rates of 112 guns, and also two powerful 98-gun Second Rates. These great ships were built either in the royal shipyard at Ferrol, in northern Spain, or in Havana. During the 18th century, no fewer than 74 Spanish ships-of-the-line were built in the Cuban port, using a combination of local hardwoods and mahogany, which was virtually impervious to damage from the *toredo* worm.

When the Spanish made peace with France in 1795, under the terms of the treaty, the Armada Real had to provide between 25 and 29 ships-of-the-line for joint service with the French Navy. After the Spanish defeat at Cape St Vincent in 1797, the Spanish remained bottled up in Cartagena, and the magnificent fleet remained in the port until the Peace of Amiens, in 1802. The resumption of war in 1803 saw the Spanish renew their alliance with France, a decision which cost them dear at Trafalgar (1805). The fleet remained blockaded in Cadiz until 1808, when the French invaded Spain. For the remainder of the war, the five remaining Spanish First Rates saw little action, as the French rarely put to sea. It was an ignominious end to a great fleet. Under more capable officers, the Armada Real might have accomplished great things. Instead, a fleet of great ships and experienced seamen was consigned to mediocrity by cautious commanders and short-sighted political masters.

# SEA BATTLE: THE BATTLE OF MOBILE BAY, 1864

During the American Civil War battle of Mobile Bay, in 1864, the Union's Flag Officer David Farragut (1801–70) passed into naval legend, thanks to a snappy retort: 'Damn the torpedoes!' By August 1864, the Confederacy was on its knees, and with the loss of the Mississippi River, Mobile, Alabama remained the last Southern port of any size on the coast of the Gulf of Mexico. Although it had been blockaded since the Civil War began, the port lay at the head of Mobile Bay, which was virtually landlocked thanks to a string of barrier islands and sandbars. It was also heavily defended – the main approaches were swept by the guns of Fort Morgan, while other smaller forts and batteries sealed off other smaller entrances. Worse, these entrances were thickly sown with mines – which were called 'torpedoes' during the American Civil War.

On 5 August, Farragut ordered his ship to storm the entrance to the bay. Before the assault, he ordered his steam-powered wooden warships to be lashed together in pairs, with a smaller vessel tied to the port side of a larger one. That way, when they passed under the guns of Fort Morgan, the larger ship should shield the smaller one from shot and shell. This vulnerable wooden fleet was screened by a squadron of four powerful monitors – two single-turreted and two twin-turreted ironclads. Each turret held two powerful guns, protected by a virtually impenetrable iron casing. These vessels – the *Manhattan*, *Tecumseh*, *Chickasaw* and *Winnebago* – were some of the most powerful warships in the Union Army – and Farragut would have need of them. If the fleet managed to fight its way into Mobile Bay, an even more powerful ironclad – the CSS *Tennessee* – would be waiting for them.

The battle started at 0647hrs, and within minutes the shot was flying in both directions. In order to see what was going on, Farragut had ordered his sailors to tie him to the rigging of his flagship, the USS *Hartford*. Suddenly, the USS *Tecumseh* struck a mine, which exploded underneath her hull. She sank within minutes, taking all but 21 of her 114-man crew down with her. Captain Alden of the wooden steam-powered warship USS *Brooklyn* stopped his ship, and signalled for fresh orders. However, Farragut saw that this wasn't a moment for caution. His flagship was next in line. He ordered Captain Drayton to swing the *Hartford* out of line, and to pass to port of the *Brooklyn*. The flagship still had the USS *Metacomet* tied to her port side. The rest of the wooden ships were ordered to follow the flagship.

This was a real gamble, as it took the *Hartford* and the *Metacomet* across the line of torpedoes strung across the entrance to the bay. When one of Drayton's officers warned the admiral of the mines, Farragut replied: 'Damn the torpedoes! Four bells, Captain Drayton! Go ahead, Jouett, full speed!' Actually, some historians doubt whether he said this at all, or if his shout was directed to Drayton and his executive officer or to Captain Alden of the *Brooklyn*. Today, the phrase which is usually quoted is a simplification of this – a simple 'Damn the torpedoes – Full steam ahead!'

The gamble paid off. The fleet passed across the line of torpedoes, passed under the guns of the fort, and broke out into the open waters of Mobile Bay. There the ships which had been tied together were unlashed, and battle was opened against the CSS *Tennessee* and her consorts. The battle ended about an hour later, when the outnumbered Confederate ironclad finally surrendered. Despite the loss of the *Tecumseh*, Farragut had won a splendid victory – an achievement he owed to his own dramatic tactics, and the most famous order in American naval history.

# THE SEVEN SEA DOGS

During the reign of Queen Elizabeth I (1558–1603), the English monarch was served by naval commanders who were celebrated for their courage and skill. These men have collectively been called her 'sea dogs'. Many were related, and most hailed from England's West Country. While all served the queen as naval commanders, they also spent much of their time in other roles – as privateers, explorers, slavers, merchants, administrators and even as pirates. Only one of those listed here actually died in his bed – and one was even beheaded for treason!

### Sir Francis Drake (c.1542–96)

The archetypal 'sea dog', Drake was a ruthless and greedy man, but a brilliant seaman and leader. In the late 1560s he sailed with John Hawkins, but in 1572 he led his own raiding expedition to the Caribbean, where he plundered Spanish treasure. In 1577 he embarked on a voyage to the Pacific, and after capturing a wealthy Spanish treasure ship he returned home by circumnavigating the globe. Drake led another expedition to the Spanish Main in 1584–85, and in 1588 he commanded part of the English fleet during the Spanish Armada campaign. He returned to the Caribbean in 1595, but died the following year, while cruising off the coast of Panama, and was buried at sea.

### Sir Martin Frobisher (c.1535–94)

This Yorkshireman spent 15 years as a privateer and trader, but he became increasingly obsessed with the quest for the North-West Passage. In 1574 he set out in search of this legendary sea route around the top of the North American continent – the first of three unsuccessful voyages. By their end he was penniless and disillusioned. He accompanied Drake on his Caribbean raid in 1584–85, and then served as a commander during the Spanish Armada campaign (1588). Further voyages against the Spanish followed, until in 1595 he was injured during a skirmish at Crozon in Brittany, and died of his wounds.

### Sir Humphrey Gilbert (1539–83)

A half-brother to Walter Raleigh, Gilbert was educated at Oxford, and then served as a soldier in Ireland. He became obsessed with the North-West Passage, and wrote a book on the subject, which encouraged Frobisher to set off in search of it. Meanwhile Gilbert developed an interest in the colonization of America. In 1578 he and Raleigh led a reconnaissance expedition to the New World, which ended in failure. Undeterred, Gilbert led a new expedition in 1583, but never made it further than Newfoundland. His ship foundered during the voyage home, and Gilbert was lost at sea.

### Sir Richard Grenville (c.1541–91)

As a young adventurer Grenville fought as a soldier in Continental Europe and Ireland. He then took part in Raleigh's expedition to colonize Virginia. In the process he attacked Spanish shipping, and plundered his way around the Azores. In 1588 he held a military command, but he returned to sea the following year, helping guard the coast against another invasion attempt. Then in 1591 he participated in an English expedition to the Azores, where the English were surprised and attacked by a larger Spanish fleet. Grenville's ship the *Revenge* was surrounded, but he fought on for 15 hours, until – mortally wounded – he was forced to surrender his sinking ship. This epic sea battle was later immortalized by the poet Tennyson.

### Sir John Hawkins (1532–95)

Hawkins was one of the first English sea captains to venture into the Caribbean. However, in 1568 his flotilla was attacked and all but destroyed by the Spanish. During the 1570s he introduced a new form of warship: the English 'race-built galleon', a vessel that was faster, more manoeuvrable and better armed than its Spanish counterpart. Hawkins served as a fleet commander during the Spanish Armada campaign (1588) and the following year he led an unsuccessful attempt to intercept a Spanish treasure fleet. He next returned to sea in 1595, sharing a command with Drake as the two sea dogs led another raid into the Caribbean. This was Hawkins' last campaign – he died off Puerto Rico, aged 63.

### Sir Richard Hawkins (c. 1562–1622)

The son of John Hawkins learned his trade under Drake, participating in his uncle's Caribbean expedition of 1584–85. During the Spanish Armada campaign of 1588 he commanded the warship *Swallow*, and he subsequently accompanied his father during the post-Armada raids on Spanish and Portuguese ports. In 1593 he began a voyage of circumnavigation. His ship the *Dainty* raided Valparaiso in Chile, but was then cornered and captured by a Spanish squadron. Hawkins spent three years in prison before his stepmother paid his ransom. He returned to sea in 1620, campaigning against the Barbary Pirates, and in 1622 – unlike most of his contemporaries – he died in his bed.

### Sir Walter Raleigh (c. 1554–1618)

Known as an explorer, a poet, a soldier and a courtier as much as a sea dog, Raleigh earned an early reputation as a soldier fighting in Ireland. Inspired by his half-brother Humphrey Gilbert, he participated in the doomed New World expedition of 1578, but returned alone the following year, and founded a colony at Roanoke (now in North Carolina). Raleigh assisted in the defence of the English coast during 1588. He became a royal favourite, but in 1592 he was imprisoned for marrying without the queen's permission. Three years later he led another failed expedition to South America, in search of El Dorado. In 1596 he served alongside the Earl of Essex – the Queen's new favourite – during a raid on Cadiz. Raleigh's fall from grace followed swiftly after the queen's death. James I accused him of conspiring against him, and Raleigh was imprisoned in the Tower of London. He spent 13 years there, where he wrote his *History of the World*. He was released in 1616, but when his next expedition to the Spanish Main ended in failure Raleigh was accused of inciting war against Spain. He was duly executed on the orders of the king.

# FIGHTING ADMIRAL: JOHN BYNG

According to François Voltaire (1694–1778), writing in his satire *Candide*, the English shoot an admiral now and again *'pour encourager les autres'* ('to encourage the others'). He was referring to the unfortunate Admiral Byng, who was shot by a firing squad on his own quarterdeck, after losing a battle to the French. In April 1756, Vice-Admiral the Honourable John Byng (1704–57) was given command of a British fleet and dispatched to the Mediterranean, with orders to raise the French siege of Minorca. At the time the island was Britain's only secure base in the Mediterranean, apart from Gibraltar.

Byng was the fourth son of George Byng, Viscount Torrington, who had been an admiral before his death in 1773. Thanks to the patronage of his father Byng rose quickly through the ranks, becoming a rear admiral while he was still in his early thirties. Before his mission to Minorca, he spent 38 uneventful years in the Royal Navy, much of it serving in administrative posts ashore. Byng's mission to the Mediterranean was to be his first real test.

When Byng arrived, he discovered that the French had already landed their troops, and that, having overrun the rest of the island, they were busy laying siege to Port Mahon. This had a small British garrison, but without Byng's intervention it was clear that it would have to surrender. The main French fleet of 12 ships-of-the-line were blockading the port, so Byng decided to attack it. Once the fleet had been driven off, he could land supplies and reinforcements, which would let the defenders hold out indefinitely. Similarly, starved of supplies from the sea, the French troops would soon be forced to surrender. It all seemed straightforward. All Byng had to do was to win the coming battle.

On 20 May Byng formed his ten ships-of-the-line into battle formation, and closed with the enemy. The French commander, Admiral Roland de la Galissonnière, ordered his own fleet to sail out to meet the British. Byng directed his line at the enemy's centre, and at the start it looked as if he would cut the enemy line. Then it all went badly wrong. The French admiral ordered the front half of his line to change course, so instead of cutting the French fleet in two, Byng's leading ships found themselves enveloped by the enemy. The leading six British ships were shot at from both sides, but they fought back bravely, and pounded the French in return. The rest of Byng's ships kept formation, and fired into the French from long range. Eventually the French fleet withdrew, but Byng's disorganized force was in no shape to pursue. It could be argued that the British had the best of the battle, but Byng had also failed to drive off the French fleet.

Instead of reorganizing his fleet and renewing the fight, Byng decided to sail back to Gibraltar, where his ships could be repaired. This of course meant that the British garrison was doomed. Port Mahon surrendered to the French nine days after the battle. The battle of Mahon might have been indecisive, but by abandoning the area Byng had effectively handed the French the island. From Gibraltar he returned to Britain, arriving back in Portsmouth in July. He had been pilloried in the newspapers, and the government needed a scapegoat to blame for the loss of Minorca. Byng was the perfect candidate.

He was duly court-martialled, charged with failing in his duty. The prosecution claimed that he had not done enough to save Minorca and, spurred on by public outrage, the result was never in much doubt. Byng was found guilty of negligence, and, unusually in such cases, he was sentenced to death. This was a political move – the government hoped that by such a draconian sentence they could avoid further scandal. Even the court added a plea that the death sentence would be revoked by the king, but the stay of execution never came. So, on 14 March 1757, Vice-Admiral Byng was shot by firing squad, as he knelt on the quarterdeck of his flagship HMS *Centurion*. While he may have blundered and been guilty of a lack of aggression, his mistakes hardly earned him a death penalty – *pour encourager les autres*.

# NAVAL DISASTER: THE SINKING OF THE USS *MAINE*

In January 1898, the American battleship USS *Maine* was sent from Key West, Florida, to Havana in Cuba, on a goodwill mission. Cuba was in a state of unrest, as a growing guerrilla movement tried to wrest the island from Spanish control. The *Maine* was there to show the flag, and to protect the interests of Havana's American community.

Then, at 2140hrs on the evening of 15 February 1898, the USS *Maine* was ripped apart by an explosion. The blast destroyed the front third of the ship, and she quickly settled on the seabed. Most of the crew were asleep when the explosion occurred, and the main crew quarters were located near the bows of the ship. These men never stood a chance, and a total of 266 sailors were killed in the blast or in its aftermath. Eight more died of their injuries over the next few days. Only 89 of her crew survived the explosion, and of these, 18 were officers, who were accommodated near the stern of the ship.

A Court of Enquiry was held in Key West, and the battleship's commander, Captain Charles Sigsbee, and his officers gave evidence. An accidental explosion was ruled out, and on 28 March the court ruled that the *Maine* had been destroyed by an underwater explosion, caused by a mine. Naturally this caused an outrage in the United States. The Spanish were blamed, and the rallying cry 'Remember the *Maine*!' was adopted as a national slogan. Spurred on by the 'yellow journalism' of William Randolph Hearst, America declared war on Spain in April 1898.

The war itself was a one-sided business. American troops landed near Santiago in Cuba, and after storming San Juan Hill they captured the city from the Spanish. On 3 July this drove the Spanish naval squadron sheltering there to sortie and do battle with the waiting American fleet. This uneven naval struggle, dubbed the battle of Santiago, ended with the complete destruction of the Spanish ships. The war extended to Puerto Rico and the Philippines, and by December a humiliated Spain was forced to sign a peace treaty, which ceded much of its overseas territory to the United States.

As soon as peace was declared another investigation was carried out, this time using the wreck as evidence. Divers were sent down, survivors were quizzed, and a more studied verdict was reached. It was discovered that the explosion took place in the forward magazines, but the inquiry was unable to explain exactly why the explosion took place. Over the years four more inquiries were held, again without reaching a definite conclusion. However, these led to a fresh theory – the idea that the explosion was accidental rather than deliberate.

The mine theory was difficult to prove. The idea was that Spanish nationalists blew up the ship to deter the United States from intervening in Cuban affairs. This was a weak political argument, as was a variant that the explosion was caused by Cuban insurgents, who wanted to embroil America in a war with Spain. A few survivors claimed they had heard two explosions, a few seconds apart. Also, part of the keel was bent upwards, suggesting an initial external blast, which then ignited the magazine. This keel damage as a possible effect of an internal explosion was later discounted. Also, nobody reported a column of water, which would indicate a mine going off.

The accidental explosion theory has more merit. Spontaneous combustion in a hot coal bunker was a fairly common phenomenon during the late 19th century, and the heat could easily have transferred through the metal bulkhead from the *Maine*'s coal bunkers into her magazine. Arguments against the theory include the fact that the coal used by the *Maine* was far less likely to spontaneously combust than other types of coal, and that the crew conducted regular bunker inspections – the latest being just hours before the explosion. Nothing untoward was discovered.

In 1976 Admiral Rickover investigated the explosion, and ruled in favour of an internal explosion. Another investigation, conducted by *National Geographic* magazine, favoured the mine theory. The cause of the explosion is still hotly debated to this day.

# PROFILE OF A WARSHIP:
# HMS *THE FORT DIAMOND*

Diamond Rock is a 574ft (175m) high rock outcrop, lying just off the south-western coast of Martinique, in the West Indies. For a few years it became one of the strangest warships in history. In 1802, Martinique was the most prosperous French colony in the Caribbean. Commodore Hood, commanding the British West Indies squadron, lacked the manpower he needed to capture the island. Therefore he came up with a plan to cripple Martinique's trade. This involved a feat of engineering only an experienced sailor could attempt – the landing of a battery of heavy guns, complete with men, stores and equipment on the top of Diamond Rock. Due to the prevailing wind, shipping bound for Martinique's capital of Port de France had to pass close to the rock, which made it the perfect place to site a gun battery. Hood's only problem was how to move the guns up a sheer cliff face.

Naval ingenuity came to the fore, and after anchoring his flagship HMS *Centaur* (74 guns) close by Diamond Rock, Hood supervised the rigging of a great line of rope between the warship and the summit. Running tackle was added, and pulleys and hauling ropes, until the whole contraption looked like a vast aerial rope runway. A naval officer recorded the way the seamen transported the guns: 'To the cable a traveller was affixed, similar in principle to that which children put on the string of a kite; to this a 24-pdr was attached, and, by means of tackles, conveyed to the top of the rock.'

Within a week, Hood managed to land two 18-pdrs and three 24-pdrs, manned by 120 men, under the command of Lieutenant (later Commander) James Maurice. The battery perched on top of the precipitous Diamond Rock was entered into the Admiralty's records as a sloop-of-war, and re-named HMS *The Fort Diamond*.

Diamond Rock was highly effective, and after a few futile attempts to run past its guns, the shipping entering or leaving Port de France was brought to a standstill. Finally, in May 1805, when Admiral Villeneuve's French fleet reached the West Indies, it ignored the threat posed by the pursuing Vice-Admiral Nelson to deal with the problem posed by Commander Maurice's garrison. Captain Cosmao-Kerjulien was detached with a squadron of 16 assorted warships, and he spent several days bombarding the rock. Of course, one of his problems was that it was extremely difficult to elevate his guns high enough to damage the gun battery on the summit.

However, gunfire cracked the stone cistern holding the battery's water supply, and most of the water drained away. Maurice was also running out of powder, and on 2 June, after three days of constant bombardment, he was compelled to surrender. The battery was dismantled by pushing the guns over the cliff. For his part, Commander Maurice was able to take pleasure from the fact that for 17 months his unusual and immobile warship had been a major thorn in the side of the French.

# THE RULES OF THE ROAD

Most countries have some form of Highway Code, designed to bring some order to the roads. They govern things like who gives way to whom, when to use headlights and how to drive in busy, wide thoroughfares. A similar set of guidelines is used at sea. The 'Rules of the Road' (or more officially the *International Regulations for Preventing Collisions at Sea*) is a set of 38 internationally recognized rules which govern the conduct of ships at sea. Their main aim is to prevent collisions, and they are divided into six groups, covering lights and shapes to be carried by night or day, sound signals, what to do in poor visibility, how to avoid collisions between two approaching ships, and what distress signals to use. Not only are they internationally recognized, but failure to comply can have serious legal consequences.

The world's navies are bound to comply with the Rules of the Road, although common sense also dictates that discretion can be used. For instance, in theory, steam-powered vessels should make way for sail-powered ones. However, if the 82,000-ton nuclear-powered supercarrier USS *Nimitz* was entering a harbour with little room for manoeuvre, she wouldn't alter course to avoid a sailing dinghy. The most basic rule to avoid a collision is that vessels approaching each other should both alter course to starboard. Also, when passing another ship, it is expedient to pass astern of her, rather than try cutting across her bows. The common sense rule is that both ships should take steps to avoid a collision, regardless of who officially has right of way. This is summed up perfectly in the little ditty:

> Here lies the body of Michael O'Day,
> Who died maintaining his right of way,
> He was right, dead right, as he sailed along,
> But he's just as dead as if he'd been wrong.

Despite the Rules of the Road, and the application of plain common sense, collisions still happen. Every year, the newspapers record that some warship or other has been involved in a collision somewhere. That of course, means a court martial for the Captain, and probably his Navigating Officer as well. Woe betide any naval officer, found guilty of breaching the most basic international rules of the road!

# MINESWEEPING FOR BEGINNERS

While most people measure the strength of a navy by the number of carriers, destroyers, frigates or submarines it has, the humble minesweeper is usually forgotten – a necessary but largely unsung tool of naval warfare. Mines (originally called 'torpedoes') have been part of naval warfare since the mid-19th century – they were first used by the Russians during the Crimean War (1854–56), but they weren't deployed in great numbers until the First World War (1914–18). By that time two main types of mine were used – 'observation mines' which could be detonated from the shore, and 'contact mines' which exploded when a ship came into contact with the 'horns' that protruded from them. 'Observation mines' (or controlled mines) were largely used to defend anchorages and naval bases – for instance, Britain's great wartime anchorage of Scapa Flow was defended by minefields, which were activated when a surface ship or a U-Boat entered them. Both types of mines were usually tethered to the seabed and deployed in minefields.

By the Second World War, magnetic, acoustic and pressure mines had all been developed. The Germans dropped magnetic mines around the coasts of Britain in 1939–40, and they were designed to explode when the steel hull of a ship passed within range. Acoustic mines were detonated when the sound of a ship's propeller passed overhead, while pressure mines reacted to changes in the density of sea water, caused by the hull of a ship. Magnetic mines could be countered by 'degaussing' – counteracting the magnetic field of a ship by passing a live wire under her hull. If this was done regularly, then the risk of detonation was greatly reduced. All other types of mines needed to be swept by minesweepers.

The first minesweepers appeared before the First World War, and were usually converted fishing boats. Their job was to tow a submerged cable behind them, which was fitted with cutting equipment. The aim was to cut the chain tethering a contact mine to the seabed. Once it floated to the surface, the mine would usually be detonated by gunfire. If two minesweepers operated together, then the wire could be trailed between them, which was far more efficient. Of course, this was extremely dangerous work, as the minesweeper was steaming through a minefield. They moved slowly, and lookouts were posted who could raise the alarm if a mine was spotted in the minesweeper's path.

Between the wars, the 'Oropesa Sweep' was invented, a device which spread the wires out behind the minesweeper, thereby allowing one minesweeper to do the job of two. The invention of new types of mines meant new mine-clearing techniques. During the Second World War, minefields frequently consisted of more than one type of mine, which made the job of clearing them even more difficult and dangerous. Magnetic mines were countered by making minesweepers out of wood or non-ferrous metal, to reduce their magnetic field. Today, most minesweepers are built using fibreglass. Acoustic mines were detonated by simulating the sound of a ship's propellers, by projecting underwater sound ahead of the minesweeper.

Magnetic mines are usually cleared by using two mine-sweepers working in tandem. Two electric cables are strung between them (a device called an 'LL Sweep'), and the electric current passed through them detonates any mines located between the two vessels. Pressure mines are the hardest of all to deal with. In most cases sonar is used to detect them, and then divers or Remotely Operated Vessels (ROVs) are sent down to defuse the mines on the seabed. Mines are rarely used today, but in any future conventional war then new, sophisticated versions of these basic mine types will be used. That means the business of sweeping the shipping lanes has to be done all over again – a thankless, dangerous but necessary task for the world's minesweeping professionals.

# SIGNALLING BY MORSE

Before the invention of the radio and Morse Code, signalling between warships was carried out using flags or lights. Then came the invention of the wireless telegraph, developed by Samuel Morse in 1837. While other forms of electric telegraph existed, the one patented by Morse was the most reliable, and he even invented a special code to use with it, which speeded up the transmission of messages. Soon afterwards the Royal Navy began experimenting with a system of transmitting Morse Code using flashing lights. But, in daylight and good visibility signalling was still largely conducted by flag, and lamp signalling was only used at night.

Then in 1905 the radio transformed naval communications. Before that, warships could only communicate with the shore by visual means, or by sending a despatch boat. The adoption of the Marconi wireless transmitter meant that radio signals could be sent by ships at sea. The use of naval radio was still in its infancy during the First World War, but by the Second World War it had come into its own. Not only did warships and merchant ships alike communicate by radio using Morse Code, but it also became the internationally recognized means of communicating from one ship to another. Naval signallers were expected to be completely conversant with Morse Code, and signals could be sent quickly and reliably from ship to ship, or from ship to shore.

Morse Code remained the international standard for maritime communication until 1999, when it was replaced by the Global Maritime Distress Safety System, which relied on radio messages using the spoken word instead. Many warships still prefer to rely on signal lamps and Morse Code, as, unlike radio, this form of ship to ship signalling cannot be intercepted, and allows the sender to maintain radio silence.

The system used by Morse has remained constant for over 150 years – a combination of dots and dashes is used to represent particular letters or numbers. Most people know the emergency distress signal 'SOS' – specifically chosen because it was easy to send – three dots, three dashes and three more dots. However, naval signalmen and aviators are among the few people who still use the whole alphabet, and can use it to signal their compatriots.

| A | · — | K | — · — | U | · · — | 1 | · — — — — |
|---|-----|---|-------|---|-------|---|-----------|
| B | — · · · | L | · — · · | V | · · · — | 2 | · · — — — |
| C | — · — · | M | — — | W | · — — | 3 | · · · — — |
| D | — · · | N | — · | X | — · · — | 4 | · · · · — |
| E | · | O | — — — | Y | — · — — | 5 | · · · · · |
| F | · · — · | P | · — — · | Z | — — · · | 6 | — · · · · |
| G | — — · | Q | — — · — | | | 7 | — — · · · |
| H | · · · · | R | · — · | | | 8 | — — — · · |
| I | · · | S | · · · | | | 9 | — — — — · |
| J | · — — — | T | — | | | 0 | — — — — — |

# FIGHTING ADMIRAL: JOHN JERVIS

Admiral John Jervis (1735–1823) was one of Britain's most gifted naval commanders during the age of fighting sail, and one of the Navy's most fearsome disciplinarians. Born into a prosperous Staffordshire family, he joined the Navy as a midshipman when he was 14 years old, and passed his lieutenant's exam six years later. This meant that he was already an experienced serving officer when the Seven Years War (1756–63) began, and Jervis played his part, participating in the capture of Quebec in 1759 – 'the year of victory'.

He became Captain Jervis in 1760, and for the next two decades he commanded a succession of warships, operating in home waters, or in the Mediterranean. He was still a captain when the American War of Independence (1775–83) began, but he never had an opportunity to distinguish himself. The only major engagement he took part in – the battle of Ushant (1778) – was indecisive, and more of a skirmish than a full-blown sea battle. However, in April 1782 he led HMS *Foudroyant* (74 guns) into action against the French 74-gun ship-of-the-line *Pégase*, and captured her after a spirited engagement. Jervis was awarded a knighthood after his victory, and five years later, in 1787, he attained flag rank, becoming a rear admiral. By now, his men had taken to calling him 'Old Jervie'.

The 1780s were a busy time for Jervis. He became a Member of Parliament in 1783, and in 1788, a year after his promotion, the 53-year old bachelor finally married his cousin, Martha Parker. His brief sojourn ashore was cut short by the outbreak of the French Revolutionary War (1793–1802). His first assignment was to the West Indies, where his squadron supported the British capture of several French-held islands. Then, in 1795, Sir John was promoted to the rank of vice-admiral, and given command of the Mediterranean Fleet. This was his first major command – his big chance.

At first, it seemed that glory would escape him. His main task was to blockade the French fleet at Toulon, which seemed reluctant to come out. In July 1795 the French and the Spanish signed a peace treaty. Then on 19 August 1796 the Treaty of Ildefonso was signed, and Spain joined the war on the side of the French Revolutionaries. Jervis had 15 ships-of-the-line at his disposal, while – if they combined – the French and Spanish had

38 major warships. His main job was therefore to prevent the two fleets from joining forces. The Spanish made their move in early 1797, when their fleet sallied out to escort a convoy from Cartagena to Cadiz. Jervis intercepted them off Cape St Vincent, and while the convoy reached Cadiz safely, the Spanish warships commanded by Don José de Cordóba decided to give battle.

Legend has it that when his flag captain on board HMS *Victory* first spotted the oncoming Spanish, he reported the news to Sir John:

> 'There are eight sail of the line, Sir John.'
> 'Very well, sir', replied Jervis.
> 'There are twenty sail of the line, Sir John.'
> 'Very well, sir.'
> 'There are twenty-five sail of the line, Sir John.'
> 'Very well, sir.'
> 'There are twenty-seven sail of the line, Sir John.'
> 'Enough, sir, no more of that; the die is cast, and if there
> are fifty sail I will go through them!'

The result was the battle of Cape St Vincent, a stunning display of British naval mastery, whose story is told elsewhere in this book (see p.48). The day ended with the Spanish in retreat, and four of their most prestigious warships in British hands. Of course, the real hero of the battle was Commodore Nelson of HMS *Captain*, who in theory disobeyed Jervis's orders in order to close with the enemy. Fortunately, Jervis recognized potential when he saw it, and recommended that Nelson should be promoted rather than castigated.

Jervis was first made a baron after his victory, and then became the First Earl of St Vincent. In this year of mutiny, while rebellion swept through the British anchorages of Spithead and the Nore, Jervis prevented any such outbreak in his own fleet, and troublemakers were dealt with severely. Flogging and hanging from the yardarm may appear draconian measures, but they helped maintain discipline within the fleet. Jervis also berated naval officers who didn't agree with his policies – one even challenged him to a duel after the Earl publicly humiliated him. However, Jervis also recognized talent, and promoted officers of ability, the most notable beneficiary being Nelson.

Jervis relinquished his command in 1799 due to failing health, but in 1801 he became the First Sea Lord, effectively running the naval war from the Admiralty. On one notable occasion he addressed the House of Lords, who were concerned about a French invasion. When asked about the seriousness of the French threat, Jervis replied, 'I do not say, my Lords, that the French will not come. I say only they will not come by sea!' He retired in 1804, but was recalled again in 1806, when he briefly commanded the Channel Fleet. He finally retired in 1811, and died 12 years later, shortly after being named Admiral of the Fleet. While historians rightly celebrate Lord Nelson, many forget that without the wisdom, skill and fighting ability of his mentor Sir John Jervis, there might have been no Vice-Admiral Horatio Nelson.

# ALFRED MAHAN: THE INVENTOR OF SEAPOWER

During the last decade of the 19th century, American naval officer and historian Alfred Thayer Mahan (1840–1914) became the unlikely leader of a naval revolution. The son of a West Point lecturer, he graduated from the US Naval Academy at Annapolis in 1859, and began his naval career on the eve of the American Civil War (1861–65). He never got the chance to shine in action as he spent the war blockading Confederate ports, or serving as a staff officer. However, this experience was very revealing – it proved that a large-scale naval campaign could have an important strategic impact. Promotion was slow – he only reached the rank of captain in 1885, after quarter of a century of service. Before this, though, he had held independent commands – he had commanded the warships USS *Wasp* and USS *Wachusett*, and developed a reputation for being an intelligent, progressive officer.

In 1883 he published a history of the Civil War, which helped earn him the post of President of the Naval War College which he took up in 1885. It was there that he wrote his masterpiece – *The Influence of Seapower on History, 1660–1783*, a seminal historical study which provoked a revolution in naval thought. He based it on a lifetime of historical research, and tried out his theories during a series of lectures. The book was first published in 1890, and its importance was immediately apparent.

Mahan argued that fleets were most effective when they were used strategically, imposing their dominance over an enemy through the pursuit of a coherent plan of campaign. He claimed that this dominance – something Mahan dubbed 'seapower' – was first developed by the Royal Navy during the late 17th century, and that it gave them a great strategic edge over their French, Dutch or Spanish rivals. He went on to claim that the US Navy could develop only if it adopted a similar strategy – the pursuit of seapower. He was also a believer of the importance of 'a fleet in being'. In time of war, even a small fleet could tie down a much larger one simply by being a latent threat, so forcing the enemy to waste precious national resources.

One of Mahan's first disciples was Theodore Roosevelt, the future President of the United States. Another was Kaiser Wilhelm II – after reading the book, he decided to embark on the building of a modern German fleet, a factor contributing to the outbreak of the First World War. Mahan's aggressive strategic stance was perfectly in tune with American opinion during the Spanish-American War of 1898. In fact, during the war, Mahan himself counselled that the United States should seize control of both Hawaii and the Philippines – useful bases if America planned to expand its influence into the Pacific.

Mahan virtually became a one-man national think-tank, producing strategic policies, representing the United States at international diplomatic conferences, and writing naval history. In 1906 he became a rear admiral, albeit one on the inactive list, and he continued to be a well-received advocate of seapower until his death, on the outbreak of the First World War. Before and after his death, his books were read in all naval staff colleges, and his views on seapower have helped to shape strategic naval thinking ever since.

# THE THEORY OF SAILING

Most people today regard the masts, sails and rigging of a sailing ship-of-war to be something of beauty, rather than a means of propelling a ship through the water. They view this mass of canvas, spar and rope as something incomprehensibly complicated, and even modern sailing boat enthusiasts would be likely to be overwhelmed by the apparent complexity of it all. However, the basic idea was pretty simple.

For a start, the wind does not simply push a boat along, unless it is sailing immediately 'before the wind'. Most of the time a sail acts as an aerofoil, generating power (or lift). This is then transferred through the spars to the hull. The shape of the boat and the resistance of the water along its hull and against its keel all contribute to turning this power into forward motion. Inevitably, some of this motion is wasted because the vessel also travels sideways (known as making leeway), or through its heeling over. However, most of the power is used to move the warship forward, through the water.

Regardless of the size or type of sailing ship, the basic principles are the same. Air (or rather wind) flows over the curved surface of the sail on the windward side (the side *from* which the wind is blowing), creating lift by building up an area of high air pressure. Air flowing over the leeward side (the side *to* which the wind is blowing) creates an area of low pressure. This was complicated slightly on a warship when several sails were used, as the wind passing between them increased the lift on the leeward side of the sail. This makes sailing ships with several sails generate more power per sail than those with a single sail. This difference in pressure is what creates the lift that drives the ship forward.

Just like an aircraft wing, the sail of a sailing ship can reach a stalling position, where the air doesn't strike the sail at an angle which will generate any lift at all. This means that the angle of attack between wind and sail is very important. The most efficient angle of attack is about 22° from the direction of the wind. Sailors therefore take a lot of care to make sure the sails are angled to make the most of the wind. In the days of sail, this was almost second nature to sailors, who knew how to coax the best possible speed out of their ships.

Of course, the wind doesn't always blow from the right direction, so sailors have to adjust their sails accordingly. This means that when the wind is blowing from behind the direction of sailing, the business of sailing is fairly straightforward. If it blows towards the ship it makes it much harder to sail in the right direction. If the wind is coming from somewhere close to dead ahead, then the boat cannot sail into the wind at all.

The closest a well-rigged sailing warship could sail into the wind was about 35–45°. In other words, it could not sail directly into the face of the wind, or on an arc to either side of it. Even beyond this arc, forward progress would be tediously slow, but it might be the only way a ship could head in the direction it wanted. If the intended course lay in the direction the wind was coming from, then the ship would have to zig-zag, moving along one arc as close to the wind as it could, then turn across the wind (a business known as 'tacking'), so that the wind would hit the sails from the other side, still as close to the wind as the captain could manage. This was (and still is) known as sailing 'close-hauled', with the sails pulled as tightly as they can be, and angled round to catch the wind. As well as being slow, sailing close-hauled also meant that more power than usual was wasted in sideways movement – making leeway.

A final factor in the age of sail was the loss of power through friction of the water and air. If a crew had not cleaned the ship's underside, then weeds, barnacles and other marine growth all worked to increase friction, and thereby reduce the amount of power which was converted into forward motion. A captain couldn't do anything about the natural resistance of wind and water, although ship designers could. Ships with low sleek hulls offered less resistance to the wind, and so were faster than larger vessels. Similarly, great care was taken to design warship hulls that were streamlined, and therefore offered the least possible amount of resistance. While all this sounds complicated, sailing a sailing man-of-war was a matter of practice. Most ship captains during the age of fighting sail knew the sailing qualities of their own ships, and could calculate the forces involved between wind and sail. The very best captains were also able to fine-tune things, so their ships made the best possible use of the wind to propel their ship faster than those of the enemy.

# THE LORDS OF THE ADMIRALTY

In accounts of the Royal Navy, historians often mention the Admiralty, as some sort of vague governing body, but few people take the time to explain what it is, and what it does. The term 'Admiralty' is used to describe the government department which was once responsible for Britain's naval affairs. In fact, until the union of Scotland and England in 1707 it was the English Admiralty, and the Scots had their own tiny version. The term is – or was – used by other countries, and of course it had its equivalents. For instance, the Admiralty had similar areas of responsibility to the US Department of the Navy, which is now part of the Department of Defense. The French equivalent was the Ministère (Ministry) de la Marine, but it is now run as part of a centralized Department of Defence. Today, Britain's naval affairs are administered by the Ministry of Defence (MoD), which controls all three services.

The origins of the Admiralty date back to the late 13th century and the reign of King Edward I (reign 1272–1307). He appointed a Lord High Admiral as the head of his small navy, and gave him a suite of offices in London. These offices became known as the Admiralty. The senior officials who ran the Admiralty were known as the Lords Commissioners of the Admiralty, and when they met for their regular meetings they were known collectively as the Board of the Admiralty. The Sea Lords were senior serving officers, who tended to handle operational matters, while the Lords of the Admiralty were civil servants or politicians, who dealt more with administration and governance. Therefore, shortly before the outbreak of the First World War, the First Sea Lord was Admiral Sir Jackie Fisher, while the Lord of the Admiralty was a politician, Winston Churchill.

This system continued in use for almost seven centuries, until the Admiralty was disbanded in 1964. From then on all three of Britain's armed services were administered by the Ministry of Defence. As a sop to tradition, the section within the MoD which deals with naval matters is administered by the Admiralty Board (or the Navy Board), although the board members – a mixture of serving naval officers and civil servants – have long since lost the title of Lords Commissioners. The Admiralty building still stands in London's Whitehall, an imposing structure that reflected the prestige of Britain's Senior Service during its heyday. In time of war its offices were a bustling hive of activity, with officers arriving in the hope of a ship, or to be court-martialled, or to receive their orders. Admirals, civil servants and politicians went about their business, holding meetings, making judgements and sending or receiving a welter of reports. The novelist Patrick O'Brian painted a vivid picture of the Admiralty during the Napoleonic wars in his superb series of historical novels, featuring Captain Jack Aubrey and his surgeon, Doctor Stephen Maturin (see p.214).

The Admiralty was more than just a place where the Royal Navy was administered. The Lords Commissioners were also responsible for legal affairs pertaining to the seas around Britain, as far as the high tide mark. That was why pirates were tried in Admiralty Courts, which had their own special powers when dealing with civil and naval cases. The ultimate legal body was the High Court of the Admiralty, which handled all of Britain's maritime cases until its disbandment in 1875. It dealt with the weighty business of deciding if captured vessels were legal prizes, and therefore it was responsible for handing out prize money to the crew of the warship that captured an enemy vessel. This was a major incentive for men of the Royal Navy during the age of fighting sail, as a seaman could easily earn the equivalent of a year's wages in a single engagement.

# PROFILE OF A WARSHIP FLEET: THE POOK TURTLES

'Pook Turtles' was the nickname given to a flotilla of seven ironclad gunboats designed to be used on the Mississippi River and its many tributaries during the American Civil War (1861–65). From the outset, the plan was for these revolutionary new warships to spearhead the Union's drive down the Mississippi River, and so cut the Confederacy in two.

Their designer was the Boston shipbuilder Samuel M. Pook (1804–78) who had built clipper ships before the war. This was going to be a challenging new departure – the creation of a flotilla of armoured river paddleboats, powered by steam and armed with powerful batteries of heavy artillery. He began the task within months of the outbreak of the war, and in August 1861 the War

Department felt ready to start building. They issued shipbuilding contracts to James B. Eads (1820–87), a civil engineer, inventor and salvage expert, based in St Louis, Missouri.

The contract called for the vessels to be built in just over two months – a near impossible target, especially as Pook was still labouring over their design. Fortunately, money seemed no object, and within two weeks, over 4,000 shipbuilders, engineers and labourers had been hired, and sub-contracts issued to shipyards in Carondelet outside St Louis, and in Mound City, Illinois. Timber was cut, shaped and then used to build their basic hulls, while steel plants rolled out the iron plate needed to protect these hulls from enemy shot. Steam engines and boilers were built, naval stores and ordnance were shipped across land to the Mississippi River, and crews were found to man these strange vessels.

The official title for these seven ironclads was the City Class of river gunboats. Unofficially they became known as 'Eads' gunboats', or – more commonly – 'Pook Turtles'. Pook's vessels were 175ft (53m) long, with a substantial beam of 51ft (15.6m), and a draught of just 6ft (1.8m). They were powered by stern paddlewheels, and were capable of a speed of up to 8 knots (14.8km/h), at least when going downstream. They were armed with 13 heavy guns (although the exact number and type varied slightly), mounted on a single gundeck, with guns pointing ahead, astern and to both sides. This gundeck was protected by an iron casemate some 2½in (6.5cm) thick, which also protected the engines and paddlewheel. The seven ungainly vessels were all named after Mississippi riverside towns in the Union – *Cairo*, *Carondelet*, *Cincinnati*, *Louisville*, *Mound City*, *Pittsburgh* and *St. Louis*. The last named was later renamed the *Baron de Kalb*.

The first of them – the *St. Louis* – was launched in mid-October 1861, which meant that Eads had more or less delivered them on time. The cost, though, was high – they had cost the US taxpayer more than $100,000 apiece. However, given what they achieved, this was money well spent. The entire flotilla was armed, crewed and ready to fight by mid-January 1862, when all seven were officially accepted into service by the War Department. They formed the Western Gunboat Flotilla, but strangely enough they were run by the US Army rather than the US Navy.

The Pook Turtles went on to achieve great things. They participated in the capture of Fort Henry and Fort Donelson; these guarded the Tennessee and Cumberland rivers, which led into the Confederate heartland of Tennessee. Next they helped capture Island No.10, which guarded the upper approaches of the Mississippi River; then in May and June 1862 they destroyed the Confederate River Defense Fleet, in a riverine campaign that culminated in the battle of Memphis. They then went on to assist in the capture of Vicksburg, Mississippi, and clear the major tributaries of the Mississippi River such as the Yazoo and the Red River. Naturally, victory came at a price. The *Mound City*, the *Cairo* and the *Baron de Kalb* were all sunk by Confederate torpedoes (mines), and at various times several of the gunboats were badly damaged by enemy gunfire. Still, they proved their worth. Thanks to Pook and his Turtles, the Mississippi River became a Union-controlled waterway, the Confederacy was split in two, and Union victory became a foregone conclusion.

# PAINTING THE SAILING MAN-OF-WAR

During the 18th and early 19th centuries, the Royal Navy (and most other navies) allowed captains a great deal of leeway in the way they painted their vessels. That way, it was easier to distinguish warships in the heat of battle. Of course, periodic attempts were made to create a more uniform appearance, but this was never enforced. For instance, as early as 1715, the Admiralty decreed that all Royal Navy warships would be painted in yellow and black, and a uniform paint colour was applied within the ship itself. While many captains conformed to this, others ignored it, and 18th-century paintings show warships painted in a range of colours, including yellow, black, red and blue. In fact, for much of the century, a light blue colour scheme for the upperworks (above the main deck) was popular, with scrollwork and decoration picked out in gold.

Another Admiralty Order of 1780 allowed captains to paint their ships black or yellow, but even then a wide variety of schemes continued to be used until the end of the Napoleonic Wars. Admiral Horatio Nelson favoured a black and yellow colour scheme – he painted the hulls of his ships yellow, then added black bands to them. He ordered the underside of his gunports to be painted black. This meant that when the gunports were closed, his ships appeared striped. However, when the gunports were opened, they appeared chequered, with the yellow lines being interrupted by the black gunports. This colour scheme became known as the 'Nelson chequer'.

Nelson's original intent was to make his flagships more distinguishable. As he put it, he wanted the ship 'to be distinguished with greater certainty in case of falling in with an enemy'. HMS *Victory* was painted in the Nelson chequer in 1800, during a refit in Chatham Dockyard. After Nelson's death at the battle of Trafalgar (1805), this colour scheme became the favoured one throughout the Royal Navy, and for the rest of the Napoleonic War most British warships were painted this way.

However, towards the end of the war, a new colour scheme gained in popularity, by which the hulls were painted black and white. This was the scheme favoured by the US Navy during the War of 1812 (1812–15), and it was slowly adopted in the Royal Navy. To confuse things, though, some American warships were also painted in the traditional Nelson chequer. After 1815, the black and white scheme became increasingly popular, and during the last decades of the age of sail, and even during the early days of steam-powered warships, this black and white version of the Nelson chequer became the standard colour scheme for Royal Naval warships.

For their part, the French and the Spanish fleets favoured colour schemes involving red and black, applied either in stripes or in solid colours. During the period before the widespread adoption of the black and yellow Nelson chequer by the Royal Navy, fleet actions were colourful affairs, with warships painted in a range of colours. The following list of colour schemes was drawn up by a Colonel Fawkes, who witnessed the battle of the Nile in 1798. It remains the most complete list of warship colour schemes from the age of fighting sail.

### The Royal Navy

*Alexander, Audacious, Bellerophon, Defence, Mutine, Orion*: plain yellow sides.

*Goliath, Leander, Majestic, Swiftsure, Vanguard* (flagship): yellow sides, with a black strake between the two rows of gunports.

*Theseus*: as above, but with the canvas covering her hammocks painted yellow, with black 'gunports' painted on it – to make her look like a three-decker.

*Culloden*: yellow sides, with two narrow black strakes between the upper and lower rows of gunports.

*Zealous*: red sides, with a yellow strake between the two rows of gunports.

*Minotaur*: red sides, with a black strake between the two rows of gunports.

Note: with the exception of the 50-gun Fourth Rate HMS *Leander*, all of these British ships were Third Rate 74-gun ships-of-the-line.

### The French Republican Navy

*Le Conquérant, Le Guerriere*: plain dark yellow sides.

*L'Aquilon*: red sides, with a black strake between the two rows of gunports.

*Le Franklin*: plain yellow sides.

*L'Orient, Le Peuple Souverain*: dark yellow sides.

*Le Tonnant*: light yellow sides, with narrow black strakes running through both rows of gunports, and a thicker black strake between them.

*L'Heureux, Le Mercure*: very dark yellow sides.

*Le Généreux, Le Timoleon*: very dark red sides.

*Le Guillaume Tell*: light yellow sides, with a black strake between the two rows of gunports.

*Artémise, Justice, Diane, Sérieuse* (all frigates): plain yellow sides.

Note: apart from the frigates, all of the French ships were 74-gun Third Rates, with the exception of the 120-gun First Rate *L'Orient*, and the 80-gun Second Rates *Franklin*, *Guillaume Tell* and *Tonnant*.

# HOW THE PRESS GANG WORKED

During the French Revolutionary and Napoleonic wars, the Royal Navy relied on three sources of manpower – volunteers, 'quota men' supplied by country magistrates, and pressed men. The Quota Act (1795) meant that each county had to supply a number of recruits, based on their total populations. Most local magistrates fulfilled their wartime quota by sending to sea convicted felons or known troublemakers. Most of these were 'landsmen', with no previous maritime experience. A much better source of trained manpower was the Press Gang.

The Impressment Service – and its tool the Press Gang – is often portrayed as a callous, brutal organization, but in fact it was as much a recruiting tool as a means of forcing seamen to join the Navy. The term 'press' comes from the French verb *prêter*, meaning to give money in return for service. It therefore stems from the payment of the king's shilling to pressed men, as a legal means of binding the sailor to Naval service.

The Impressment Service usually set up recruiting stations in ports and even inland towns, and pressed men were usually a mixture of men forced into service and those who were naïve enough to approach the recruiters to ask for more details. These men were usually taken to a receiving ship moored offshore, where they were evaluated according to their ability, physical stature and intelligence. It was common to release up to a quarter of these pressed men, as they were either physically or mentally unfit for service. For the most part the press gangs targeted seamen, and certain professions or classes of society were exempt from impressment. Finally, individual captains often sent their own press gangs ashore in an attempt to recruit sailors, and it was these part-time press gangs – the 'hot press' rather than the professionals of the Impressment Service – who earned the worst reputation for seizing 'recruits' by force.

# SEA BATTLE: THE BATTLE OF MANILA BAY, 1898

In 1898, the United States went to war with Spain, prompting a naval war in two oceans. The war began after the explosion of the USS *Maine* in Havana harbour that February, as the US government laid the blame for the tragedy at the door of the Spanish. While the bulk of the US Navy blockaded Cuba, and prepared for a naval battle against the Spanish Atlantic Squadron, Commodore George Dewey's American Asiatic Squadron was ordered to the Philippines, where it was ordered to seek out and destroy the Spanish Pacific Squadron.

The two sides were far from evenly matched. Admiral Patricio Nontejo y Pasarón commanded a collection of eight small, obsolete and unarmoured light cruisers and gunboats, and flew his flag in the slightly more modern cruiser *Reina Cristina*. All of them were based in the Philippine port of Manila, where at least they had the benefit of protection, supplied by four equally obsolete shore batteries.

Commodore Dewey's American Asiatic Squadron was a lot more powerful. His flagship was the powerful cruiser USS *Olympia*, and it was accompanied by two other modern cruisers, and four assorted gunboats. In late April Dewey sailed from Mirs Bay (Tai Pang Wan), Hong Kong, and he arrived off Manila Bay early on 1 May. He entered the bay in line astern, with his flagship leading. The *Olympia* struck two mines during its approach towards the Spanish, but neither of them exploded, and the fleet passed over them without incident. Then, just before 0500hrs, the Spanish shore batteries and warships opened fire at extreme range. The Spanish ships were clustered close to their main naval base at Cavite, a few miles down the coast from Manila City.

Dewey still hadn't given the order to fire on the Spaniards, as he wanted every shot to count. Finally, at 0541hrs, he gave the *Olympia*'s commander – Captain Gridley – the order the entire squadron had waited for: 'You may fire when you are ready, Gridley'. The *Olympia* concentrated its fire on the *Reina Cristina*, and the wooden-hulled old cruiser *Castilla*. The rest of the fleet joined in when their guns had a clear shot, as Dewey led his squadron back and forth, bombarding the Spanish ships at a range of 2,200 yards (2,000m). Soon Cavite Bay was blanketed with gunsmoke. With his ships running low on ammunition, Dewey gave the order to cease fire and withdraw, at least until the smoke cleared. In the meantime the commodore and his men ate a hearty breakfast. He was worried though – it seemed that his guns had been having little effect on the Spanish ships, and that the enemy were still in action.

Dewey needn't have worried. When the smoke cleared, and he closed with the Spaniards again, the full extent of the American gunnery was revealed. The *Reina Cristina* and the *Castilla* had both been sunk, while the rest were either sinking or on fire. Still, Dewey wanted to make sure. At 1116hrs he gave the order to resume firing, until within an hour every Spanish ship lay on the bottom of the harbour.

With hindsight, it is easy enough to dismiss Dewey's victory as a one-sided affair – a turkey shoot against a far weaker opponent. In fact, Dewey and his men had no real idea how powerful the Spanish squadron was before the battle began, and then there was the very real danger of loss through mines or from the Spanish shore batteries. Commodore Dewey must have been a very relieved man when the smoke cleared after breakfast, and he realized he had won. The US Navy's victory at Manila Bay opened the way for an American invasion of the Philippines – Manila was captured on 13 August, and the islands fell soon afterwards. By capturing Spain's possessions in the Pacific, the United States had begun the process of becoming a global power.

# RUM RATIONS IN THE AGE OF SAIL

During the age of sail, a ship's company in the Royal Navy could expect a fairly plentiful supply of alcohol to help them through the day. Until the mid-17th century sailors were given a beer ration, or else French brandy. Then, in 1655 the English captured Jamaica, and rum became available as an alternative, first in ships serving in the Caribbean, and later throughout the whole fleet. It was thought that rum was a cure for scurvy, but by the time that theory proved false, sailors had come to expect their rum ration, regardless of any dubious medicinal qualities it might have. Actually, the first rum issues involved either serving it neat or mixing it with lime juice, which later became the principal maritime protection against scurvy.

A rum ration was issued twice a day: at noon, accompanying dinner (the main meal of the day), and at 1800hrs, to accompany a light supper of ship's biscuit and either butter or cheese. Usually, the issue was accompanied by the playing of the tune 'Nancy Dawson'.

From 1740, before being issued, the neat rum was diluted to produce 'grog', a mixture of one part of rum to two parts of water. This watering down was an attempt to reduce drunkenness at sea. This was a relative improvement, as from 1740 onwards the ration of neat rum per man was laid down as a half quart (a pint, or just over half a litre) a day, mixed with a quart (two pints or just over a litre) of water. Half of this quantity was issued at a time, one issue with each of the two meals. Occasionally the Captain would give the order to 'splice the mainbrace', which involved an extra rum issue, usually given as a reward for a particularly hard and gruelling task, such as raising a new mast, or manning the pumps on a badly damaged ship.

Watering the rum down to create 'grog' first started on the instigation of Admiral Edward Vernon, who was operating in the Caribbean at the time. He ordered that the mixing was to be done on the open deck, under the watchful eye of the officer of the watch. By the time of the Seven Years War (1756–63) the issuing of rum as 'grog' had become the standard form of alcohol issue in the Royal Navy.

When rum wasn't available, the crews were issued with whatever the ship's captain could procure – brandy being a popular substitute. In home waters beer was issued as well – each man receiving a daily ration of up to 8 pints (4.5 litres) a day. This, though, was 'small beer', which had a low alcohol content, and was issued more as an alternative to drinking water than anything else. For the most part this 'small beer' was brewed in the Navy's own brewery in Portsmouth. Warships on the North American station were often given a variant called spruce beer. In the Mediterranean wine was plentiful, so it was sometimes issued in lieu of beer, and once again it was watered down slightly, to make it less potent. The quantities are still surprising – as much as 2 pints (over 1 litre) of wine could be issued a day.

In the Royal Navy the rum ration continued until 1970, although from 1850 onwards the size of the issue was reduced to a mere one gill (½ pint, 28cl) of neat rum per day, diluted with three parts of water. By 1970 this had been reduced even further, to ½ gill (¼ pint, 14cl), The Canadian Navy followed suit two years later, in 1972. In the US Navy rum was originally issued in similar quantities to the Royal Navy, but the American rum ration came to an end in September 1862, soon after the start of the American Civil War. Alcohol was still available on board US warships until June 1914, when the Secretary of the Navy Josephus Daniels issued General Order 99, which prohibited the drinking of any form of alcohol on board American warships, so creating a 'dry fleet'.

# FIGUREHEADS

As early as the 13th century, the bows of warships were decorated with figureheads – ornamental carved and painted figures, usually in the shape of a human or an animal. In fact, figureheads are even older than that, as the Ancient Egyptians, the Phoenicians, the Greeks and the Romans were all fond of decorating their ships in this manner, usually with the image of a deity of some kind. The Vikings used dragon carvings on the stem posts of their longships, while the mid-11th-century Bayeux Tapestry shows William the Conqueror's own ship decorated with a lion's head on its prow.

However, the first figureheads to appear in the historical records date from the 14th century. This is when the first proper figureheads appear – carved figures attached to the bows of the ship, rather than just carved pieces of ship's structure. Records from the time of King Henry VIII of England provide us with useful titbits of information – for instance in 1546 the warships *Salamander* and *Unicorn* had figureheads depicting these two mythical creatures. It was during this period that the bow of the sailing ship evolved to create the shape it would retain until the end of the age of sail. Most of the larger sailing warships in the world's navies boasted figureheads from the mid-17th century onwards.

Certain carvings were more popular than others. For instance, the English and Dutch favoured figureheads depicting lions, while the Spanish preferred religious figures, and the French created elaborate statues, frequently based on the gods of antiquity. Often these were political as well as decorative. The figurehead of the *Naseby* during the 1650s portrayed an equestrian Oliver Cromwell, riding down his Royalist, Scottish, Irish, Dutch, French and Spanish foes.

By the 18th century it had become more common to use the figurehead to reflect the name of the ship itself. Thus the *Edgar* (1779) featured the head of the Anglo-Saxon king of the same name, the *Agamemnon* (1781) was decorated by a bust of the Greek hero, the *Hannibal* (1786) portrayed the Carthaginian general, and the *Brunswick* (1790) carried a figurehead depicting the Duke of Brunswick, a relative of King George III. In fact, during the battle of the First of June (1794), a French roundshot hit the figurehead, knocking off the cocked hat worn by the duke. Captain Harvey took off his own hat, and ordered it to be nailed in place, to cover the wooden duke's head.

The French often hired well-known artists and sculptors to produce designs for their naval figureheads, and during the reign of King Louis XIV the French monarch was often depicted on his throne, flanked by the figures of Fame and Victory. Once again, though, politics intervened – during the French Revolutionary Wars the frigate *Carmagnole* carried a figurehead carving of a guillotine on her bows. The Emperor Napoleon refused to let his image be used as a figurehead, mainly because there was no guarantee a ship would not be captured. Other leaders were less reserved: in 1834 the USS *Constitution* was adorned by a full-length statue of President Jackson.

After the Napoleonic Wars, post-war parsimony meant that warship figureheads tended to be less lavish and imaginative than before. However, the Scottish-born naval artist John Shetky was appointed as a drawing master to the Navy, and under his tutelage figureheads became more exotic. Nevertheless, the general trend was to make figureheads less obtrusive, and far less decorative.

The introduction of steam-powered warships made figureheads no longer necessary. In fact, although HMS *Warrior* (1860) carried a splendid figurehead depicting an ancient soldier, most later warships were given little more than a shield. By the end of the century figureheads had almost completely disappeared from the world's warships, reflecting a new age where firepower and armour were more important than ostentation. Fortunately many of the world's maritime museums contain some fine examples of naval figureheads, dating back to a time when no self-respecting sailing warship would put to sea without one.

# THE GUNBOATS OF LAKE TANGANYIKA

One of the most bizarre naval encounters of the First World War was fought on a freshwater lake, some 2,500ft (760m) above sea level, and 500 miles (800km) from the ocean. It also involved the transport of two tiny gunboats – *Mimi* and *Toutou* – across half of Africa, by a naval officer who wore a skirt and was worshipped as a god.

During the last decades before the First World War, Germany played her part in the European 'scramble for Africa' by carving out her own enclave, known as German East Africa (now Tanganyika). It stretched from the Indian Ocean to Lake Tanganyika, in the Rift Valley. Over 400 miles (740km) long and 45 miles (72km) wide, Lake Tanganyika (or the Tanganjikasee) was the largest freshwater lake in the world. The Germans transported two large gunboats to the lake, and used them to police the colony's western borders.

In August 1914, the Germans destroyed a Belgian gunboat, giving them complete naval mastery of the lake. In fact, the Germans had three gunboats – the *Graf von Götzen* and the slightly smaller *Hedwig von Wissman*, plus a smaller patrol boat, the *Kingari*. This force meant that the British and the Belgians were unable to attack German East Africa from their own colonies, as they needed control of the lake to transport men and supplies. Back in London, the Admiralty vowed to do something.

The result was that, in June 1915, a group of 28 British sailors were sent from Britain to South Africa by steamer, led by an eccentric and accident prone naval officer, Lieutenant Commander Spicer-Simpson (1876–1947). The steamer's cargo consisted of two 40ft (12m) motor launches, each armed with a 3-pdr and a machine gun. Spicer-Simpson tried to name them *Dog* and *Cat*, but when the Admiralty rejected the names, he renamed them *Mimi* and *Toutou* instead – French slang for 'miaow' and 'woof'! They arrived in Cape Town in mid-July, and the boats were transferred onto a train, which transported them to the Belgian Congo, where the railway ended. The boats were then taken across land, dragged on wheeled carriages by a combination of oxen, steam engines and African labourers.

Finally, on 26 October, the expedition reached the western shore of Lake Tanganyika. By that time, Spicer-Simpson had taken to wearing a skirt, specially made for him by his London tailors. The eccentric commander and his men prepared the boats, and two months later they were ready for action. On 26 December they spotted the *Kingari*, gave chase, and captured her after a short, sharp battle. Spicer-Simpson repaired her and renamed her the *Fifi*.

Then, on 9 February 1915, the British flotilla encountered the *Hedwig von Wissman*. Spicer-Simpson attacked her in the *Fifi*, supported by *Mimi*. After a lengthy chase a lucky shot from the *Fifi* holed the German gunboat, and she sank an hour later. Bizarrely, now that the odds were stacked in the British favour,

Spicer-Simpson refused to attack the remaining German gunboat. Instead he used his ships to support Belgian land operations, and avoided the *Graf von Götzen*. She was eventually scuttled by the Germans, when they were forced to abandon their last port on the lake in late July. She was salvaged after the war, and still plies the waters of Lake Tanganyika, serving as a passenger ferry.

As for *Mimi* and *Toutou*, the two launches were abandoned, and Spicer-Simpson and his men were recalled to Britain. Despite avoiding a final battle, Spicer-Simpson and his men had accomplished a great deal. Spicer-Simpson served in naval intelligence for the rest of the war. Back in East Africa, it was claimed that some tribes on the edges of the lake worshipped the effigy of a kilted figure, wearing a skirt and a pith helmet. In Africa, truth is sometimes much stranger than fiction.


# WHAT IS THE WEATHER GAGE?

In most accounts of naval battles during the age of fighting sail, a lot of emphasis seems to be placed on one side or other having the weather gage (or gauge). It was of crucial importance, as the ship or fleet with the weather gage had the ability to break off the fight, or to dictate the pace of the action.

Essentially, a ship or a fleet which is to windward of the enemy is deemed to have 'the weather gage'. Windward, of course, is the side from which the wind blows; the other ship or fleet – without the weather gage – is deemed to be to leeward. The ship or fleet to leeward is sometimes described as having 'the leeward gage'.

During an engagement, the side without the weather gage would find it far harder to come to grips with the enemy than the fleet to windward of them. They would have to tack slowly towards the enemy, all the time exposing themselves to gunfire. The fleet with the weather gage could also move further to windward, and so keep its distance, and thereby avoid battle. It would also find it relatively easy to close with the enemy, as all it had to do was to sail downwind.

One final advantage was that if two sailing ships were parallel to each other, and one had the weather gage, then both ships would heel over slightly, but the one to leeward would have its guns pointing upwards at the opposing fleet, while the guns of the ships to windward would point down at the enemy. This made it far harder for the leeward ship to depress its guns far enough to fire into the hull of the enemy. By contrast, the ship with the weather gage would find it comparatively easy to fire at the enemy's hull.

When sail gave way to steam, having the weather gage was no longer of critical importance. In fact, it can be argued that the ship to leeward had a slight edge, as its smoke blew away from the enemy, making it slightly easier to come in range and hit the enemy ship to windward. Set against this was the possibility that spray and enemy smoke might obscure the target slightly. However, all these advantages and disadvantages were pretty minor, compared with the edge the weather gage gave to warships in the age of fighting sail.

# PROFILE OF A WARSHIP: USS *MONITOR*

The outbreak of the American Civil War in 1861 found both sides unprepared for the conflict. The Union possessed a sizeable navy of wooden screw warships, but no ironclads. Prompted by rumours that the Confederates were building an ironclad, the Secretary of the Navy Gideon Welles commissioned Swedish-born designer John Ericsson to construct a small ironclad vessel armed with two guns, mounted in a revolving turret. The result was the USS *Monitor*, which was completed in February 1862.

Unlike previous warships the tiny *Monitor* was completely armoured, with her turret sitting on an iron-plated hull that barely rose out of the water. Her engines and magazines were all below the waterline. She was just 179ft (55m) long at the waterline, with a 41½ft (12.6m) beam, and a draught of 10½ft (3.2m). However, she had a freeboard – the distance between the waterline and the upper deck – of just 18in (45cm). This made the hull very difficult to hit, but it also made the ship unsuitable for operations in anything other than the calmest of waters.

The most striking thing about the *Monitor* was her 20ft (6m) diameter circular turret. It contained two 11in smoothbore guns, mounted on a revolving platform. It was open-topped – only a wire grill protected it from the elements – but its sides were heavily armoured, with 8in (20cm) of iron plate. Apart from her freeboard, the weakest feature of the *Monitor* was her engines. While they and her propeller and rudder assembly were protectively sited beneath her armoured deck, they weren't particularly powerful, and the ironclad had a top speed of just 9 knots (16.7km/h).

The new vessel was so ungainly that critics doubted that she would ever work. The newspapers dubbed her 'Ericsson's Folly', and an observer described her as looking 'like a cheesebox, mounted on top of a raft'. However, in the spring of 1862 she was all that stood between the Union Navy and disaster.

On 8 March, 1862, the ironclad CSS *Virginia* steamed out of Norfolk into Hampton Roads. In the next four hours she demonstrated the superiority of the shell gun and the resilience of her armour, destroying two Union wooden warships before returning to a hero's welcome. The following morning she tried to complete her destruction, but found herself facing the USS *Monitor*, which had only reached Hampton Roads the night before. In what was the first fight between two ironclads, the *Virginia* and the *Monitor* hammered each other at close range, but failed to damage their opponent. Although the battle of Hampton Roads was a stalemate, it changed the course of naval warfare forever. Wooden warships were clearly redundant, and the future lay in armour plate and large guns. 'Ericsson's Folly' had proved its worth.

Subsequent ironclads produced by both sides were based on their respective prototypes, and all future turret ironclads produced for the US Navy were given the typological name 'monitor'. Both monitor and casemate ironclads proved invaluable warships during the American Civil War, but they were exclusively coastal vessels, far smaller than the seagoing ironclads of Britain and France. While the USS *Monitor* broke new ground by taking part in history's first fight between ironclad warships, and although Ericsson's turret design eventually led to the powerful turrets used in later battleships, she also represented a dead end in warship evolution. The future of naval warfare lay in much bigger blue-water ironclads, and an evolutionary line which led to the great battleships of the 20th century.

# NELSON'S 'BAND OF BROTHERS'

During the Mediterranean campaign of 1798, Rear Admiral Nelson referred to the British captains under his command as his 'band of brothers'. He took the phrase from William Shakespeare's *Henry V* (Act IV, Scene III), and the speech given by the English king on the eve of the battle of Agincourt:

> This story shall the good man teach his son;
> And Crispin Crispian shall ne'er go by,
> From this day to the ending of the world,
> But we in it shall be remembered, —
> We few, we happy few, we band of brothers;
> For he to-day that sheds his blood with me
> Shall be my brother; be he ne'er so vile,
> This day shall gentle his condition.

Nelson used the phrase to bolster morale among his 15 captains during the weeks preceding the battle of the Nile (1798). He invited them to dine with him, they discussed strategy and tactics together, and – above all – he was able to imbue them with his own ideas about how to come to grips with the enemy; something the press dubbed 'the Nelson spirit'. The result was the creation of a tightly knit community of naval commanders, whom Nelson felt he could rely upon in battle. This fostering of 'the Nelson spirit' played a significant part in the decisive victory Nelson inflicted on his French counterpart at the Nile. Nelson's foray into what now would be called 'team building' paid off handsomely.

Nelson used the term in his reports, claiming that, 'I had the happiness to command a band of brothers'. While this original 'band of brothers' dispersed at the end of the campaign, their commander resurrected the phrase again, most notably during the Trafalgar campaign of 1805. During the months before his final battle, Nelson held regular meetings with his captains, and used the words to foster the same team spirit. Of course, he also imbued his subordinates with his own views on naval tactics.

As Nelson himself put it, 'When I came to explain to them the "Nelson Touch", it was like an electric shock. Some shed tears, all approved, and from Admirals downwards it was repeated; "It must succeed, if ever they allow us to get at them! You are, my Lord, surrounded by friends whom you inspire with confidence."' After Nelson's death at Trafalgar, the term 'band of brothers' cropped up regularly, usually when referring to a close-knit group of servicemen.

# NAVAL POWER IN 1862

The start of the 1860s was a fascinating time in naval history. For a start, the world's first sea-going ironclad – the French warship *Gloire* – entered service in August 1860, and by 1862 she had been joined by five more French ironclads. This threatened to upset the naval status quo, so the Royal Navy commissioned its own class of ironclad warships – the first of which was HMS *Warrior*. This initiated an ironclad-building race between Britain and France – one that the British won handsomely.

Then, on the far side of the Atlantic, the United States was riven by Civil War. Her fleet was small by comparison with the British or French fleets, but in 1862 the Union Navy was undergoing a rapid expansion, having embraced the technology of the ironclad warship. The battle between the USS *Monitor* and the CSS *Virginia* on 9 March 1862 demonstrated the effectiveness of the ironclad as a warship, and so a large-scale ironclad-building programme was put into operation. Unlike the warships in other navies, these ironclads were designed for use in rivers or shallow coastal waters, rather than on the high seas. Therefore a direct comparison between the US Navy and its European counterparts is a little misleading.

The other point of interest is the large number of obsolete wooden-hulled warships which still remained in service. Both the British and the French had substantial fleets of these, which had been rendered extremely vulnerable by the new invention of the shell gun. These wooden hulls offered little or no protection against modern naval artillery, and consequently they were of little use in a future naval war.

In the list below, the totals have been altered slightly, the effect of which is to boost the smaller navies, as for the sake of clarity, steam-powered and sailing frigates in the British and French navies have been omitted. For the record, the French had 15 steam-powered frigates, and 27 sail-powered ones. The British had almost phased out their sailing fleet, so most of their vessels were on the inactive list. That still left a total of 44 steam-powered and five sailing frigates, the latter being used for training purposes rather than as active warships. This meant that, in numbers, the Royal Navy was still by far the largest naval force in the world. Thanks to the introduction of the ironclad, in terms of combat effectiveness the British and the French were pretty much on par in 1862.

**Royal Navy**

4 ocean-going ironclads (15 building)
62 steam-powered ships-of-the-line
10 sailing ships-of-the-line

**Imperial French Navy**

6 ocean-going ironclads (10 building)
36 steam-powered ships-of-the-line
8 sailing ships-of-the-line

**United States Navy**

1 ocean-going ironclad
4 riverine ironclads (23 building)
8 steam-powered frigates
6 sailing frigates

**Imperial Russian Navy**

0 ocean-going ironclads (3 building)
18 steam-powered ships-of-the-line (9 were frigates)

**Italian Navy**

2 ocean-going ironclads (2 building)
6 steam-powered ships-of-the-line (8 building)
3 sailing frigates

**Austro-Hungarian Navy**

0 ocean-going ironclads (3 building)
4 steam-powered ships-of-the-line (all but 1 were frigates)
2 sailing frigates

**Prussian Navy**

3 steam-powered frigates
2 sailing frigates

# PAY AND PRIZE MONEY IN THE AGE OF FIGHTING SAIL

At the start of the French Revolutionary War in 1793, seamen serving in the Royal Navy hadn't had a pay rise for a little over a century. Their complaints were ignored, and in April 1797 the frustration and resentment resulted in mutinies at Spithead and the Nore. Although the mutinies were quelled, the Admiralty saw reason, pay was increased, and conditions were improved. From late 1797 on, 'seamen' were given a monthly wage of around £1 15s a month (the equivalent of a farm labourer's wages), while 'landsmen' earned around £1 (20s).

Clearly these wages were minimal, so most sailors hoped to augment their income through prize money – the bounty issued on capturing an enemy ship. This was a major spur for seamen, and encouraged ferocity in boarding actions or when manning the gun deck. The value of a prize was decided by the Admiralty prize court, and the total was usually equivalent to the value of the ship and its cargo if a merchantman, or a ship and its armament if a warship.

Prize money was allocated by eighths. Two-eighths went to the captain of the warship that captured the prize, while another eighth went to the admiral who controlled the ship. If the warship was operating under Admiralty orders rather than those of an admiral, then this eighth devolved to the captain, giving him three-eighths. One-eighth was divided among the remaining commissioned officers (lieutenant, surgeon, purser etc.), while a further two-eighths went to the non-commissioned officers on board (the midshipmen, the petty officers and marine sergeants). That left two-eighths to be divided among the rest of the crew. A slightly larger proportion was given to seamen than landsmen. This complex system was changed slightly in 1808, but the basic divisions remained the same. A successful prize might earn a seaman a year's worth of wages in a day, or give a non-commissioned officer a handy retirement nest – enough to buy him a pub or inn when he retired from the service.

# PROFILE OF A WARSHIP:
## CSS *HUNLEY*

In 1863, during the American Civil War, the Confederacy was at a low ebb. Its ports were blockaded, Union fleets had joined forces on the Mississippi River, and its armies were suffering bloody defeats at Gettysburg and Vicksburg. The Confederacy needed a miracle to restore its fortunes, or a secret weapon. Earlier in the war, half-hearted attempts had been made to build a submarine capable of single-handedly breaking the Union blockade. A consortium of four entrepreneurs decided to build a new submersible, basing its design on an existing cylindrical boiler, 4ft (1.2m) in diameter.

Tapering bow and stern sections were added, and each of these contained the water-filled ballast tanks that would be used to make the boat capable of submerging. Ballast weights were clamped to the outside of the hull, and a couple of small hatches on the upper deck provided a means of getting in or out of the submarine. The whole boat was just 30ft (9m) long. She was powered by means of a hand-turned crank which ran the length of the boat, and turned a propeller. Steering was achieved by pulling on levers which moved a small rudder. The finished boat was named the CSS *H. L. Hunley*, after one of its four builders.

She was built in Charleston, South Carolina, and launched in July 1863. Lieutenant Dixon − a veteran of the battle of Shiloh − was named as her commander, and he was joined by seven volunteers. Sea trials began, and she demonstrated her effectiveness by sinking a coal barge. Her offensive weapon was a torpedo (mine), mounted on the end of a long pole. It was used as an explosive ram, fitted with a contact ignition system. Amazingly, this primitive and highly dangerous warhead proved highly effective. A later modification involved a spiked barb, which was designed to be rammed into the side of the enemy ship. The torpedo could then be detached, and detonated from a safe distance by means of a lanyard. Everything seemed to be working well.

Then, in August 1863, politics got in the way. Dixon and his volunteers were dismissed, as the Confederate Navy wanted to crew her themselves. Unfortunately, on 30 August, her new commander, Lieutenant Payne, accidentally stepped on the dive plane lever while the boat lay alongside Charleston quayside and she submerged before the hatches could be closed, drowning five of her crew. This time the four builders chose a new crew from their engineering works in Mobile, Alabama, and Hunley himself took command. The submarine was back in service by late September.

Then, on 15 October, disaster struck again. The *Hunley* sank during a diving exercise, taking her namesake and seven crewmen to their deaths. She was raised, the bodies were buried, and she again returned to service. Lieutenant Dixon returned to be her commander, and another volunteer crew was raised. By this stage of the war the Confederates were becoming desperate, and they were ready to try anything to break the blockade of Charleston. However, it wasn't until February 1864 that Dixon and his men were ready.

On 17 February 1864, the *Hunley* was towed round to Sullivan's Island, on the south side of Charleston Bay, so she could begin her attack as close as possible to the blockading Union fleet. It was a moonlit night, and the sea was calm. Dixon set a course for the steam sloop USS *Housatonic*, one of the most powerful warships in the Union fleet. Just after 2100hrs, the officer of the watch on the warship spotted what he thought was a log in the water. It was the *Hunley*. Realizing his mistake, he raised the alarm, but it was too late. The *Hunley* had already attached her torpedo, and was backing away. They were about 50ft (15m) from the *Housatonic* when Dixon detonated the torpedo, and the explosion ripped a hole in the warship. She sank in minutes.

As for the *Hunley*, she never returned. Her wreck was discovered in 1995, four miles (7.5km) from the shore, in 30ft (9.1m) of water. She had survived the explosion of the torpedo, but for some reason she succumbed as she began her voyage back to base. The remains of Lieutenant Dixon and his crew were recovered, and in 2004 they were buried with full military honours. Historians are still trying to piece together what happened during the final moments of this brave but unfortunate little craft.

# MUTINY!

Technically, a mutiny involves a group conspiring to disobey orders that they are legally and duty-bound to obey. Mutinies aren't exclusively a naval phenomenon – for instance the Indian Mutiny began hundreds of miles from the sea. The term is typically applied to servicemen who rebel against authority, although it is most commonly bestowed on rebellious seamen. In most countries, a mutiny was a serious business, as it usually involved the death penalty for those mutineers who were caught. It was in the interests of naval power to inflict draconian punishments for mutiny, simply to discourage others from rebelling.

It was often said that you could tell if a crew on board a sailing ship-of-war were mutinous, as they became sullen and secretive. Traditionally, an early sign of dissent involved the rolling of roundshot across the decks in the middle of the night, usually immediately above the cabins of the Captain or his officers. Crews were sometimes driven to mutiny by harsh captains, who flogged and punished a crew to the point of rebellion. Naval mutinies also came in different forms, as reflected in the following selection of mutinous outbreaks.

## HMS *Hermione* (1782)

The bloodiest mutiny in British naval history took place in September 1782, when the crew of the frigate *Hermione* rebelled against the harsh and sadistic Captain Pigot. During his nine months in command he flogged half the crew, killing two sailors in the process. Finally the crew had had enough, and rose in revolt when the warship was patrolling the West Indies. The final straw came when the Captain ordered his crew to set the sails, threatening to flog the last man aloft. As a result, three young seamen fell to their deaths, and Pigot ordered his crew to 'throw the lubbers overboard'.

That night, Pigot was attacked and stabbed in his cabin, then thrown overboard, together with nine of his officers. The 210 crew who remained sailed the *Hermione* to Venezuela, where they handed the ship over to the Spanish. The Admiralty was furious, and put a lot of effort into tracking down the mutineers. In the end, 33 sailors were recaptured, and, of these, 24 were hanged for their crime. In 1799 the *Hermione* was recaptured by the Royal Navy and, appropriately, she was renamed HMS *Retribution*.

## HMS *Bounty* (1789)

Probably the most famous mutiny in history was the one against Captain William Bligh, of the British warship *Bounty*. She had sailed to the South Pacific to collect breadfruit, which it was hoped could be replanted in the West Indies. Bligh spent five months on Tahiti, and when he finally left, his crew mutinied, preferring the delights of the island to the monotony of a sea voyage home.

The mutiny was led by Acting Lieutenant Fletcher Christian, who bundled Bligh, the Master, two midshipmen and 15 loyal sailors into the ship's launch. Four more loyalists were forced to stay on board, to help Christian and his mutineers sail their ship. Bligh survived, after a remarkable 3,600-mile (5,700km) voyage to the Dutch East Indies – a masterpiece of navigation.

As for the mutineers, they were unwelcome in Tahiti, as the islanders feared retribution, so Christian, some of his supporters and their Tahitian wives sailed on to Pitcairn Island, where they established a colony. Several of the mutineers who remained on Tahiti were subsequently recaptured by the Royal Navy, and three of them were eventually hanged. Christian burned the *Bounty* to cover his tracks, and spent the rest of his days on his harsh and remote island home.

## The Spithead and the Nore (1797)

These two rebellions by sailors in the Channel fleet were not so much full-blown mutinies as a succession of strikes, in order to improve pay and living conditions. At the time, though, Britain was at war with Revolutionary France, and the mutinies fuelled fears of a general insurrection, of the kind so recently seen in France.

The mutineers allayed fears by offering to sail at once if the French fleet put to sea, and in Spithead the diplomatic Admiral Howe managed to calm the situation down. Some grievances were addressed, and the mutiny petered out. The mutiny at the Nore was more serious, particularly as the mutineers blockaded the port of London. Eventually the ringleader, Richard Parker, overreached himself when he ordered the mutinous ships to sail to France. As a result the mutiny failed, and Parker was eventually hung from the yardarm, along with 29 of his supporters.

## The USS *Somers* (1842)

In September 1842, the brand-new sailing brig USS *Somers* sailed on her first major voyage, from New York to West Africa and back. She was acting as an experimental training ship for naval cadets. She returned by way of the West Indies, but it was clear that morale on board was extremely low. Commander Mackenzie identified the source of the unrest – Midshipman Spencer, the 19-year-old son of the US Secretary of War. In late November Spencer and two seamen were arrested, and charged with inciting mutiny.

An investigation was held, and the ship's officers declared that Spencer and his accomplices were guilty. Mackenzie ordered them to be hanged from the yardarm. An inquiry was held when the USS *Somers* returned to New York, but Mackenzie's verdict and his draconian punishment were upheld.

## The *Potemkin* (1905)

In June 1905 the crew of the Russian battleship *Potemkin* mutinied and took over their ship. At the time she was part of

Russia's Black Sea fleet, based in the port of Odessa. The catalyst came when the crew were threatened with punishment for refusing to eat maggot-infested meat. Fearing a mass execution, the crew rushed at the officers, and threw several of them overboard. The battleship then returned to port, flying the red flag.

The burial of a sailor killed during the mutiny prompted a popular demonstration, which was broken up by Cossacks. When the rest of the fleet were called on to recapture the *Potemkin*, the fleet's crews refused to open fire on the mutineers. The battleship steamed to Romania, where it surrendered to the authorities. After the Russian Revolution, the *Potemkin* became a Soviet symbol, and her exploits were recounted in Sergei Eisenstein's cinematic masterpiece *Battleship Potemkin*.

# RELATIVE BEARINGS

If a sailor spots something like an enemy warship, or a headland, he expresses its position as a 'relative bearing', which means its position relative to the direction his own ship is pointing. This is usually expressed in one of two ways. In the past century, it has become common to give relative bearings in degrees. For instance, if a lookout spots an enemy warship off the port beam, he'd describe its position as 'red 90' or 90° from the direction of travel, with red representing port, and green standing for starboard. These two colours are drummed into sailors throughout their careers, as they're also the colours used by port and starboard navigation lights.

In the age of fighting sail relative bearings were given a different way. They were given as general bearings, either 'ahead', 'astern', 'abeam', 'on the bow' or 'on the quarter'. 'Ahead' and 'astern' are self-explanatory. 'Abeam' was directly to one side – the equivalent of red or green 90. 'On the bow' was the 45° angle between ahead and abeam, while 'on the quarter' was the similar angle, midway between abeam and astern.

These general relative bearings were effectively compass bearings, relative to the direction the ship was travelling in, each given in 45° increments. They could also be fine-tuned, down to roughly 22½°. For instance, a lookout on a sailing ship might describe an enemy vessel as being 'fine on the port bow', which meant she was off the port side, somewhere between ahead and on the bow. The word 'fine' was also used for targets spotted between astern and on the quarter. If a target was spotted midway between abeam and on the quarter, or abeam and on the bow, then it would be described as being 'broad'. Therefore, a lookout might describe an enemy as being 'broad on the port beam' (the equivalent of 'red 67.5'), or 'broad on the starboard quarter' (midway between being on the starboard beam and on the starboard quarter, the same as 'green 112.5').

The aim was to create a system where anyone on board a warship knew exactly where to look in order to spot the enemy vessel. If a lookout yelled out 'sail fine on the port bow', the captain shouldn't have to yell 'where does she bear?', as he'd already have trained his telescope in the right direction, and was probably giving the orders to send the ship to action stations.

# FIGHTING ADMIRAL: ANDREW CUNNINGHAM

During the dark days of 1941, Admiral Andrew B. Cunningham (1883–1963), or 'ABC' to his contemporaries, gave the British people hope and victory when they needed it most. Born outside Dublin, he joined the Royal Navy in 1897, and saw action on land during the Boer War. In 1908 he was given his first command – a torpedo boat – and he remained with small ships, commanding the destroyer HMS *Scorpion* throughout the First World War.

Between the wars he rose steadily through the ranks, seeing service against the Bolsheviks in the Baltic, then commanding a destroyer flotilla in Home Waters, before being attached to the staff of the brilliant but irascible Admiral Cowan in the West Indies. In 1932 'ABC' was promoted to flag rank, becoming the rear admiral in charge of destroyers in the Mediterranean Fleet. Further promotion in 1936 led to other plum commands and by the outbreak of the Second World War he had been appointed the commander of the Mediterranean Fleet, which he described as 'the finest command the Royal Navy has to offer'.

His first big test came in June 1940, when he had to capture and intern a French squadron in Alexandria. He managed this with minimal casualties. Then the Italians entered the war, and the strategic balance changed dramatically. Cunningham had expected this, and was eager to bring the Italians to battle. When they declined a fleet engagement, 'ABC' sent in the Fleet Air Arm. The raid on Taranto in November 1940 was a stunning success – the first successful naval air strike of the war. One Italian battleship was sunk, and two were seriously damaged.

He finally achieved the fleet engagement he longed for in March 1941. The battle of Matapan was a spectacular success, and his fleet sank three Italian heavy cruisers during a dramatic night-time action. This was his second spectacular victory in five months – after that, the Italians remained in port, which meant that Cunningham won the battle for naval supremacy. From that point on, British seapower would dominate the Mediterranean.

His biggest challenge yet came in April 1941, when the Germans invaded Greece. Over the next two months, Cunningham had to evacuate the British and Commonwealth Army, first from Greece, and then from Crete. Without air cover the task was near suicidal. He replied to doubters by saying that the Navy must not let the Army down. However, by late May the situation had become critical. The Germans had landed in Crete, and a full-scale evacuation became vital. Warship losses mounted, and Cunningham's political and military superiors in London questioned whether the operation was worth the heavy cost. Cunningham responded by saying; 'It takes three years to build a ship; it takes three centuries to build a tradition.' This was his finest hour. Despite the loss of nine warships and the damage of several more, his fleet successfully transported over 16,000 soldiers to safety.

By 1942, Cunningham was back on the offensive. That April he headed a naval staff mission to the United States, to discuss strategy with the hard-spoken Admiral King, who masterminded America's naval war effort. Cunningham then supervised the naval side of the landings in North Africa, and struck up a firm friendship with General Eisenhower. He returned to his beloved Mediterranean Fleet in February 1943, and supervised the interception of Axis' attempts to evacuate its troops from North Africa. There would be no Crete-style evacuation for Rommel's veterans. Cunningham's orders to his commanders were to 'Sink, burn and destroy: Let nothing past.' This is exactly what they did. In July he supervised the naval landings on Sicily and three months later he took the surrender of the Italian fleet – a personal triumph for the man who had led the fight against them for the past three years.

Cunningham became the First Sea Lord in October 1943, and ended the war as a grand strategist, directing British naval efforts, and representing her interests at the conferences of Tehran, Yalta and Potsdam. He finally retired in 1946 – a much loved and highly respected fighting commander, and a man who upheld the finest traditions of the Service.

# NAVAL STRATEGY:
# THE CHANNEL FLEET

For much of the age of sail the Channel Fleet represented Britain's front line, her bulwark against foreign invasion. In effect, Britain's survival depended on the efficiency of her Channel Fleet. The strategic picture was simple. In a war, if the British managed to defeat the French, Spanish or Dutch fleet, the result would be a respite, while the enemy rebuilt their fleet. Britain didn't have an army large enough to fight on the European continent, unless it enjoyed the support of Allies. This meant that the British could never really follow up a great naval victory by launching an invasion of an enemy country.

By contrast if the Channel Fleet were destroyed, the southern coast of England would be left defenceless. Britain's polyglot collection of regular troops, militiamen and conscripts, and her limited coastal defences, would all be hard pressed to resist a determined invasion by the veterans of the French Army, or a similarly professional military force. This meant that the Channel Fleet was a priceless asset. Its defeat would be a disaster. Its mere existence was a guarantor that Britain wouldn't be invaded. Risking it simply to win a battle wasn't an option. Its real job was to remain in existence – a 'fleet in being' – a strategic asset rather than a tactical tool.

During the French Revolutionary and Napoleonic Wars, Britain was threatened by French invasion in 1804–05, when Napoleon massed his Grand Armée on the coast of the English Channel. Invasion barges were built, supplies were gathered, but the threatened invasion never came. The reason was that the French and their Spanish allies never managed to remove the latent threat posed by the Channel Fleet.

Of course, this isn't to say that the Channel Fleet was a purely defensive entity. The Admiralty adopted a policy of distant blockade of the main enemy ports, such as Brest, Cherbourg, Le Havre,

Boulogne and La Rochelle. Observation squadrons kept watch on enemy ports in all weathers and seasons, while the main battlefleet cruised over the horizon in the English Channel. More frequently it rode at anchor in Torbay, its main place of refuge, replenishment and reinforcement. The Channel Fleet remained a powerful entity, and a floating bastion. Critics of what seemed like naval inactivity couldn't understand that it was virtually impossible to maintain a close blockade of the enemy coast for years at a time. Warships needed to be refitted, their tired crews needed to rest, and long months of inactivity on blockade sapped the fighting spirit of the men. Just as importantly, the prevailing wind direction in the English Channel blows towards France rather than away from it, meaning that the French coast is a 'lee shore'. In the event of a major storm, the fleet had little option but to lift the blockade, and to take refuge in a safe anchorage such as Torbay or Yarmouth Roads. As soon as the storm passed, fast ships were sent to lie off the enemy ports again, followed by the observation squadrons.

An example of how the system worked is the Camperdown campaign of October 1797. When Vice-Admiral Duncan received news that the Dutch Admiral de Winter had sailed from the Texel in Holland with 16 ships-of-the-line, he set course to intercept him. A small inshore squadron had brought Duncan news that the French had sailed, and this squadron then shadowed the Dutch, keeping Duncan updated on any developments. As a result Duncan's fleet was able to intercept the Dutch with comparative ease. The result was a hard-fought but decisive British victory – the battle of Camperdown.

This policy of distant blockade was modified slightly during the long years of the French Revolution and the Napoleonic Wars, but it essentially remained the Royal Navy's main strategy. While inshore or observation squadrons patrolled off the enemy ports, the main fleet – the Channel Fleet – remained a powerful fleet in being, ready to counter any attempt at invasion, and safeguarding the country from attack.

# THE KING OF THE CORSAIRS

One of the most successful privateers of the age of sail was Robert Surcouf (1773–1827), a man dubbed the 'King of the Corsairs' by a delighted French press. Surcouf was born in the privateering port of St Malo in Brittany, and at the age of 15 he became a sailor, serving on board a slave ship bound for the Indian Ocean. He spent five years as a slaver, before returning to St Malo in 1792 – the year the French Revolutionary War began. He returned to sea, and was in the Île de France (now Mauritius) in the Indian Ocean early the following year, when Britain declared war on France.

Surcouf helped drive off two British blockading warships, making him a local hero, a success he repeated in the summer of 1794 when he captured another British warship. By this time he had command of his own ship, but he was still denied a 'letter of marque' by the local governor. Therefore he returned to France, determined to acquire his privateering licence. He became a properly authorized privateer, and in August 1798 he made his first independent cruise, in the 18-gun *Clarisse*, of Nantes. He captured ten ships in the South Atlantic and the Indian Ocean before returning to the Île de France as a successful privateer.

In May 1800 he took command of a new ship – the 18-gun *Confiance* – and sailed the Indian Ocean in search of prey. He captured ten British ships off India, and on 17 October he captured the 38-gun East Indiaman *Kent* in the Bay of Bengal, one of the richest privateering prizes of the war. It also made Surcouf a national hero. He evaded British patrols and returned to France in April 1801. The sale of his plunder made him an extremely wealthy man, and he retired to St Malo, where with the coming of peace in early 1802 he established himself as a shipowner and businessman.

During his career, Robert Surcouf was known for his humane treatment of prisoners and for the discipline of his men. He was also a gifted tactician. For instance, he used deception and speed to bring his small ship alongside a larger enemy before the latter's guns could inflict much damage. He then relied on specially trained marines and large numbers of boarders to overwhelm the enemy.

During the Napoleonic Wars (1805–15) Surcouf sent 14 privateers to the Indian Ocean, but they met with mixed success, and several were captured. In 1807 he returned to sea in his own purpose-built privateer *La Revenant*, which captured 20 British ships during a year-long cruise. After his ship was commandeered by the governor of the Île de France he seized one of the governor's own frigates, and returned to France. He was subsequently ennobled as a baron by the Emperor Napoleon. Surcouf ended his days as a wealthy shipowner, in his native St Malo.

# NAVAL GUN CREWS IN THE AGE OF SAIL

During the heyday of the sailing ship-of-war, most navies agreed about certain things, such as the number of men it took to raise or lower a sail, or the crew needed to man a particular size and type of naval gun. It was all a matter of organization. Every ship had a 'quarter bill', which laid out the action station of every man on board. It covered the men allocated to crew the guns, those who formed boarding parties, the powder monkeys who brought up powder and shot from the magazines, and the damage control parties, ready to repair any emergency damage, put out fires or deal with flooding. Most, though, would be serving the guns.

First of all, each gun crew was actually responsible for two guns – one on each side of the ship. Naturally enough, the size of a gun crew varied considerably, depending on the size of the gun. The rule of thumb was that each man was expected to haul 500lb (227kg) of gun and carriage. Naval 12-pdrs required a crew of ten, 24-pdrs were served by 12 men, and 32-pdrs needed a 15-man crew. These gun crews usually consisted of two captains, two loaders and two spongers, while the rest of the crew were deemed auxiliaries, who were expected to pull on the ropes and tackles used to run the gun in and out. These gun crews were deliberately overmanned, having two men covering each task. This meant that if anyone was killed, then another trained man would be available to take his place. It also meant that, if needed, half of the crew could be taken away to work the other gun on the opposite side of the ship.

Here is the 12-man gun crew allocated to a 24-pdr during the Napoleonic Wars, the largest gun carried on a 74-gun ship-of-the-line:

| | |
|---|---|
| Gun captain | In charge of the gun, and supervises its firing, and the safety of his crew. |
| Deputy gun captain | Primes the gun, takes command of the second gun when required to fight both sides of the ship at once. |
| Loader | Loads the powder cartridge, shot and wadding. |
| Rammer | Rams home the charge, shot and wadding. |
| Deputy rammer | As above, but acts as the rammer for the second gun. |
| Sponger | Swabs the gun barrel after firing. |
| Deputy sponger | As above, but acts as the sponger for the second gun. |
| Powder man | (usually a task given to a marine) Passes the powder cartridges to the loader, and protects the box containing the cartridges from fire. If fighting both sides he supplies cartridges to both guns. |
| Gun crew (x4) | Man the gun tackle, to run the gun in and out. |

When running the gun in and out, everyone apart from the gun captain would be expected to man the gun tackle, and help the rest of the gun crew perform the job as quickly and efficiently as possible. A well-trained crew could prepare a gun for action in six minutes; its rate of fire was one round every two minutes, although some ship captains managed an even faster rate, through constant practice.

Other ship captains were less enthusiastic about gunnery practice, as there was no budget for practice gun-firing, so ship captains were expected to pay for the powder out of their own pocket. Others still were reluctant to fire their guns except in anger, as it might damage the paintwork or mess up the decks. The rate of fire also depended on whether there was a full or half crew working the gun, and the number of casualties.

# BOARDERS AWAY

During a boarding action during the age of sail, sailors fought with whatever weapons they had to hand. Marines in the tops poured musket fire down onto the enemy deck, but in a general boarding action pistols and edged weapons were much more useful. Before a boarding party attacked an enemy, the crew would try to kill as many of the opposition as they could using swivel guns, grapeshot, grenades or musketry. Next, grappling hooks would be thrown, and the two ships locked together. Sailors would then clamber on board the enemy ship, and fight it out hand-to-hand.

The following selection includes most of the sailors' weapons of choice:

**Long arms:** While muskets and their attendant bayonets were usually the preserve of the marines, these single-shot flintlock weapons could also be used by sailors, if they had access to them. In trained hands they had an effective range of around 100 yards (90m). In the hands of the average sailor, the range would have been considerably less. Far more suitable in a boarding action were shorter, more lethal firearms such as blunderbusses and volley guns. Both were single-shot weapons, but they fired a scatter of shot at the enemy – perfect for a first shot during a boarding action.

**Pistols:** Sea Service pistols were often carried for use during boarding actions. These heavy weapons were single-shotted and hard to reload. However, after being discharged, they could be turned around and used as improvised clubs.

**Boarding pikes:** 'Half pikes' were similar to the pikes which had once been commonplace on land, only they were much shorter – usually around 7ft (2.1m) long. Their wooden hafts were tipped with a steel point, and their long reach made them useful defensive weapons if a ship was being attacked by enemy boarders.

**Swords and cutlasses:** Cutlasses were thick, robust swords, designed as cutting or slashing weapons rather than thrusting ones, although the point could be used if required. Although sailors practised cutlass drill, there was little finesse to them, and in a swirling mêlée the large guard protecting the swordsman's hand could be used as a large knuckle-duster, making it almost as useful a part of the weapon as the blade itself. Officers tended to use swords, which were often quite ornate. While these could be used to cut, it was more common to thrust with them, using the point rather than the edge of the blade.

**Knives and axes:** Most seamen carried knives, and these were useful as a weapon of last resort. Similarly, midshipmen carried dirks – miniature versions of full-sized swords, which were little more than ornate knives. In a knife fight a seaman's knife became a useful offensive dagger, or a foil to parry an enemy's blow. Boarding axes could be wielded with great effect on board a ship, and these were usually double-headed, with a curved blade on one side and a vicious metal spike on the other. Of course, regular axes could also be used as improvised boarding weapons.

# PEARL HARBOR HERO: DORIS MILLER

Doris 'Dorie' Miller (1919–43), an African-American from Waco, Texas, was a mess attendant (2nd class) on board the battleship USS *West Virginia* when the Japanese attacked Pearl Harbor. On the morning of 7 December 1941 he was collecting laundry for the galley when the Japanese planes first appeared, and like the rest of his shipmates he was completely taken by surprise. The battleship was hit several times in as many minutes, and Miller dropped his laundry and hurried topside to his action stations on the amidships AA battery. It had been knocked out. However, he saw that the bridge had been hit, so he continued upwards, to see what he could do to help.

He discovered the gravely wounded Captain Bennion and, as a keen boxer, he had the strength to carry his captain to safety. However, despite Miller's pleas, the dying skipper refused to leave his stricken bridge. Miller helped load a machine gun, and then manned another and opened fire on the Japanese. Despite his lack of training he fired off everything he could at the enemy aircraft before the Japanese flew off, leaving devastation in their wake. Unfortunately Miller did not shoot any of the planes down, and the doomed battleship began to settle on the seabed. He abandoned ship, and swam to safety.

'Dorie' Miller was duly awarded the Navy Cross, the first African-American to win the coveted medal for bravery. He was also promoted – although only to mess attendant (1st class). His face was used on a US Navy recruiting poster, under the heading 'Above and Beyond the Call of Duty'. The Pittsburgh Courier expressed its outrage at this menial promotion by running his story under the caption 'He fought – keeps mop'. After more press coverage a chastened Navy sent Miller on a war bond tour, where he drummed up support for America's war effort.

In June 1943 Miller was promoted to petty officer (officers' cook, 3rd class), and assigned to serve on board the new escort carrier USS Liscome Bay. On 20 November the carrier was operating off Tarawa, when she was hit by a torpedo fired from a Japanese submarine. She sank within minutes, and 'Dorie' Miller never made it to safety. However, his achievements did much to raise public awareness of the lowly status of African-Americans within the US military, and three decades after his death the US Navy celebrated his heroism by naming a warship after him.

# PROFILE OF A WARSHIP: *HUASCAR*

The British naval officer and warship designer Captain Cowper Coles (1819–70), impressed by the USS *Monitor*, was determined to design a similarly working turreted ironclad warship for the Royal Navy. The result was HMS *Captain*, a turreted ironclad which entered service with the Royal Navy in 1870. Before her commission the Admiralty was concerned by her low freeboard, and rightly so. On the night of 7 September 1870, the *Captain* foundered in a squall in the Bay of Biscay, and went down with almost all hands. Those lost included Captain Coles, who was on board to evaluate his design.

However, several years before the *Captain* was launched, Coles designed and built another ironclad, which still exists today. In 1864 he supervised the building of the small ironclad *Huascar*, which was armed with two main guns, mounted in a revolving turret. The *Huascar* wasn't such a radical design as the *Captain*, which meant that she was much more seaworthy, and had a much higher freeboard. She entered service with the Peruvian Navy, and for the next 12 years she served as its flagship – the pride of the Peruvian fleet.

In 1877 a civil war was raging in Peru, and political tensions were running high. The crew of the *Huascar* mutinied, and declared themselves for the Peruvian rebels. After appointing their own captain, they used the powerful ironclad to attack shipping all along the Pacific coast of Peru. In effect, she had turned to piracy. Her victims included several British clipper ships, so warships of the British Pacific Squadron were dispatched to deal with her.

On 29 May two British warships – the steam-powered frigate HMS *Shah* and the steam corvette HMS *Amethyst* – finally cornered the ironclad off the Chilean port of Ilo. In the battle that followed she was hit over 60 times, but none of the shots managed to penetrate her armour, or inflict any serious damage. At one stage the *Shah* even fired a torpedo at her, from a range of just 400 yards (370m) – the first time in history a self-propelled torpedo was launched in anger against an enemy warship. It missed. The *Huascar*'s own guns were highly ineffective, and the battle ended when the shallow-drafted ironclad escaped from the British by anchoring close to the shore where the deep-drafted British ships could not reach her. The ironclad survived to continue her piratical rampage.

The *Huascar* was eventually recovered by the Peruvian Navy when her crew deserted her. During the Chilean-Peruvian War (1879–84) that followed, the ironclad was used to raid the Chilean coast. This time it was the Chilean Navy who pursued her, and she was eventually forced into battle by a squadron of five Chilean warships, which included the powerful unarmoured steam-powered warships *Almirante Cochrane* and *Encelda*. This time there was no escape. The well-armed Chilean warships closed to within point-blank range, and pounded the *Huascar* with solid shot. At that range their fire was able to inflict damage, and the ironclad's turret was disabled early on in the fight. After an hour of this uneven pounding the surviving crewmen surrendered by waving white towels. The Chileans boarded her, just in time to prevent her one remaining officer from scuttling the ship. The little ironclad is now a historic visitor attraction, and is still officially a warship of the Chilean Navy.

# INJURY AND DISEASE IN THE AGE OF SAIL

A healthy crew was vital to the efficiency of a warship. A crew wasted by disease was in no condition to operate something as complex as a sailing man-of-war, let alone fight in her. During the 18th century, over two in every five deaths in the Royal Navy were caused by disease, while most of the rest were the result of accidents such as drowning, tumbling down hatches or falling from the rigging. Less than one in twenty deaths was actually caused by the enemy. For instance, while the decks of the ships-of-the-line that took part in the battle of Trafalgar (1805) might have resembled a charnel house by the end of the fighting, on board HMS *Victory*, which was in the thick of the fighting, only 7 per cent of its crew were actually killed during the battle.

As well as death, injuries were commonplace, particularly those resulting from falls, immersion in the sea or lifting weights. A naval surgeon had to be able to deal with hernias and back injuries with as much skill as he applied to amputation after a battle, or treating venereal disease after a visit to a port. He also had to cope with diseases such as typhus, malaria or yellow fever; in warmer climes these could devastate the crew, leaving the ship too short-handed to operate effectively.

In cases like these the surgeon would often clear the ship, sending his worst cases to a naval hospital on shore, or even housing them in tents on the beach, while the ship was disinfected using vinegar and brimstone. While diseases of this kind were not fully understood during this period, it was felt that a clean ship was at least a good start. Scurvy was another major threat, a disease caused by a deficiency of vitamin C. Cases often appeared after six weeks at sea, if the diet of salt beef was not augmented by healthier fare. Symptoms included swelling of the gums, blotching of the skin and extreme lethargy. From the early 18th century scurvy had been dealt with by providing the crew with fruit (usually given in the form of lime juice) and vegetables (known as 'green stuff'). From 1795 on, lime juice was a compulsory part of a sailor's ration on board a British man-of-war.

By the end of the 18th century advances in medical science meant a general improvement in treating injuries and diseases on board men-of-war. Thanks to the publication of treatises on naval medicine, naval surgeons knew more about the diseases they faced, and were better prepared to deal with the shattering injuries encountered on board a sailing warship. Dedicated sick bays were created, which improved the supervision of the wounded and helped slow the spread of disease through the ship.

New drugs also appeared during the French Revolutionary and Napoleonic Wars, and surgeons were generally better trained (and accorded a higher status) than their counterparts of the previous century. Slowly, disease became less of a threat, although injury in battle or by accident was often something few naval surgeons could do much about, apart from resorting to the usual staples of amputation, bleeding and waiting for nature to take its course.

# FLOGGING

During the age of fighting sail, the ultimate naval punishment was hanging from the yardarm (or guillotining in the French Revolutionary Navy). The hanging was always conducted on the larboard (port) side of the ship, where a noose was placed around the seaman's neck and the end of a rope suspended from the mainmast yardarm. A party of seamen then hoisted him up, and left him there until he died. However, the death sentence was given after the deliberation of a court martial. So too was 'flogging round the fleet', a punishment which was simply a more prolonged form of execution, involving anything from 100 to 1,000 lashes. The man was tied to a cross formed from capstan bars in a longboat, and rowed around the fleet, and was whipped beside each warship in the anchorage. Few victims even survived the experience.

An individual ship's captain was unable to order an execution himself, with the exception of the US Navy in time of war. However, he could order a man to be flogged – anything up to 100 lashes, which was more than capable of killing the unfortunate miscreant. In theory a captain could only order punishments of a dozen lashes on his own authority, but after the mutinies of 1797 (see p.154) this rule was relaxed, and far more severe punishments were regularly meted out.

Floggings were carried out using a cat-of-nine-tails (a nine-stranded whip), and were conducted in front of the entire ship's company. Marines with loaded muskets would be on hand to deal with any attempt to free the prisoner, while the captain and all his officers lined the quarterdeck, to add an air of authority to the proceedings. The reason for the punishment was read out, including the Articles of War the offender had contravened. The most common punishments were for disobedience, fighting, drunkenness, insolence, sleeping on duty and theft. The average punishment was either 12 or 24 lashes, but theft was particularly disliked on board, so this usually incurred the heaviest punishments – 48 or even 96 lashes being commonplace.

After the punishment was ordered the prisoner was led forward and tied up, either to a vertically rigged grating or to the capstan. He was stripped to the waist beforehand, and a leather gag was placed in his mouth. The punishment was carried out by a boatswain's mate, or by several acting in relays if the punishment involved more than a dozen strokes.

Punishments were rarely prolonged – they were conducted quickly, efficiently and with the least possible disruption to the daily routine of the ship. Most captains held 'defaulters' once a week, when minor misdemeanours were dealt with by stoppage of grog or fines, and more serious crimes by flogging. This meant that flogging was carried out weekly, and on a large ship-of-the-line several punishments might be carried out, one after the other. Other minor punishments such as 'starting' – hitting a sailor with a cane or a rope's end – took place on a daily basis, at the whim of the First Lieutenant and the Boatswain.

# THE ARTICLES OF WAR

During the era of the sailing warship, the 'Articles of War' were read out to the ship's company of every Royal Naval warship when it was first commissioned, before serious punishments were meted out, and at least once a month, usually on a Sunday, when the ship was rigged for church service. In effect the Articles of War represented the law on board a British warship, and were regarded with the same seriousness as holy writ. They were certainly Old Testament in character – most punishments listed involved flogging, hanging, or both. The Articles of War were first introduced to Cromwell's Navy in the mid-17th century, and they were revised in 1749, and again in 1757. This was the draconian version which remained in use throughout the Napoleonic Wars. A few of the most interesting of the 35 articles are given here:

**Article 2:** All flag officers, and all persons in or belonging to His Majesty's ships or vessels of war, being guilty of profane oaths, cursings, execrations, drunkenness, uncleanness, or other scandalous actions, in derogation of God's honour, and corruption of good manners, shall incur such punishment as a court martial shall think fit to impose, and as the nature and degree of their offence shall deserve.

**Article 19:** If any person in or belonging to the fleet shall make or endeavour to make any mutinous assembly upon any pretence whatsoever, every person offending herein, and being convicted thereof by the sentence of the court martial, shall suffer death: and if any person in or belonging to the fleet shall utter any words of sedition or mutiny, he shall suffer death, or such other punishment as a court martial shall deem him to deserve: and if any officer, mariner, or soldier on or belonging to the fleet, shall behave himself with contempt to his superior officer, being in the execution of his office, he shall be punished according to the nature of his offence by the judgment of a court martial.

**Article 20:** If any person in the fleet shall conceal any traitorous or mutinous practice or design, being convicted thereof by the sentence of a court martial, he shall suffer death, or any other punishment as a court martial shall think fit; and if any person, in or belonging to the fleet, shall conceal any traitorous or mutinous words spoken by any, to the prejudice of His Majesty or government, or any words, practice, or design, tending to the hindrance of the service, and shall not forthwith reveal the same to the commanding officer, or being present at any mutiny or sedition, shall not use his utmost endeavours to suppress the same, he shall be punished as a court martial shall think he deserves.

**Article 22:** If any officer, mariner, soldier or other person in the fleet, shall strike any of his superior officers, or draw, or offer to draw, or lift up any weapon against him, being in the execution of his office, on any pretence whatsoever, every such person being convicted of any such offence, by the sentence of a court martial, shall suffer death; and if any officer, mariner, soldier or other person in the fleet, shall presume to quarrel with any of his superior officers, being in the execution of his office, or shall disobey any lawful command of any of his superior officers; every such person being convicted of any such offence, by the sentence of a court martial, shall suffer death, or such other punishment, as shall, according to the nature and degree of his offence, be inflicted upon him by the sentence of a court martial.

**Article 27:** No person in or belonging to the fleet shall sleep upon his watch, or negligently perform the duty imposed on him, or forsake his station, upon pain of death, or such other punishment as a court martial shall think fit to impose, and as the circumstances of the case shall require.

**Article 35:** All other crimes not capital committed by any person or persons in the fleet, which are not mentioned in this act, or for which no punishment is hereby directed to be inflicted, shall be punished by the laws and customs in such cases used at sea.

# NAVAL ARMS TREATIES

When the First World War ended in November 1918, most of the countries involved were virtually bankrupt. Britain and her Empire had spent over £20 billion, while the United States and France had each spent the equivalent of £12 billion on their war effort. The British were still paying off their war debts when the Second World War began, over two decades later. Britain still had the largest battlefleet in the world with 45 dreadnought battleships and battlecruisers. The United States Navy had 16 dreadnoughts, the French had 12, the Italians five and the Japanese four. This didn't even take into account obsolete pre-dreadnought battleships.

Following the first World War, which was meant to have been 'the war to end all wars', it made sense to scale down the size of everyone's national battlefleets. Unfortunately, not all nations felt that way. In 1920 the United States declared it planned to produce a navy 'second to none', and ordered 15 new capital ships. The Japanese countered this by embarking on their own ambitious plan to build 16 modern battleships and battlecruisers. By 1921 it seemed clear that the world was embarking on a new and extremely costly naval arms race. However, the US government saw that by joining in the arms negotiations proposed by Britain, all countries involved could avoid the need to embark on costly shipbuilding programmes just to maintain their strategic position.

The result was the Washington Conference, attended by representatives of the United States, Britain, France, Japan and Italy. All five naval powers wanted to reduce their naval budgets, and to protect their own position in the naval status quo. The talks began in November 1921, and after much 'horse trading', the five powers approved limits to both the size of existing fleets and the construction of new warships. The total tonnage of capital ships in each fleet was set at 525,000 tons for the British and the Americans (with an additional 135,000 tons allocated for aircraft carriers), 315,000 tons for the Japanese (plus 81,000 tons for carriers), and 175,000 tons (plus 60,000 tons) for both France and Italy. In addition, no single ship could exceed 35,000 tons or carry anything larger than a 16in gun. The Washington Treaty was signed in February 1922.

The big loser was the Royal Navy, whose strength was greatly reduced. However, the British government saved money, and the naval status quo was maintained. The treaty was partly renewed in 1930 (The London Treaty), but it soon became clear that Japan, Italy and the new naval power of Germany weren't willing to abide by international restrictions. By 1937 all existing treaties were scrapped, and the navies of the world were able to build whatever warships they wanted, limited only by national budgets and available technology.

# PROFILE OF A WARSHIP:
## *ADMIRAL POPOV*

The *Admiral Popov* was probably one of history's strangest looking warships. She was named after her Russian designer, and was built in Nicolaev on the Black Sea coast in 1875. Vice-Admiral Andrei Popov thought that a circular-shaped hull would make an ideal gun platform, and would be relatively stable, whatever the sea conditions. She was armed with two 12in guns, mounted in a rotating circular barbette (open-topped turret), which sat in the centre of the circular upper deck. The bridge superstructure was placed behind the turret, and a tall funnel was placed on either side of the guns, on what would normally be the centreline of the ship. She was powered by eight steam engines, which operated six propellers. The whole ship was 101ft (30.8m) in diameter, and had a displacement of 3,533 tons.

The whole thing looked like a floating dinner plate, with a mast, funnels and a gun turret on it. The world's navies were amazed by her, and more than a little sceptical about her performance.

However, Popov had so much faith in his design that another identical circular battleship was ordered, and named the *Novgorod*.

In fact, the sceptics were proved right. The two strange warships proved surprisingly reliable, but they proved useless in anything other than a flat calm. In rougher seas their decks were constantly awash with water because of their low freeboard, and the flat circular hulls were unable to cut through the waves like normal ships, so instead they floated over them. This meant that the waves were constantly pounding the hulls, making the vessels extremely uncomfortable to sail in. Worse, when the Russian Navy tried them out on the broad Russian rivers, it was discovered that although they could steam upstream fairly happily, they became virtually uncontrollable when they went downstream again, spinning like tops in the current! This revolutionary experiment was never repeated, and the two warships were never used in anger.

# NAVAL TECHNOLOGY: THE CORVUS

During the mid-third century BC, the Roman Republic fought the first of three wars against the Carthaginians. This struggle – the First Punic War (264–241 BC) – began as a conflict between two very different forces. The Carthaginians had an unbeatable navy, but their army was mediocre. The Roman Army, while not the veteran force it would become, was still more powerful, and could guarantee victory in a land battle. Unfortunately for the Romans, the battleground was Sicily, and as the Carthaginians controlled the seas, they could strike where they wanted, relieving besieged cities or cutting off the Romans from their supplies. In order to win, the Romans needed to control the sea.

When the war began, Roman naval experience was minimal, but they were able to build a powerful fleet of galleys, based on captured Carthaginian warships. These were *triremes* and *quinquiremes* – with either three or five banks of oars on each side. Still, the Romans knew they were unable to face the Carthaginian fleet without finding a way to tip the balance in their favour.

Their battle-winning device was the *corvus* ('raven' in Latin). It was aptly named – a beak-like boarding bridge, which was fitted onto the bow of every major Roman warship in the fleet. The Greek historian Polybius (c.203–120 BC) described the new invention. A pole was erected in the bow of the galley about 23ft (7m) high. A gangway was secured to its base by a hinge, while the top of the gangway was linked to the top of the pole by rope and a pulley. This meant that the gangway could be lowered like the drawbridge of a castle when the Romans wanted to board an enemy ship. The gangway itself was 36ft (11m) long and 4ft (1.2m) wide – providing enough space for a file of Roman soldiers two men abreast to race along it onto the enemy deck. The leading pair held up their shields, while those behind them covered each flank as they charged, protecting the boarding party from enemy missiles. Better still, the corvus could be dropped on either side of the Roman galley, or even straight ahead, giving the Romans tactical flexibility in the midst of a battle.

The corvus proved an immediate success. From 260 BC onwards the Romans won a string of naval battles, most notably at Mylae (260 BC) and Ecnomus (256 BC). As a result the Carthaginian fleet was destroyed as a fighting force. The main advantage of the corvus was that it allowed the Romans to make the best possible use of their one great asset – their soldiers. Each of their galleys carried a large contingent of veteran marines, and when the corvus was dropped, these marines swarmed onto the Carthaginian ship, and victory was virtually assured.

Of course, it also had its drawbacks. It couldn't be used in any sort of rough sea, as the two galleys were moving around too much. It also weighed upwards of a ton, which didn't help the speed and stability of the Roman warships. Consequently, after Ecnomus the corvus was removed. By that time, the Carthaginians were weakened, and the Romans had gained enough experience to win their battles without resorting to gimmicks.

# NAVAL DISASTER: THE SINKING OF THE *ROYAL OAK*

When the Second World War began, the British Home Fleet moved north to its wartime anchorage in Scapa Flow. This great natural harbour lay in the Orkney Islands, off the north of Scotland. It had served the Grand Fleet well during the First World War, although the remote and often windswept harbour proved less than popular with the sailors whose ships were stationed there. Although the defences of the anchorage had been quite formidable in 1918, during the two decades of peace they had been largely dismantled. Consequently, during the late 1930s the British did what they could to make the anchorage defensible again, but the work was still far from finished by the outbreak of war.

On the evening of Friday 13 October 1939 most of the Home Fleet was at sea – of the major capital ships, only the venerable battleship HMS *Royal Oak* was still in the harbour, anchored in the northern part of Scapa Flow. She wasn't a modern battleship – she had entered service just before the battle of Jutland in 1916. She hadn't really been modernized since, and even the Navy saw her as a second rate battleship. Still, she carried a powerful armament of eight 15in guns, and she remained a useful asset to the fleet.

That night, a U-Boat sneaked its way through an unguarded channel called Kirk Sound, on the eastern side of Scapa Flow, and by picking its way through the blockships meant to block the channel, she found herself inside Britain's main wartime anchorage. A week before, German reconnaissance aircraft had spotted that Kirk Sound was unguarded, and so Korvetten-Kapitän Gunther Prien was given the challenge of breaching the defences of Scapa Flow. After passing through Kirk Sound, Prien's *U-47* was like a wolf loose in the fold – only all the sheep seemed to be gone. After scouring the main anchorage *U-47* turned north, and she soon spotted the *Royal Oak*, lying a few miles from Scapa Bay, at the head of Scapa Flow. She was illuminated by light from the *Aurora*

*Borealis* – the 'Northern Lights'. Gunther Prien had found his victim.

The U-Boat closed to within 2,200 yards (2,000m) of the Royal Oak, and fired a spread of four torpedoes. One misfired, and the rest missed their target. Prien calmly turned his boat around, and fired his two stern torpedoes. One missed; the other hit something, but not the battleship. The likelihood is that it struck her anchor chain. On the battleship, the crew spilled out of their bunks, but they found the ship was largely undamaged. The duty crew went to investigate a mysterious fire in the store rooms at the bow of the ship, while everyone else went back to their bunks. Incredibly, nobody suspected the battleship had received a near hit from a torpedo. Instead, it was thought the muffled explosion was called by an accidental fire breaking out in a paint store.

While all this was going on, Prien's crew were busy reloading the bow tubes. Prien leisurely turned the boat around, and almost 13 minutes after the previous torpedoes were fired, *U-47* let loose another salvo. This time at least two torpedoes slammed into the starboard side of the battleship. This was a mortal wound, and the *Royal Oak* slowly filled with water and capsized. She sank in less than quarter of an hour, taking almost 800 men down with her.

While the ship sank, Prien headed back towards Kirk Sound and safety. The anchorage was in an uproar, with warships searching for the intruder, and searchlights sweeping the water. Somehow *U-47* not only evaded pursuit, but also managed to thread her way back through the blockships of Kirk Sound, to reach the safety of the North Sea. The U-Boat returned to her base in Kiel, where she received a hero's welcome. It was an incredible propaganda coup – a humbling of the Royal Navy, and a feat of naval prowess which ranked among the great raids in history.

Within weeks, the Kirk Sound channel was blocked, and within a few months Scapa Flow had been rendered impregnable. However, it was too late for the crew of the *Royal Oak*. As for Gunther Prien, he became Germany's most celebrated U-boat commander, until his death in 1941, when *U-47* was lost with all hands.

# PROFILE OF A WARSHIP FLEET: THE FIRST TORPEDO BOATS

When the British inventor Robert Whitehead (1823–1905) pioneered the use of the torpedo as an offensive weapon in 1866, he revolutionized naval warfare. Unlike mines or 'moored torpedoes', his 'locomotive torpedo' could be used against specially selected targets, such as enemy battleships and large cruisers. His first weapon was powered by compressed air, and had a speed of 6 knots (11.1km/h) and a range of less than 500 yards (450m). However, by the time he offered his design to the world's naval powers three years later, his design was much more powerful, and boasted a device which kept it on a relatively steady course and depth.

The British were the first to adopt the torpedo, and in 1876 they produced HMS *Lightning*, the world's first torpedo boat. Other nations followed Britain's lead, and as both torpedoes and torpedo boats improved, naval tactics developed to cope with the new device. By the 1880s the weapon had gained a loyal following among naval theorists, particularly the adherents of *la jeune école* ('the young school'), who adopted the doctrines espoused by the French Admiral Aube. He argued that the torpedo meant that the days of the battleship were over, as one of these prestigious and expensive warships could be sunk by a relatively inexpensive torpedo boat, thereby obviating the need for the battleship. Torpedo boats could dominate coastal waters, rendering a country immune from amphibious attack or enemy bombardment.

This view was the antithesis of that held by Captain Alfred Mahan, an American naval historian and theorist who advocated the pursuit of 'seapower' (see p.124). Mahan saw the battleship as the arbiter of naval victory, and this view was shared by both the United States Navy and the Royal Navy. After all, they had the battleships. The experiences of both Britain and US in the First World War only served to underline their belief in the Mahanian doctrine of seapower, as it was by the use of the British battlefleet that the Germans were eventually brought to bay, their coastline blockaded and their population starved into surrender.

The *jeune école* doctrine only made its mark in the use of submarine warfare to threaten the sea lanes of the large maritime powers. After the war, while the British were willing to develop their own small submarine fleet, they appeared to ignore the possibilities of developing their own fleets of small torpedo boats. After all, they had experimented with these craft before, and had found the vessels wanting in strategic purpose.

In 1887, however, the US Navy's first torpedo boat, USS *Stiletto*, had entered service, followed by several more vessels or classes in the decades which followed. During this period naval designers invented the 'torpedo boat destroyer' as an antidote to the torpedo boat – small warships which could screen the main battlefleet from attack by torpedo boats, and sink the attackers through gunfire. Inevitably, the distinction between torpedo boat and torpedo boat destroyer became blurred, and by the First World War most 'destroyers' were also fitted with torpedoes.

This development was coupled with a general increase in the size of the destroyers, and an increase in their armament from light quick-firing guns to weapons with a calibre of 3in or more. This effectively meant that torpedo boats had become obsolete, replaced by the larger and more versatile destroyer. Of course, during the First World War several naval powers also experimented with small torpedo boats – the forerunners of the PT Boats, MTBs and E-Boats of the Second World War. However, these fast, nippy little vessels were a far cry from the torpedo boats of *la jeune école* in the 19th century.

# JOSIAH TATTNALL – US NAVAL HERO

The popular saying 'Blood is thicker than water' is usually taken to mean that the bonds between members of a family are stronger than those between friends and acquaintances. Traditionally, it comes from a German proverb, the translation of which became popular in the English-speaking world. The phrase cropped up regularly in poetry and literature over the centuries, but in the US Navy, the expression is attributed to one man – Commodore Josiah Tattnall (1795–1871). For them, it sums up the close links between the US Navy and the Royal Navy.

Josiah Tattnall was an interesting character. As a midshipman he fought against the British during the War of 1812 (1812–15), and he later fought against the Barbary Corsairs in the Mediterranean, and hunted pirates in the Caribbean. He was wounded during the Mexican-American War (1846–48), and was presented with a sword by his home state of Georgia as a token of esteem.

In early 1856 Tattnall assumed command of the US Navy's East India Squadron, flying his flag in the steam frigate USS *San Jacinto*. Two years before, Chinese troops had seized a British-registered sailing ship and her cargo. An international incident blew up, and by the start of 1856 it was clear that Britain and France were prepared to go to war with China, in order to preserve their trade. This conflict became known as the Second Opium War (1856–60).

In May 1858, Rear Admiral Sir James Hope arrived off the Peiho (now the Hai) River which linked Peking (now Beijing) with the Yellow Sea. The river mouth was guarded by the Taku Forts – a sprawling defensive network consisting of five large fortifications and numerous smaller batteries. Hope's job was to capture them, in an attempt to force the Chinese to the negotiating table. After some futile negotiations, Hope launched an attack. On 25 June he sent his gunboat flotilla up the river, but the Chinese fire proved far more deadly than anyone had expected. By the time he called off the assault, four steam gunboats had been sunk and two more were badly damaged.

Commodore Tattnall was anchored off the river mouth in the chartered steam gunboat *Toeywan*. As America remained neutral, he took no part in the attack – he was merely an observer. However, when he saw that two British gunboats – *Plover* and *Cormorant* – had drifted onto the Chinese-held shore, he decided to intervene. He ordered the *Toeywan* to sail up the river, and while under fire from the Chinese forts, he successfully towed the two stricken British gunboats to safety. In fact, at one stage some of his men even clambered on board the *Plover*, and fired on the Chinese batteries, before the gunboat was towed out of range.

Naturally enough the Chinese government was furious, as were many politicians back in Washington. When asked to justify his intervention, Tattnall replied that 'Blood is thicker than water'. A few years later, in 1861, Tattnall resigned his commission, and served in the Confederate Navy during the American Civil War (1861–65). Despite this lapse, he is remembered as a US Naval hero, and an early advocate of the Anglo-American 'special relationship'.

# THE GUNS OF THE *VICTORY*

The armament of most sailing warships was rarely constant. Ships were refitted, improvements were attempted, and individual captains added or removed guns almost at will, in an effort to improve the firepower or seakeeping qualities of their ships. A prime example of this is the armament of HMS *Victory*, which changed frequently during her four decades of active service.

For instance, the *Victory* was originally designed to carry a lower deck armament of huge 42-pdr guns, some of the largest cast-iron weapons of their day. Before she entered service, however, it was decided that the weight of this armament would adversely affect the sailing performance of the ship. Consequently, when she was commissioned in 1778, she was fitted with 32-pdrs instead of the larger and heavier guns, saving a total of 60 tons to her displacement. Just as importantly, her first commanding officer, Admiral Keppel, felt that 32-pdrs were superior guns, as they could be reloaded faster, but had a similar penetrating power to the larger 42-pdr pieces. He was right, and during tests held before the French Revolution, it was proved that the 32-pdr was the optimal heavy naval gun. The 42-pdr guns were tried out on board the *Victory* in 1780, but the experiment wasn't a success, and they were replaced with 32-pdrs in 1788.

Similarly, the development of the carronade around 1780 saw the replacement of the *Victory*'s lighter quarterdeck and forecastle guns with powerful carronades, which weighed roughly the same as the guns they replaced, but packed a far greater close-range punch. Also, some of her original upper deck and quarterdeck guns were bronze, but by 1782 these had been removed to make way for these new carronades, meaning that by 1782, at the latest, all her guns were made from cast-iron. The greatest fluctuation in the armament of the ship came from these carronades, as heavier guns were added, or small batteries were replaced by composite ones. Whatever she was armed with, she remained one of the most efficient and deadly warships in the Royal Navy until she was withdrawn from active service after the end of the Napoleonic Wars.

## On entering service, 1778

Lower deck: thirty 32-pdrs
Middle deck: twenty-eight 24-pdrs
Upper deck: thirty 12-pdrs
Quarterdeck: ten 6-pdrs
Forecastle: twelve 6-pdrs
*Total number of guns: 110*
*Weight of broadside: 1,062 pounds (482 kg)*

## During the American Revolutionary War, c.1780

Lower deck: thirty 42-pdrs
Middle deck: twenty-eight 24-pdrs

Upper deck: thirty 12-pdrs
Quarterdeck: ten 6-pdrs
Forecastle: two 6-pdrs, two 24-pdr carronades
Poop deck: six 18-pdr carronades
*Total number of guns: 108*
*Weight of broadside: 1,260 pounds (558 kg)*

## During the French Revolutionary War, c.1796

Lower deck: thirty 32-pdrs
Middle deck: twenty-eight 24-pdrs
Upper deck: thirty 12-pdrs
Quarterdeck: twelve 12-pdrs
Forecastle: two 24-pdr carronades
*Total number of guns: 102*
*Weight of broadside: 1,092 pounds (495 kg)*

## At Trafalgar, 1805

Lower Deck: thirty 32-pdrs
Middle Deck: twenty-eight 24-pdrs
Upper Deck: thirty 12-pdrs
Quarterdeck: twelve 12-pdrs
Forecastle: two 68-pdr carronades, two 24-pdr carronades
*Total number of guns: 104*
*Weight of broadside: 1,160 pounds (526 kg)*

## During the later Napoleonic Wars, c.1812

Lower deck: twenty-eight 32-pdrs
Middle deck: twenty-eight 24-pdrs
Upper deck: thirty 12-pdrs
Quarterdeck: eight 32-pdr carronades
Forecastle: two 12-pdrs, two 32-pdr carronades
*Total number of guns: 98*
*Weight of broadside: 1,136 pounds (515 kg)*

# THE MOST TREACHEROUS
# WATERS IN THE AGE OF SAIL

During the French Revolutionary War (1793–1802) the Royal Navy lost 204 warships of various sizes. A few of these were captured by the enemy, others were lost in accidental fires or by being 'expended' as too rotten to continue sailing. The remaining 118 were lost at sea, either by being wrecked or by foundering in mid-ocean. By looking at the locations of these warship losses, we can see which areas were highly dangerous during the age of fighting sail. The following ten regions proved the most treacherous for the Royal Navy during this period:

1   **The Caribbean** (22 ships lost): an area known for its hurricanes, the Caribbean also contained numerous uncharted reefs, making safe navigation difficult.

2   **The English Channel** (20 ships lost): a lack of sea room made operating in the Channel difficult, and numerous warships were wrecked along England's southern coast.

3   **The French Ports** (13 ships lost): maintaining a blockade off ports such as Brest and Cherbourg was extremely dangerous, as the French coast near these ports was a treacherous maze of rocks, shoals and headlands.

4   **The North Sea** (12 ships lost): most of these warships were lost on the moving and largely uncharted sandbars off the Dutch coast.

5   **The Iberian Peninsula** (11 ships lost): the northern coast of Spain and the southern tip of Portugal were known as maritime graveyards during the age of sail.

6   **The Mediterranean** (7 ships lost): most British warships were lost off the Italian coast, or off Sicily.

7   **Newfoundland** (6 ships lost): the fog banks, ice and storms off the Grand Banks and Newfoundland made navigation hazardous in these North American waters.

8  **Ireland** (5 ships lost): most of these were driven onto the western Irish coast by Atlantic storms.

9  **Channel Islands** (4 ships lost): most of these losses were warships which were driven onto the islands from the blockading fleets off Brest and Cherbourg.

10 **American Seaboard** (4 ships lost): the sandbanks and islands of the Outer Banks proved particularly treacherous for sailing warships, earning the area a reputation as 'the graveyard of the Atlantic'.

# THE WORLD'S MOST POWERFUL BATTLESHIP

The Second World War was the last hurrah of the battleship. The development of naval airpower and the increasing effectiveness of submarines both put paid to the supremacy of the big gun in naval warfare. Ever since, naval enthusiasts have debated which of these battleships was the most powerful. Some point to the Japanese *Yamato* and her sister ship the *Musashi*, armed with nine 18in guns apiece. Others argue on behalf of the later American battleships such as the Iowa Class, with their combination of nine 16in guns apiece, backed up by the latest in radar fire control. Others could argue that all-round fighting ability was more important than armament.

The truth is, battleships were designed as a compromise – a balance between speed, firepower and protection. The relative importance of the holy trinity of naval design – guns, propulsion and armour – is subjective. Other factors are worth considering as well. For instance, how well were the battleships protected against a hit by an enemy torpedo? How well could they defend themselves against air attack? Fire control was also of crucial importance, both by visual means and by radar. After all, however powerful a gun might be, it was only effective if its fire could be skilfully directed onto its target. Then there were the other tactical considerations, such as how long the battleship could steam without refuelling, and the reliability of its systems or its damage control organization.

The *Yamato* had more powerful guns than the *Iowa*, and slightly better armoured protection. Both outclassed other contenders such as the *Bismarck* or the *King George V*. Surprisingly, despite its reputation, the German battleship was less well protected than many of its contemporaries. The same was true of its underwater protection, and particularly of its fire control. The Germans never perfected an effective radar fire control system, and the Japanese only introduced radar fire control in 1944. The visual and radar fire control available to American and British battleships was far superior to those of their Axis counterparts, and although it is subjective, the British King George V Class probably enjoyed better fire control than the battleships of the Iowa Class. That said, the *Iowa* had an extremely effective propulsion system, and was a full 6 knots (11.1km/h) faster than her Japanese rival.

Taking everything into account, the most powerful battleship in the world during the Second World War was the American Iowa Class – the battleships USS *Iowa* (BB61), USS *New Jersey* (BB62), USS *Missouri* (BB63) and USS *Wisconsin* (BB64). A combination of superb fire control, powerful armament, high speed and excellent protection (both above and below the waterline) make these battleships the most powerful all-round gun-armed fighting vessels of the war. The Yamato Class may have had bigger guns and been slightly larger, but their fire control and their speed were decidedly inferior to their American counterparts. British battleships were highly effective, but they were often limited by the constraints of pre-war treaties, or they lacked the extensive anti-aircraft protection of their American or Japanese counterparts.

The armament of the Iowa Class battleships didn't remain static. They were placed in reserve after the war, but brought back into service twice, for the Korean and Vietnam wars. Despite the development of other, more modern forms of warships, there was still a need for big guns, used for naval gunfire support. Then in 1975 the US Navy decided to re-arm them, as the centrepiece of US Surface Action groups (SAGs), and after a costly and controversial programme the *Iowa* and the *New Jersey* returned to front-line service. The big difference was that instead of some of their secondary armament, the battleships now carried 32 Tomahawk cruise missiles, as well as Harpoon anti-ship missiles (SSMs). The battleships were decommissioned during the 1990s, and now all three are earmarked as or already have been turned into museum ships – a lasting legacy to the heyday of the big gun.

# THE CAPTAIN – A MAN APART

While a captain is certainly a naval rank – the equivalent of a colonel in the army – it is much more than merely a step on the naval ladder of rank. Today, most warships are commanded by officers with the rank of commander. The rank of captain is reserved for the largest, most prestigious naval commands. However, all these warship commanders, whatever rank they are, are addressed as 'Captain'. According to naval custom it is a title which accompanies the command of a ship, regardless of the actual rank held by the warship commander.

A captain is responsible for the ship under his command. Even if a more senior officer is on board, these higher-ranking officers can't order the captain what to do when it comes to the operation or safety of his ship: he, and he alone, is responsible for it, and for the men under his command. The title was first introduced during the 16th century. Before then, the term 'master' was more commonly used. By the 18th century, this term was more commonly used to refer to a warrant officer, responsible for seamanship on board a vessel. A captain was either called a 'master and commander' if the vessel was unrated or termed a 'post captain' if the vessel was the size of a frigate or larger.

A guidebook to naval service, compiled by the Royal Navy during the Second World War, defined the nature – and the loneliness – of a naval captain's role. It said:

The captain carries the ultimate responsibility for every word spoken by, and for every action of, an individual on board his ship. He also has the most immediate responsibility for her safety and war efficiency. For conduct in war he is guided by the *Articles of War*, which enjoin that he shall 'use his utmost exertion to bring his ship into action, and during such action, in his own person, encourage his inferior officers and men to fight courageously'.

Here you will see that two of his responsibilities, the safety of his ship and the taking of her into action, must be balanced one against the other. In some cases the latter outweighs the former, as in the case of HMS *Jervis Bay*, whose captain, by fighting to the last against hopeless odds, saved most of his convoy from destruction.

Consider for a moment this taking of a ship into action by the captain. He is on the compass platform. The navigating officer and the officer of the watch are there too, but they are there to obey his orders: in as much as he must make every decision himself, and has to bear full responsibility for it, he is completely alone. The ship is moving through the water at whatever speed he alone has ordered.

The guns' crews are all at their stations. When he gives the order they will open fire. When they fire, whether they hit the enemy or not will depend upon the training he has ensured these crews have had, and whether the whole enormously complex mechanism of fire control and guns has been maintained to produce its maximum efficiency at this moment.

And lastly, he has to consider the moment ahead when the enemy's shells will burst on board his ship. How his ship's company will react to that almost inevitable moment, how much or how little it will affect their morale, will depend upon things almost indefinable, upon 'all their yesterdays', upon the spirit that he has instilled throughout his ship.

This loneliness of high command accompanies him wherever he may be, on board, at sea or in harbour, in peace and in war. He lives alone, in fact as much as in spirit. If he paces the quarterdeck he selects the starboard side, by the custom of the Service, and anybody who happens to be there immediately vacates it for the port side. There is nothing of the cold shoulder about it; it is the tradition of the sea.

# THE U-BOAT ACES

During the Second World War, the Germans sent just over a thousand U-Boats out on patrol, and while ultimately most of these boats were sunk, the U-Boat fleet proved to be the most successful arm of the Kriegsmarine. Almost 3,000 Allied ships were sunk by U-Boats during the war, amounting to over 14 million tons of shipping. However, almost three out of every four U-Boat crews were lost – over 28,000 German men. This was a high price to pay for an ultimately unsuccessful campaign of attrition. During the war, a handful of U-Boat commanders proved to be far more aggressive, lucky or successful than their fellow skippers. These twelve 'aces' were the elite of the U-Boat arm – the men who almost single-handedly brought Britain to the verge of ruin. The top dozen listed here are presented in order of the tonnage of Allied shipping they sank during their brief careers.

1.  **Otto Kretchmer (1912–98)**
    Tonnage sunk: 273,043 Ships sunk: 46 Patrols: 16
    U-Boats: *U-23*, *U-99*
    The highest-scoring U-Boat ace, Kretchmer was an aggressive, determined commander, who preferred to attack at night, on the surface. He was captured when *U-99* was damaged and forced to surface in March 1941, and he ended the war as a prisoner-of-war. He subsequently served in the post-war German Navy.

2. **Wolfgang Lüth (1913–45)**

   Tonnage sunk: 225,204 Ships sunk: 46 Patrols: 16

   U-Boats: *U-9*, *U-138*, *U-43*, *U-181*

   One of the most highly decorated German naval officers of the war, Lüth was also an ardent Nazi. In early 1944 he was selected to spearhead the training of new crews. He was accidentally shot by a German sentry just a few days after the end of the war.

3. **Erich Topp (1914–2005)**

   Tonnage sunk: 197,460 Ships sunk: 35 Patrols: 12

   U-Boats: *U-15*, *U-552*, *U-2513*

   Topp's 'Red Devil' (*U-552*) specialized in attacking shipping off the American coast, sinking eight ships in one patrol. He was one of the only commanders to lead Germany's most modern U-Boat – the Type XXI – in action. After the war he became an architect, before rejoining the Navy in 1958.

4. **Heinrich Liebe (1908–97)**

   Tonnage sunk: 187,267 Ships sunk: 34 Patrols: 9

   U-Boats: *U-2*, *U-38*

   A commander with pre-war U-Boat experience, Liebe's most successful patrol was his last one, when he sank eight ships off Freetown, on the West African coast. From July 1941 onwards he held staff appointments ashore.

5. **Viktor Schütze (1906–50)**

   Tonnage sunk: 180,073 Ships sunk: 35 Patrols: 7

   U-Boats: *U-25*, *U-103*

   Schütze mainly operated in the North Atlantic and off the West African coast, achieving considerable success before he was transferred to training and command duties in August 1941.

6.  **Heinrich Lehmann-Willenbrock (1911–86)**
    Tonnage sunk: 179,125 Ships sunk: 25 Patrols: 10
    U-Boats: *U-5*, *U-96*, *U-256*
    A successful commander, Lehmann-Willenbrock's last boat was sunk during an Allied bombing raid on Wilhelmshaven in 1945. The activities of *U-96* in 1941 were recounted in the film *Das Boot*. Unlike his film counterpart, Lehmann-Willenbrock survived the raid, and the war.

7.  **Karl-Friedrich Merten (1905–93)**
    Tonnage sunk: 170,151 Ships sunk: 27 Patrols: 5
    U-Boats: *U-68*
    Merten patrolled as far as the Indian Ocean and the Caribbean, but his most profitable hunting ground was off the South African coast, where he sank over 100,000 tons in two months during late 1942.

8.  **Herbert Schultze (1909–87)**
    Tonnage sunk: 169,709 Ships sunk: 26 Patrols: 8
    U-Boats: *U-48*
    Schultze was the first U-Boat commander to surpass the 'ace' target of 100,000 tons, and was known as a humane and honourable man, who even transmitted radio coordinates to the Allies to help them locate survivors of ships he sank.

9.  **Günther Prien (1908–41)**
    Tonnage sunk: 162,769 Ships sunk: 30 Patrols: 10
    U-Boats: *U-47*
    Prien is best remembered as the man who penetrated the defence of Scapa Flow, sinking HMS *Royal Oak* (see p.180). His U-Boat was sunk during a convoy attack in the North Atlantic, in March 1941.

10. **Georg Lassen (1915–unknown)**
Tonnage sunk: 156,082 Ships sunk: 26 Patrols: 4
U-Boats: *U-160*
Lassen sank six ships on his first patrol, and he sank as many again in a single day in March 1943, off the South African coast. On his return he was transferred to training duties.

11. **Joachim Schepke (1912–41)**
Tonnage sunk: 155,882 Ships sunk: 37 Patrols: 14
U-Boats: *U-100*
Schepke was one of Germany's most successful and promising U-Boat aces, until his boat was rammed and sunk by HMS *Havoc* in March 1941.

12. **Werner Henke (1909–44)**
Tonnage sunk: 155,714 Ships sunk: 24 Patrols: 7
U-Boats: *U-515*
In May 1943, Henke sank eight ships in eight hours off the West African coast. He was captured by the US Navy when his boat was damaged in April 1944, and he was subsequently shot while trying to escape from a prisoner-of-war camp in Virginia.

# NELSON AND OTHER LIMBLESS ADMIRALS

Vice-Admiral Horatio Nelson (1758–1805) is remembered as much for his injuries as for his great victories. He lost his right eye during a shore action at Calvi in Corsica in 1794, when a cannonball landed beside him and debris struck the young captain in the face. He was injured again three years later. As a rear admiral, Nelson led an amphibious attack on Santa Cruz de Tenerife in the Canary Islands (1797). As he stepped ashore, a musket ball struck his right arm, just above the elbow. He was taken back to HMS *Theseus*, where his arm was amputated. Soon afterwards he wrote: 'a left-handed Admiral will never again be considered as useful, therefore the sooner I get to a very humble cottage the better.' Within a year the limbless admiral led a fleet to victory at the battle of the Nile (1798).

Nelson was wounded in this great battle, but his injuries were superficial. His injuries did not prevent him from taking a mistress – Lady Hamilton – and causing a major scandal. However, his reputation was saved by another victory at Copenhagen (1801), when he used his one eye to good advantage. When his superior ordered him to withdraw he put his telescope to his injured eye, and turned to Captain Foley, his flag captain: 'You know, Foley, I have only one eye. I have a right to be blind sometimes. I really do not see the signal.' Nelson was mortally wounded four years later, at the battle of Trafalgar (1805).

The battered, limbless admiral became a national hero, and his statue – with one eye and one arm – still dominates London's Trafalgar Square. However, he wasn't the only limbless admiral in history – only the most famous. The following limbless admirals all led their ships into action against the enemy, regardless of their disability:

### Don Blas de Leso (1688–1741)

This highly respected Spanish admiral lost his left leg to an English roundshot during the battle of Velez-Malaga, fought off Gibraltar in 1704. He recovered from his injuries, and three years later he helped a Franco-Hispanic force defend Toulon against an Allied attack. It was there that he lost his left eye, during an attack on the fortified heights of Santa Caterina. Despite his injuries he returned to service, and in 1714 he was injured again, this time during the siege of Barcelona, when he lost his right arm. To his men, the one-eyed, one-armed and one-legged commander was known as *Patapalo* ('Pegleg'), or even *Mediohombre* ('Half a Man'). However, he still went on to become an admiral, his most notable achievement being the defence of Cartagena des Indies against Admiral Vernon in 1737.

### John Benbow (1653–1702)

This English admiral was more fortunate than Don Blas de Leso, as he never received a serious injury until his final sea battle. He earned his reputation fighting the Barbary Pirates during the 1670s, but his performance during the War of the Grand Alliance (1688–97) earned him his promotion to flag rank. Then, in 1702 he led a squadron to the West Indies, in an attempt to intercept a Spanish treasure fleet. Instead he encountered a French squadron off the coast of Hispaniola. In the ensuing action Benbow was hit by a chainshot, which all but severed his leg. After having his wounds dressed, he returned on deck, and supervised the rest of the battle. He died three months later, not from his wounds, but from melancholia. His exploit was remembered in *Brave Benbow*, a popular song of the 18th century:

> Brave Benbow lost his legs
> By chain shot, by chain shot
> Brave Benbow lost his legs by chain shot.
> Brave Benbow lost his legs,
> And all on his stumps he begs,
> Fight on my English lads,
> 'Tis our lot, 'tis our lot.
> The surgeon dress'd his wounds,
> Cries Benbow, cries Benbow
> The surgeon dress'd his wounds, cries Benbow.
> Let a cradle now in haste,
> On the quarterdeck be placed
> That the enemy I may face
> 'Til I die, 'til I die.

### Andrew Chan Chak (Chau Shek) (1894–1949)

Admiral Chan Chak commanded the miniscule southern fleet of the Chinese Navy during the Second Sino-Japanese War (1937–45). He lost his leg in his youth, during naval operations against Chinese river pirates. In December 1941 he was based in Hong Kong, and commanded the city's National Military Council. He worked closely with the small British garrison there, and on 25 December 1941, as commander of Anglo-Chinese naval forces in the port, he led the British 2nd MTB Flotilla in an escape bid, to avoid these five small warships falling into the hands of the Japanese. After running a gauntlet of fire the boats made good their escape, and eventually reached the temporary safety of Rangoon. Known as 'the Nelson of the East', Chan Chak was awarded a knighthood by the British, before returning to serve the Chinese nationalist government as Mayor of Canton until his sudden death in 1949.

### Cornelis Jol (1597–1641)

This Dutch sea captain served the Dutch West India Company as a privateer, and during the 1620s and 1630s he led several expeditions against Spanish and Portuguese settlements in Brazil and the Caribbean. His leg was amputated following a land battle with the Portuguese on the island of Fernando de Norhona in 1631, and consequently his men gave him the nickname *Houtebeen* ('Pegleg'). By 1639 he had become a rear admiral, and his squadron helped defeat the Spanish in the battle of the Downs (1639). He died of malaria off the West African coast while trying to seize the island of São Tomé (Principe) from the Portuguese.

# ANGLO-AMERICAN FRIGATE DUELS

During the War of 1812 (1812–15) between Great Britain and the United States of America, the two navies fought a string of single-ship actions on the high seas. After a century of near-constant victories against the French, the Dutch and the Spanish, the Royal Navy expected the US Navy to be just as lacklustre an opponent as their European rivals had been. The British were in for a shock – not only was the US Navy highly efficient, ship for ship it was also more than a match for the largest naval force in the world. While the typical British 38-gun frigate of the time carried a broadside weight of metal of around 528lb (240kg), the American 44-gun heavy frigates threw broadsides of 864lb (392kg), which gave them a decided advantage. The Americans also had the edge in training over their war-weary British counterparts. Regardless of these arguments, the British public were outraged. The run of American victories was finally ended by Captain Broke of HMS *Shannon*, and after that the naval war swung in the favour of the British. However, by the end of the war honours in frigate actions were roughly even. After the war, both navies retained a healthy respect for each other.

## The *Constitution* and the *Guerrière*

The 38-gun frigate HMS *Guerrière* was captured from the French in 1806, and her French name (meaning 'Warrior') was retained. On 19 April 1812, the frigate – commanded by Captain James Dacres – was in mid-Atlantic, some 400 miles (740km) east of Nova Scotia. She was attacked by the USS *Constitution* (44 guns), commanded by Captain Isaac Hull. After trading broadsides for half an hour the British frigate lost her mizzen mast, allowing the *Constitution* to manoeuvre round her, and rake her stern. Dacres thwarted a boarding attempt, but more American broadsides soon brought down both her remaining masts. The unfortunate Dacres had little choice but to surrender. The *Guerrière* was too badly damaged to save, so after her crew were taken aboard the *Constitution* as prisoners, Hull ordered her to be set ablaze.

## The *United States* and the *Macedonian*

On the morning of 25 October 1812, the 38-gun frigate HMS *Macedonian* under the command of Captain John Carden encountered the USS *United States* (44 guns) near Madeira. The larger American frigate was commanded by Captain Stephen Decatur, a friend of the British commander. The battle was a one-sided affair. The *Macedonian* was dismasted by the *United*

*States'* first broadsides, and when Decatur moved into a position to rake his opponent, Carden struck his colours. The captured *Macedonian* was escorted to Newport, Rhode Island, to great national acclaim.

## The *Constitution* and the *Java*

In September 1812, Captain William Bainbridge succeeded Isaac Hull as the commander of the USS *Constitution*, and he sailed her south, to cruise the busy shipping lanes off the coast of Brazil. On 29 December he encountered the 38-gun frigate HMS *Java*, commanded by Captain Henry Lambert. At first the British got the better of the exchange, wounding Bainbridge and damaging the *Constitution*'s rudder. Then, though, the American broadsides brought down the *Java*'s foremast and bowsprit, which fell over her gun decks, obscuring most of her guns. Bainbridge poured shot into the hull of the British ship, bringing down her remaining masts, and mortally wounding the British captain. He pulled away to repair his own damage, and then returned for the kill. At that point Lambert's deputy Lieutenant Chads surrendered the ship, to avoid further bloodshed. Like the *Guerrière*, the shattered *Java* was scuttled after the battle.

## The *Chesapeake* and the *Shannon*

By 1813 the British had imposed a blockade of the American ports, and the 38-gun frigate HMS *Shannon* was ordered to patrol off the port of Boston. Her commander, Captain Philip de Vere Broke, knew that an American frigate of a similar size – the USS *Chesapeake* (38 guns) lay inside the harbour, so he issued a personal challenge to her commander, Captain James Lawrence. On 1 June the *Chesapeake* sailed out to do battle, and the two frigates exchanged broadsides at close range. Both ships were badly damaged in the exchange, and Lawrence was mortally wounded. As he was carried below, his last order was 'Don't give up the ship. Fight her till she sinks!' However, Broke set his frigate alongside the American warship, and his men boarded her. Although Broke was badly wounded in the mêlée, his men prevailed, and, despite Lawrence's dying wish, the *Chesapeake* was captured. She was taken to Halifax, where the news of the British victory delighted the British and Canadian public.

## The *Essex* and the *Phoebe*

In January 1813, the frigate USS *Essex* (46 guns), commanded by Captain David Porter, sailed into the Pacific, to disrupt the lucrative British whaling trade. However, she was trapped in the port of Valparaiso by two British warships – a frigate and a sloop. On 28 March 1814 Porter sailed out to give battle, and the challenge was taken up by the frigate HMS *Phoebe*, of 36 guns. Unusually, the *Essex* was almost entirely armed with carronades – ideal for a close-range battle, but with less than half the range of conventional naval guns. Captain James Hillyar kept his distance, and after two and a half hours of pounding the *Essex* was too badly damaged to continue, and Porter was forced to surrender. The American frigate was later taken into British service.

## The *President* and the *Endymion*

On 13 January 1815 Captain Stephen Decatur, commanding the 44-gun frigate USS *President*, attempted to break the British blockade of New York, under cover of a blizzard. Despite briefly running aground in the darkness she made it out to the open sea, but at dawn she was spotted, and pursued by four British frigates. By evening she had outpaced them all apart from the 38-gun frigate HMS *Endymion*, which managed to come within range. The two ships raced on through the night, exchanging fire from bow and stern. Occasionally, the faster British ship would yaw round and fire a full broadside into the *President*, before continuing the chase. Decatur was unwilling to risk an all-out engagement, as that would allow the other British frigates to catch up. Eventually, the two ships were so battered that one of the other frigates,

HMS *Pomone*, managed to overhaul the *President*. She fired two broadsides into the American frigate, and, realizing the battle was lost, Decatur hauled down his colours.

# SHIPS' MASCOTS

During the Second World War and its aftermath warships of various nations often carried an animal on board, as a way of bolstering morale. These were usually dubbed ship's mascots. Here are some of the better-known examples.

'**Simon**': A ship's cat on board the sloop HMS *Amethyst*, when the British vessel was shelled by Communist Chinese batteries on the Yangtze River in 1949. Simon was awarded the PDSA Dickin medal in recognition of his courage. He was later buried with full naval honours.

'**Whisky**': A tabby cat carried on board HMS *Duke of York*. During the battle of North Cape (1942) when the guns of the British battleship pummelled the German battlecruiser KMS *Scharnhorst*, Whisky remained asleep throughout the entire engagement. Whisky was renowned as a rat catcher on board the battleship.

'**Olga**': A reindeer given to Rear Admiral Burnett by the Soviet authorities in Murmansk. Olga was kept in the hangar of HMS *Belfast* during the battle of North Cape. Unfortunately she was driven berserk by the gunnery, and had to be put down.

'**Oskar/Oscar**': The feline mascot of the KMS *Bismarck*. He was on board the German battleship when she made her famous sortie into the North Atlantic. He survived the sinking of the ship, and was pulled out of the water by British sailors on HMS *Cossack*. Oscar was cast into the sea again when *Cossack* was sunk later that year. He was taken to Gibraltar where the colony's governor took him in. It was later claimed that Oscar was given to the crew of HMS *Ark Royal*, and consequently was shipwrecked a third time in November

1941, but this version of his story has never been corroborated. A painting of Oscar now hangs in the National Maritime Museum in Greenwich, London.

**'Mary' and 'Mack':** Two ship's cats, appropriately named 'Mary' and 'Mack', carried on the fleet oiler USS *Merrimack*. The vessel served in both the Atlantic and the Pacific theatres during the Second World War, and won eight battle stars.

**'Blackie/Churchill':** The ship's mascot of HMS *Prince of Wales*, a large cat called Blackie. He was photographed being stroked by Churchill when Britain's wartime prime minister met President Roosevelt in Newfoundland in August 1941. Blackie was duly renamed Churchill. The *Prince of Wales* was sunk off Malaya in December 1941, but Churchill managed to swim ashore, where he was found by British servicemen. He was left in Malaya when Singapore fell in February 1942.

# RAISING THE V*ASA*

On 10 August 1628, the Swedish warship *Vasa* capsized and sank in Stockholm harbour, less than an hour into her maiden voyage. During the subsequent inquest it was revealed that the stately 64-gun ship-of-the-line was dangerously top-heavy, and when she heeled over in the wind the water poured in through her open gunports. After a few salvage attempts the wreck was abandoned and she remained undisturbed for another three centuries. Then in August 1956 the Swedish engineer Anders Franzén rediscovered her, lying in 100ft (30m) of water in Stockholm's main deep water channel. Franzén was delighted to find that her remains were very well preserved, and, after he and his supporters lobbied the Swedish government, the official decision was made to raise her.

Nothing like this had ever been attempted before. Swedish Navy divers tunnelled through the mud beneath her hull using high-pressure water jets, before slipping steel cables around her.

The work was dangerous and slow, and was carried out in pitch darkness. It was finally completed in late 1959, without any diver losing their life.

The idea was that the cables would form a lifting cradle. These were attached to two salvage barges. The first move would be just a few feet, so the hull was lifted clear of the mud. This worked perfectly, and her hull now hung above the mud of the seabed.

Then the salvagers moved her slowly into shallower, clearer water. Once she was there, divers went to work on the hull itself, sealing up gunports, filling in holes left by corroded iron fasteners, and patching up the damaged stern with timber. The work took another year. Eventually, everything was ready for the final raising.

The final lift took place on 24 April 1961, and after 333 years the *Vasa* was raised from the depths. As soon as her deck appeared Anders Franzén jumped on board – the first man to walk her deck in a third of a millennium. Then the business of pumping out the water began. The salvagers discovered that the *Vasa*'s hull was so well preserved that she was able to float unaided. It was therefore with great dignity that she completed her 'maiden' voyage, and she was towed into a waiting dry dock – the place that would become her permanent home.

For the next four decades, the hull was cleaned and preserved, her guns and decks were restored, and thousands of objects were conserved. Today the *Vasa* is one of the most popular tourist attractions in Scandinavia – the only original 17th-century ship-of-the-line in the world. Just as importantly, the ship and the artefacts found inside her have given us a unique opportunity to understand what life was like on board these beautiful sailing ships of war, and to see how they were built, sailed and fought.

# THE MOST SUCCESSFUL ADMIRALS IN HISTORY

Any list of this kind is bound to be subjective, but it remains a valuable exercise in showing which naval commanders had a decisive impact on world history as a result of their naval victories. In this list, the admirals have been rated according to the level of their achievement, and linked to one of their victories which played a major part in the shaping of events.

1. **Lord Horatio Nelson (Trafalgar, 1805)**
   The greatest of Nelson's victories, Trafalgar ensured Britain's mastery of the seas during the Napoleonic Wars, and ushered in a century of British naval dominance. Nelson himself was an inspirational commander, who was willing to take risks in the pursuit of a decisive victory.

2. **Chester Nimitz (Midway, 1942)**
   During the battle of Midway, Nimitz made good use of intelligence reports to place his carriers in exactly the right place to ambush the Japanese carrier fleet. His victory turned the tide in the Pacific campaign, and allowed him to mastermind the great Allied counter-offensive that led to the defeat of Japan. The battle firmly established the US Navy as the dominant naval power, if not in the world, then at least in the Pacific.

3. **Themistocles (Salamis, 480 BC)**
   This Athenian politician and commander had to command a disparate allied naval force, which he held together through a mixture of diplomacy and coercion. His victory over the Persians at Salamis ensured the survival of Athens and the mastery of the Greeks over the Persians, and ushered in a century of Athenian naval supremacy in the Aegean.

4. **Don Juan de Austria (Lepanto, 1571)**

The illegitimate son of the Emperor Charles V of Spain and the Holy Roman Empire, Don Juan led a coalition of Christian naval powers to victory at Lepanto, and ended Ottoman Turkish expansion in the Mediterranean. This was the ultimate clash between the two religions, and one of the greatest and most decisive naval battles in history.

5. **Lord Howard of Effingham (Gravelines, 1588)**

Charles Howard commanded the English fleet during the Spanish Armada campaign, which reached its climax in the battle of Gravelines. Having used fireships to drive the Spanish fleet from the Flemish coast, Howard attacked and battered the Spanish, driving them into the North Sea. As a result, the Spanish invasion attempt was foiled, and England rather than Spain became the dominant naval power in Europe.

6. **Comte de Grasse (Chesapeake Bay, 1781)**

It can be argued that the indecisive naval battle fought between De Grasse and his British counterpart Rear Admiral Sir Thomas Graves helped decide the fate of a continent. As the result of what was effectively a drawn battle, the British fleet withdrew to New York. This meant the French remained on station off the Virginia Capes, guarding the entrance to Chesapeake Bay. Consequently, the isolated British Army at Yorktown was forced to surrender. While De Grasse showed little tactical genius, the strategic implications of his drawn battle make his action one of the most decisive naval encounters in history.

7. **Togo Heihachiro (Tsushima, 1905)**

By inflicting a crushing defeat over the Russian Navy at Tsushima, Togo established Japan as the dominant military and naval power in Asia. His fleet virtually annihilated its opponents, demonstrating the effectiveness with which the Japanese had embraced modern technology. For the next four decades, the Imperial Japanese Navy would be a naval force of international repute.

### 8. Yi Sun Sin (Hansando, 1592)

This Korean admiral used a form of armoured warship – the 'turtle ship' – to inflict a decisive defeat over the Japanese in several battles, the most important of which was Hansando. As a result, Japanese attempts to intervene in Korean and Chinese affairs were thwarted for the best part of three centuries. At the time of his death in late 1592, Yi Sun Sin had won a string of 23 successive naval victories.

### 9. John Jellicoe (Jutland, 1916)

While Jutland could never be described as a decisive battle in its own right – the result was effectively a draw – its strategic implications were immense. After Jutland the German fleet never tried to fight another general engagement, and British control of the seas was assured. A British defeat would have been a disaster – Churchill described Jellicoe as the one man who could lose the war in an afternoon. By simply not doing so, he ensured a great strategic victory for the Royal Navy.

### 10. Wilhelm von Teggethoff (Lissa, 1866)

While the naval clash at Lissa was decisive – Teggethoff's Austrian steam-powered fleet decisively beat its Italian opponents – the strategic impact of the battle was minimal. However, the tactics, ships and weapons used by Teggethoff would influence warship design for another half a century.

# NAVAL POWER IN 1914

When the First World War began in 1914, the Royal Navy was by far the largest naval power in the world. Of course, this numerical superiority was misleading, as her forces were spread across the globe, protecting the sprawling sea lanes which bound together the British Empire. However, the majority of her most powerful warships – principally her dreadnought battlefleet – were concentrated in home waters. In contrast the Germans positioned the bulk of their fleet in the North Sea, while both the Americans and the French had to split their navies between two theatres of operations – the Atlantic and the Pacific for the Americans, and the English Channel and the Mediterranean for the French.

Of the warships listed, the total of light cruisers includes a range of different vessels, including protected and unprotected cruisers and scout cruisers, all of which might have had different definitions, but ultimately they all performed the same role. This was to patrol the sea lanes, to scout for the enemy, and to counter the threat of enemy light forces to the main battlefleet.

Pre-dreadnought battleships were virtually useless, save as a tool with which to bombard the enemy coast, or to support an amphibious landing. They were also used to protect convoys, and to support the dreadnought battlefleets if required. Destroyers were in their infancy, and while they had originally been designed as 'torpedo boat destroyers', protecting the fleet from attack by torpedo-firing light vessels, by 1914 they had become little more than larger and better-armed versions of the vessels they were designed to destroy.

Submarines were in their infancy, and the First World War would prove the first real test of their effectiveness. Of all the maritime powers, it was the Germans who made the best use of their submarine fleet, harassing British sea lanes, and tying down significant quantities of Allied ships in the process.

|  | Britain | Germany | USA | France | Italy | Japan |
|---|---|---|---|---|---|---|
| Dreadnought battleships | 22 | 15 | 10 | 4 | 3 | 2 |
| Pre-dreadnought battleships | 40 | 22 | 23 | 20 | 8 | 10 |
| Battlecruisers | 9 | 5 | – | – | – | 1 |
| Armoured cruisers | 34 | 7 | 22 | 19 | 7 | 12 |
| Light cruisers | 87 | 33 | – | 9 | 14 | 21 |
| Destroyers | 221 | 90 | – | 81 | 33 | 50 |
| Torpedo boats | 109 | 115 | 23 | 187 | 71 | – |
| Submarines | 73 | 31 | 50 | 67 | 20 | 12 |

In addition, the British had 13 more dreadnought battleships under construction, while the Germans were building five of their own. Of the world's other navies, only Austria-Hungary possessed dreadnought battleships, three of which entered service before the war began.

# NAVAL DISASTER: ARCTIC CONVOY PQ-17

The invasion of the Soviet Union by Nazi Germany in June 1941 caused consternation in Britain, particularly when it appeared that the Red Army was being dismembered by the German Panzers. Stalin appealed to Britain for aid and, despite his personal reservations, Churchill saw no alternative but to offer whatever military assistance he could to his new-found ally. Supplies could only be sent northwards to the ports of Murmansk and Archangel, through the waters of the Arctic. Unfortunately, since the summer of 1940 Norway was in German hands, which meant these convoys would have to run the gauntlet of aircraft, submarine and surface ship attacks launched from northern Norway.

The first convoy sailed for Russia in August 1941, just two months after the German invasion. It made it through with relatively light losses, but during the winter the Germans reinforced their air bases and naval squadrons. By the spring they were ready to strike back. In March 1942, Convoy PQ-13 was attacked by a flotilla of powerful German destroyers, and although the convoy was saved, the escorting cruiser HMS *Trinidad* was badly damaged during the action. The following month another cruiser – HMS *Edinburgh* – was sunk.

The Admiralty decided that the long hours of daylight during the summer made the convoys far too vulnerable to German air attacks. It was decided to halt the convoys until the return of the winter darkness. However, pressure from the Soviet Union meant that for the moment, the convoys would continue, regardless of the risk. The result was the disaster of Convoy PQ-17.

The convoy of 34 merchantmen and their escorts sailed from Iceland on 27 June, bound for Archangel. The escorting forces were divided into two groups: Commander Broome's close escort (six destroyers, four corvettes and two AA ships) was designed to protect the merchantmen from aircraft or submarines, while the covering force of four cruisers and three destroyers kept its distance from the convoy, and provided protection against any sudden sortie by German surface ships. Larger and heavier warships of Admiral Tovey's Home Fleet provided distant support, and could be called in to assist if the Germans attacked with anything larger than a destroyer.

A German spotter plane sighted the convoy on 1 July, off Jan Mayen Island, and a German battlegroup was ordered to intercept it. This force consisted of the battleship *Tirpitz*, the pocket battleships *Admiral Scheer* and *Lützow*, the heavy cruiser *Admiral Hipper*, and a flotilla of destroyers. The *Lützow* ran aground and had to return to its base in the Altenfjord, and the rest failed to locate the convoy. By 4 July they were back in the Altenfjord. However, the British Admiralty knew that the Germans had sailed, and they realized that the convoy escorts were no match for this assembly of German naval firepower. It was then that Admiral Dudley Pound made the fateful decision to scatter the convoy.

By ordering the merchantmen to disperse he hoped to reduce Allied losses. After all, if this powerful German battlegroup sighted the closely packed convoy, then very few of the ships would survive. The order reached the convoy at 2215hrs on 4 July. At that stage the convoy was just to the south of Spitzbergen, and still 800 miles (1,500km) from the safety of a Russian port. The covering force headed back to its base in Scapa Flow, off the north of Scotland. Of course, by that time the threat of surface attack had evaporated. Unfortunately, the scattered merchantmen were easy prey for German U-Boats and aircraft. On 5 July 14 merchant ships were sunk. Another six merchantmen were lost over the following two days, and three more succumbed to German torpedoes before the survivors reached Archangel. A total of 23 merchant ships were lost – just over two-thirds of the convoy.

It was an unmitigated disaster. As well as the huge loss in ships and merchant seamen, some 99,000 tons of vital war supplies had been sent to the bottom of the Barents Sea. In addition nearly 4,000 tanks, trucks, artillery pieces and aircraft had been lost – enough to make a real difference in the Soviet Union's fight for survival. All further convoys were cancelled, and the Allies spent the long days of summer trying to improvise new plans, which would ensure that a disaster of this magnitude would never happen again. The convoys would run again, but from now on the merchant ships sailed during the long arctic winter, where the near-constant darkness and bad weather helped to keep the enemy at bay.

# PROFILE OF A WARSHIP: Q-SHIPS

During the First World War the Royal Navy used decoy ships to lure enemy submarines within range of their hidden guns. These vessels were called 'Q-Ships'. They should not be confused with German commerce raiders or well-armed merchantmen. These were warships which were disguised as harmless merchant vessels.

If a German U-Boat came across a lone merchantman it would save its torpedoes, and use its deck gun to sink its target instead. This meant the U-Boat had to surface, and to close within easy gunnery range. A Q-Ship would wait until the German crew were ready to open fire, and then it would abandon its disguise. Concealed guns would be uncovered, and the U-Boat would be ambushed. Sometimes these Q-Ships even sailed under false colours, using the flags of non-combatants. That way, the U-Boat might surface for news, and it wouldn't even be in a position to fire back.

The first decoy vessels entered service in November 1914, within three months of the outbreak of war. However, it wasn't until July 1915 that a Q-Ship was attacked. Then, the British collier *Prince Charles* was approached by *U-36*, just off Orkney. The trap was sprung, and *U-36* became the first victim of a Q-Ship ambush. A month earlier the disguised trawler *Taranaki* had also lured a U-Boat within range, but her ploy was a little different. She was working in consort with the British submarine *C-24*, and the submarine was used to sink the unfortunate *U-40*, which had unsuspectingly surfaced close to the trawler.

In fact, Q-Ships were never very successful. Early on in the war, there were not enough Q-Ships available to make a difference to the U-Boat campaign. By late 1915, when more Q-Ships became available, the Germans recognized the threat, and changed their tactics. For a start, U-Boat commanders became increasingly suspicious, and if there was any doubt, they tended to sink their victim without warning, using their torpedoes.

During the First World War just under 200 Q-Ships entered service, but altogether they managed to account for only 11 U-Boats. Worse, 29 of them were sunk by German torpedoes from U-Boats which never surfaced. Two more were lost in gunnery duels with U-Boats or German surface warships. In the winter of 1917 the remaining Q-Ships were withdrawn from service. By that time, the U-Boat threat had diminished, and the gun crews were better employed on board more conventional warships.

The British briefly revived the Q-Ship idea during the Second World War, but this time they were even less successful. During this later conflict, U-Boat commanders tended to fire their torpedoes rather than rely on gunnery to sink their targets, partly because most ocean-going merchantmen were larger and harder to sink than their First World War predecessors. The last Q-Ships were withdrawn from service in early 1941.

# THE NAVAL WORLD OF PATRICK O'BRIAN

Over the years there have been numerous naval fiction writers. Perhaps the most famous of these is C. S. Forester (1899–1966), whose series of Hornblower novels set in the Napoleonic Wars was beloved by millions. Forester's admirers included Winston Churchill and Ernest Hemingway, both of whom considered him the best naval writer there was. Since his death other writers have followed in his wake, most notably Alexander Kent (aka Douglas Reeman), Dudley Pope, C. Northcote Parkinson, James L. Nelson and more recently Julian Stockwin. However, few of these writers surpassed Forester's portrayal of life at sea during the age of fighting sail. One novelist does, however, stand out from the crowd – a writer who breathed life into the period like no other.

Patrick O'Brian (1914–2000) was born Richard Russ, and led an unremarkable and somewhat secretive early life, until 1946, when he changed his name. He began writing, and in 1949 he and his new wife moved to France, where he lived until his death. In the late 1960s he began writing the first of his Aubrey-Maturin novels of naval fiction, and the result was *Master and Commander*, first published in 1969. Over the next 30 years he wrote another 20 novels in the series, which proved increasingly popular. Today he is widely regarded as the greatest naval fiction writer of all time, a novelist whose work far surpasses that of Forester or any of his nautical rivals.

His books follow the naval career of Jack Aubrey, a bluff, engaging and highly competent naval officer, whose skills at sea are matched only by his inability to manage his affairs on dry land. The other main character is Stephen Maturin, an Irish (and part Catalan) naval surgeon, who is also involved in naval intelligence. What really sets these books apart is O'Brian's mastery of the world these characters inhabit, particularly his superb portrayal of life at sea on board a sailing man-of-war.

The novels are also noted for their humour, the accuracy of the contemporary language and the way O'Brian entwines his story with historical events, without their presence influencing the historic outcome. O'Brian has a distinctive literary style, which makes the books as highly readable as they are technically and historically accurate.

One minor criticism is the telescoping of time. *Master and Commander* is set around 1800, and is based on Lord Cochrane's activities in the Mediterranean. The sixth novel, *Fortune of War*, centres on the War of 1812 (1812–15), and ends with the action between the *Shannon* and the *Chesapeake* in June 1813. However, 12 books further on, *The Yellow Admiral* is clearly set in November and December 1813. O'Brien himself admitted that he, 'made use of hypothetical years … an 1812a as it were or even an 1812b'! Of course, this does nothing to distract from the delight of his narrative.

### The Aubrey-Maturin Books

1. *Master and Commander* (1969)
2. *Post Captain* (1972)
3. *HMS Surprise* (1973)
4. *The Mauritius Command* (1977)
5. *Desolation Island* (1978)
6. *The Fortune of War* (1979)
7. *The Surgeon's Mate* (1980)
8. *The Ionian Mission* (1981)
9. *Treason's Harbour* (1983)

# PEARL HARBOR – FACTS AND FIGURES

While most people know the basics about the unprovoked Japanese attack on Pearl Harbor on 7 December 1941, many of the more unusual facts, events and statistics surrounding the event are less widely remembered.

🐚 The naval base at Pearl Harbor lay on the southern side of the island of Oahu, a little to the west of the city of Honolulu. The bay there was originally called *Wai Momi* ('Bay of Pearl' in Hawaiian).

🐚 In 1889 *Wai Momi* was ceded to the US Government, which created a naval base there, and named it Pearl Harbor. The islands were formally annexed by the United States of America nine years later, in 1898.

🐚 One of the main reasons behind the Japanese pre-emptive strike was the belief that war was inevitable. This attitude had been fostered as a result of a trade embargo in 1940, and a growing fear of American naval expansion.

🏮 As well as attacking Pearl Harbor with carrier-launched aircraft, the Japanese also deployed five midget submarines off the entrance to the harbour. One of these was sighted, attacked and sunk by the destroyer USS *Ward* just hours before the Japanese aircraft attacked Pearl Harbor. This was the first shot fired in anger by an American serviceman during the Second World War. A second midget submarine was sunk by the USS *Monaghan* after the air attacks began. The further three midget submarines were destroyed in the immediate aftermath of the attack, one of which ran aground.

🏮 Six Japanese aircraft carriers were involved in the attack (*Kaga*, *Akagi*, *Soryu*, *Hiryu*, *Shokaku* and *Zuikaku*). Between them they carried 408 aircraft. Of these, 360 were earmarked to take part in the attack, while the remainder maintained a defensive 'Combat Air Patrol' over the Japanese carriers.

🏮 The Japanese attempted to make a formal declaration of war before the attack was launched. However, delays in decoding the message by Japanese Embassy staff meant that the attack took place before the declaration of war could be delivered.

🏮 The first wave of 183 aircraft led by Captain Fuchida was split into three groups. The main body of 50 dive-bombers and 40 torpedo-bombers attacked the fleet itself. Meanwhile 54 dive-bombers attacked the airfield at Wheeler Field, and the naval air station on Ford Island. A further 45 fighters provided air cover, and strafed aircraft on the ground.

🏮 The approaching Japanese aircraft were detected on radar, but due to confusion over identity and numbers the alarm was never raised.

The first Japanese planes appeared over Pearl Harbor at 0748hrs. The alarm was finally raised by the US Army Air Force, which sounded air raid warnings, followed by the announcement 'Air Raid Pearl Harbor. This is no drill.'

The second wave of 171 Japanese aircraft commanded by Lieutenant-Commander Shimazaki arrived over the island minutes later. Of these, 81 dive-bombers attacked the fleet, while 54 more concentrated on the airfields. Another 36 fighters strafed targets of opportunity.

The entire air attack lasted just 90 minutes. In that time 2,331 American servicemen died, as well as 55 civilians. Five of the eight battleships anchored in the base (*Arizona*, *California*, *Nevada*, *Oklahoma* and *West Virginia*) were either sunk or forced to beach to avoid sinking as a result of the attack. Three others were damaged, along with three cruisers. Two destroyers (*Cassin* and *Downes*) were also sunk, as was the auxiliary vessel *Oglala*.

Of 402 American aircraft present in Hawaii, 188 were destroyed, and a further 159 were damaged. Most of these were damaged or destroyed on the ground. Five US Navy aircraft were shot down by 'friendly fire' as they attempted to land, having been flown from the USS *Enterprise* earlier that morning.

No American carriers were present in Pearl Harbor when the Japanese attacked. Admiral Halsey's carrier force – USS *Lexington* and the USS *Enterprise*, carrying a total of 139 aircraft – were at sea when the Japanese struck. Similarly the carrier USS *Saratoga* had still not joined the fleet by 7 December. The loss of these carriers would have crippled the American war effort.

A total of 27 Japanese aircraft were shot down during the attack, and a total of 55 aviators were killed, and one was captured.

Of all the battleships which were sunk or damaged, only the *Arizona* and the *Oklahoma* were never salvaged, repaired and sent back into service. The *Arizona* is now a war memorial, maintained by the US Park Service.

# THE NAVY IN THE MOVIES

A list of the top ten naval films would be a pointless exercise, as any such list is subjective, and would vary so much from person to person that it would be rendered meaningless. Instead, here is offered a list of ten naval films which this author found particularly good because of their historical accuracy, their depiction of naval life or historic events, or simply because they provided excellent seafaring entertainment. The films are listed in alphabetic order, to avoid accusations of favouritism.

*The Battle of the River Plate* **(Britain, 1956)**
(Distributed in the USA as *The Pursuit of the Graf Spee*)
**Directors:** Michael Powell & Emeric Pressburger
**Leading actors:** John Gregson, Anthony Quayle, Peter Finch
This gripping retelling of the last battle of the German pocket battleship SMS *Graf Spee* paid great attention to detail. The heavy cruiser USS *Salem* stood in for the German battleship, and other British warships stood in for HMS *Exeter* and HMS *Ajax*. HMS *Achilles* played herself, although by 1956 she had been handed over to the Indian Navy, and re-named INS *Delhi*. The main historical inaccuracy is that the *Salem* didn't really look like the *Graf Spee*, and her crew weren't allowed to wear German helmets, so were filmed wearing their own American ones instead.

*Das Boot* **['The Boat'] (Germany, 1981)**
**Director:** Wolfgang Peterson
**Leading actor:** Jürgen Prochnow

This highly accurate film covers a wartime patrol by the German U-Boat *U-96*, and captures the mixture of tedium, excitement and fear that was the lot of the U-Boat crew during the Second World War. Heinrich Lehmann-Willenbrock, the real skipper of *U-96*, served as a consultant during the filming, which helped ensure it was as accurate as possible. The film was based on the bestselling book by Lothar-Günther Buchheim.

### The Caine Mutiny (USA, 1954)

**Director:** Edward Dmytryk

**Leading actor:** Humphrey Bogart

Based on the Pulitzer Prize-winning novel by Herman Wouk, the story was based on the author's own experiences on board a destroyer-minesweeper during the Pacific War. The plot concerns a mentally unstable captain, who is eventually relieved of his command by his own crew – a legal rather than a violent mutiny. The climax of the film, though, takes place on dry land, during the subsequent court martial. It remains a superb account of the tribulations and responsibilities of naval command.

### The Cruel Sea (Britain, 1953 B&W)

**Director:** Charles Frend

**Leading actor:** Jack Hawkins

From its opening credits, played against a rough Atlantic swell, this film captures the nature of the lonely fight between man and the sea that characterized the battle of the Atlantic. It tells the story of the corvette HMS *Compass Rose*, and her struggle against the elements and, occasionally, against the Germans. It remains one of the most atmospheric naval films, and perfectly captures the tedium and sacrifice of this hard-fought and unglamorous campaign. This very British film was based on the bestselling book by Nicholas Monsarrat.

### HMS Defiant (Britain, 1962)

(Distributed in the USA as *Damn the Defiant!*)

**Director:** Lewis Gilbert
**Leading actors:** Alec Guinness, Dirk Bogarde

A Napoleonic naval adventure, the film captures a struggle of wills between a humanitarian captain and a sadistic first lieutenant. This story is played out against the backdrop of a naval campaign in the Mediterranean, and the British mutinies of 1797. While it might appear dated, it remains a spirited depiction of naval life during the age of fighting sail.

### *The Hunt for Red October* (USA, 1990)

**Director:** John McTiernan
**Leading actors:** Sean Connery, Alec Baldwin

Based on the bestselling thriller by Tom Clancy, the film tells the story of a Soviet submarine commander who defects, taking the Soviet Union's latest stealth nuclear submarine with him. While the plot itself is far-fetched, the submarine sequences are well done, and what the film lacks in realism, it makes up for in atmosphere.

### *In Which we Serve* (Britain, 1942 B&W)

**Directors:** Noël Coward and David Lean
**Leading actors:** Noël Coward, John Mills

This was produced as wartime propaganda, and while the screenplay by Noël Coward might seem extremely clichéd and very British, David Lean turned it into a cinematic masterpiece. Its stark realism and spirit of shared sacrifice struck a chord with wartime audiences, and it remains just as powerful today.

### *Master & Commander* (USA, 2003)

**Director:** Peter Weir
**Leading Actors:** Russell Crowe, Paul Bettany

Despite its title, this atmospheric film was an adaption of Patrick O'Brian's tenth Aubrey-Maturin novel, rather than the first. For box office reasons it also had the British pursue a French frigate across the Pacific, rather than an American one. It still remains a fairly faithful adaptation, and possibly the most realistic film about the sailing navy that has ever been made.

### Sink the Bismarck (Britain, 1960 B&W)

**Director:** Lewis Gilbert

**Leading Actor:** Kenneth More

This account of the pursuit of the German battleship *Bismarck* is seen through the eyes of a Captain in naval operations, based in a bunker beneath the Admiralty. The film contains several minor inaccuracies, but it remains a tense and moving account of this vital naval campaign, shown from the point of view of the naval strategists as well as the men on board the *Bismarck* and her British adversaries. Two moments stick out – the gut-wrenching moment when HMS *Hood* blows up, and the ending, an understated paean to British seapower.

### Tora! Tora! Tora! (USA, 1970)

**Directors:** Richard Fleischer, Kinji Fukasaku and Toshio Masuda

**Leading Actors:** Sô Yamamura, Martin Balsam

The film's title comes from the Japanese codeword meaning 'attack with torpedoes', which was the signal for their successful attack on Pearl Harbor. The film is a detailed and accurate documentary-like portrayal of the attack from both sides, but when it was released it was a box office flop. One critic even called it one of the deadliest, dullest blockbusters ever made. He obviously wasn't a naval history enthusiast – for us it remains a fascinating and realistic account of the events of 7 December 1941.

# SEA BATTLE: THE BATTLE OF MIDWAY, 1942

The battle of Midway was the turning point of the War in the Pacific, and probably the most decisive naval battle of the Second World War. The earlier carrier battle in the Coral Sea was a stalemate that decided nothing. The main Japanese thrust would be eastwards towards Midway and Hawaii, finishing the job it started at Pearl Harbor. The operation was the brainchild of Fleet-Admiral Yamamoto, Commander-in-Chief of the Japanese Navy. He realized that, in the long run, the production capacity of the United States would ensure an American victory over Japan, and saw that his country's only hope was to destroy the American fleet. With the American western seaboard exposed to attack, the United States would be forced to sue for peace.

His plan was overly complicated, involving several separate task forces. Admiral Nagumo commanded the main Carrier Group, charged with bombing Midway before Admiral Tanaka's amphibious force landed on the island. Yamamoto himself commanded the main battlefleet, while a fifth group under Admiral Kondo supported the landing by bombarding the island. Submarines were stationed to intercept the Americans if they tried to counter-attack. On paper the plan looked foolproof.

Unfortunately for Yamamoto, American naval intelligence broke the Japanese codes, and so Admiral Nimitz knew what was coming. He divided his fleet into two groups – a task force commanded by Admiral Spruance centred on the carriers *Enterprise* and *Hornet*, and Admiral Fletcher's task force which included the carrier *Yorktown*. The two groups would support each other. Nimitz himself coordinated the battle from Pearl Harbor. Fletcher and Spruance waited for the Japanese at 'Point Luck', to the north of Midway.

At dawn on 4 June a seaplane spotted Nagumo's Carrier Group, and reported their position. The Americans steamed south to intercept, and launched a strike. The two carrier fleets were 200 miles (320km) apart. At 0600hrs, Nagumo attacked Midway with half of his 225 aircraft, the few defending aircraft were brushed aside, and the island was bombed. However, the runway at Midway was still serviceable, so Nagumo decided to arm his remaining aircraft, and send them out as a second strike. It was just after 0700hrs.

Minutes later a small wave of ten torpedo-bombers from Midway attacked the Japanese carriers, but they were cut to pieces. Then, at 0728hrs, a Japanese scout plane spotted the American task forces, but failed to report the presence of carriers. It was too late – 106 American aircraft were heading Nagumo's way, in four waves. An unsuspecting Nagumo then made his big mistake. His torpedo-bombers preparing to strike Midway were armed with bombs. He ordered them to be re-armed with torpedoes instead. Shortly before 0800hrs a second larger wave from Midway arrived – 43 aircraft, including 16 B-17 heavy bombers. No hits were scored, and Nagumo felt he had weathered the storm. His second strike would deal with the Midway threat once and for all.

At 0830hrs the Midway strike returned, and Nagumo made his second blunder. He decided to land them first, before launching his second strike against Midway. By re-arming them, he could then launch an overwhelming strike around 1030hrs. This meant that the decks and hangars of the Japanese carriers were crammed with aircraft. The first American aircraft arrived over the Japanese Carrier Group at 1000hrs. Unfortunately the waves had become strung out, and the attackers lacked fighter cover. The first wave of 15 Dauntless dive-bombers was shot down, and the next wave was equally unsuccessful. Then, at 1024hrs the third wave appeared, when the Japanese fighters were distracted. These Dauntless dive-bombers from *Enterprise* and *Yorktown* were more successful. The carrier *Kaga* was hit by a 1,000lb (450kg) bomb, which exploded in her crowded hangar. She quickly became a blazing wreck. Two bombs hit the *Akagi*, detonating a stack of torpedoes. Her flight deck became a blazing inferno. Next it was the turn of the carrier *Soryu*, which was hit by the fourth wave – torpedo-bombers from *Yorktown*. She was hit three times, and was stricken and set ablaze. Within minutes three Japanese carriers had been put out of action, and turned into floating wrecks. All three sank or were scuttled that evening. Only the carrier *Hiryu* remained. However, her pilots were eager for revenge.

Its strike of 18 'Val' dive-bombers and six 'Zero' fighters reached the American fleet at noon, just as the surviving American planes were landing. Although 11 of the dive-bombers were shot down, the remaining seven attacked *Yorktown*, and she was hit three times. The carrier was crippled. Just before 1430hrs a second wave from the *Hiryu* appeared, and this time the *Yorktown* was struck by two Japanese torpedoes. She was abandoned, but she refused to sink, and was taken under tow, only to be sunk the following morning by a final torpedo, launched by a Japanese submarine.

The final act in the drama came at 1700hrs, when 41 dive-bombers from *Enterprise* and *Hornet* attacked the *Hiryu*, hitting her with four bombs. The blazing wreck sank the following day. When he learned of the disaster, Yamamoto ordered an immediate retreat. With four carriers lost, the Japanese had suffered a crippling defeat, and had lost the initiative in the Pacific. From that point on, it would be the Americans and their allies who would do the attacking, a campaign that would take them from Guadalcanal to Okinawa, and on to Japan. Midway was regarded as something of a miracle – the complete reversal of the strategic situation, and an almost flawless American victory. Above all, it demonstrated just how effective naval air power could be.

# THE NAVY AND THE PIRATES

The first quarter of the 18th century has often been dubbed 'The Golden Age of Piracy' – this was the time when some of the most notorious cutthroats in history were preying on their victims, including pirate captains such as 'Black Bart' Roberts, 'Black Sam' Bellamy, 'Calico Jack' Rackam and his female accomplices Anne Bonny and Mary Reade, and 'Blackbeard', the most notorious pirate of them all.

This pirate scourge was eventually ended by force, through a combination of strong-arm tactics by colonial governors and the actions of the Royal Navy. During this period, three sea battles stand out as milestones in the fight to subdue these pirates.

## Lieutenant Maynard versus Blackbeard

*22 November 1718 Ocracoke Island, North Carolina*

In November 1718, the pirate Edward Teach ('Blackbeard') was operating from a base on Ocracoke Island, in North Carolina's Outer Banks. Governor Spotswood of Virginia sent a small naval expedition to deal with him, led by Lieutenant Maynard of the Royal Navy, who commanded 50 sailors, in two hired sloops. Maynard launched his attack at dawn on 22 November. Blackbeard had just 25 men on board his sloop – the *Adventure* – but she was armed with eight guns. Maynard's sloops – the *Ranger* and the *Jane* – had no guns, but were crewed by 50 well-armed veteran sailors. As the sloops approached the *Adventure* they were both raked by gunfire, which killed several crewmen, and forced the *Jane* to drop out of the fray. Blackbeard taunted his enemies, and he must have been convinced he could defeat Maynard. However, by the time the two ships collided Maynard had hidden most of his men below decks. They surged up out of the hold, taking the pirates by surprise.

A furious hand-to-hand battle followed, and Blackbeard and Maynard sought each other out. Maynard wounded Blackbeard twice with his pistols, but the pirate got the better of the sword duel that followed. Then, just as Blackbeard was about to deliver a killer blow, a seaman slashed at him with his cutlass, cutting the pirate's throat. With his next stroke he severed Blackbeard's head from his body. With their captain dead, the pirate crew quickly surrendered, and Maynard was victorious. He returned to Virginia in triumph, with Blackbeard's severed head hanging from the bowsprit of his sloop.

## Colonel Rhett versus 'The Gentleman Pirate'

*27 September 1718 Cape Fear River, North Carolina*

For the best part of a year, Stede Bonnet, dubbed 'The Gentleman Pirate', had operated alongside Blackbeard. Eventually, though, Blackbeard double-crossed him, and sailed off with all the plunder. Bonnet then hunted alone, and in the late summer of 1718 he entered the Cape Fear River to repair his sloop, the *Royal James*. Around that time two pirate-hunting sloops under the command of Colonel William Rhett left Charles Town, South Carolina. On the evening of 26 September the *Henry* and the *Sea Nymph* approached the mouth of the Cape Fear River, where they spotted Bonnet's sloop. It was already growing dark, so they blockaded the river, and prepared for a battle the next morning.

Bonnet was outnumbered, so his big hope was to surprise the enemy, race past them with guns blazing, and head for the open sea. However, just as the *Royal James* came within range of the two pirate-hunting sloops she ran hard aground on a sandbank. Then, when the *Henry* and the *Sea Nymph* moved in for the kill, they both ran aground as well. All three ships were stranded within musket range of each other, exchanging fire while waiting for the tide to come in. This strange battle lasted for five hours, but it was the *Henry* which was the first to float free. With her guns threatening to sweep the decks of the *Royal James*, Bonnet had little choice but to surrender. He was then taken to Charles Town, where he was tried, convicted and hanged.

## Captain Ogle versus 'Black Bart'

*10 February 1722 Off Whydah, West Africa*

For more than two years, the pirate Bartholomew Roberts ('Black Bart') had cruised the waters of the Atlantic and the Caribbean, capturing over 100 ships, including a Portuguese treasure galleon. By January 1722 he had arrived at Whydah, on the coast of West Africa, and captured 11 more ships – all slavers. Then his luck ran out. On 5 February a ship appeared off Whydah, and Roberts sent his smaller consort the *Great Ranger* out to investigate. The newcomer fled over the horizon and the pirate ship gave chase. Then, out of sight of land, the stranger turned round and gave battle. She turned out to be the 50-gun warship HMS *Swallow*, commanded by Captain Challoner Ogle. The *Swallow* captured the *Great Ranger* after a two-hour battle, and locked the survivors of her pirate crew in the warship's forecastle. Ogle then set a course for Whydah, where 'Black Bart' was waiting.

Roberts realized what had happened when the *Swallow* reappeared on 10 February. The pirate captain dressed in his finest clothes, and sailed his 40-gun pirate flagship *Royal Fortune* out of the anchorage, to do battle. However, the *Swallow* fired first, and the conspicuous Roberts was killed in the first broadside. His men threw the body of their captain over the side, and kept fighting. Eventually, though, they proved no match for Ogle's well-trained gunners. Within an hour the pirates surrendered, and *Royal Fortune* was captured. The pirates were thrown into the cells of Cape Coast Castle, and in late April 1722 some 54 of them were sentenced to death, and hanged on the seashore. The rest were either sold as slaves or transported to the West Indies. This mass hanging marked the end of the 'Golden Age of Piracy'.

# HISTORIC SHIPS: OUR INTERNATIONAL NAVAL HERITAGE

Around the world, hundreds of historic warships have been saved from the scrapyard, and are preserved as a lasting legacy to our maritime heritage. The following selection includes some of the most important, the most impressive, and the best-preserved of these naval treasures. All the vessels listed here are owned by museums or historic trusts, and are open to the public.

- **HNLMS *Abraham Crijnssen* (1936) Dutch Navy Museum, Den Helder, Netherlands:** This little Dutch minesweeper escaped from the Japanese in 1942, disguised to look like an island.
- ***Aurora* (1900) St Petersburg, Russia:** This is the protected cruiser that fired the opening shots of the Russian Revolution (1917). She is also a veteran of the battle of Tsushima (1905).
- **HMS *Belfast* (1938) London, United Kingdom:** This Town Class light cruiser played a prominent part in the battle of North Cape (1943), and the sinking of the German battlecruiser *Scharnhorst*.
- **USS *Cairo* (1861) Vicksburg Military Park, Tennessee, USA:** This 'Pook Turtle' (see p.130) sank in late 1862, but she was rediscovered in 1956, raised and preserved. She remains a unique example of an American Civil War ironclad.
- **USS *Cod* (1943) Cleveland, Ohio, USA:** This Gato Class submarine is a well-preserved survivor of the US Navy's submarine fleet during the Pacific War.
- **USS *Constitution* (1797) Boston Naval Shipyard, Massachussetts, USA:** 'Old Ironsides' – the veteran of the War of 1812 (1812–15).
- ***Georgios Averof* (1910) Faliro, Athens, Greece:** The only surviving armoured cruiser, the *Averof* saw action during the First Balkan War (1912–13).
- ***Huascar* (1865) Talcahuano, Chile:** This 'pirate ironclad' has been preserved, and is now a museum ship.
- ***Jylland* (1860) Ebeltoft, Denmark:** This screw frigate took part in the battle of Heligoland (1864), during the Second Schleswig War.
- ***Mikasa* (1902) Yokosuka, Japan:** The last surviving pre-dreadnought battleship, the *Mikasa* was Admiral Togo's flagship at the battle of Tsushima (1905).
- **USS *Nautilus* (1954) US Navy Submarine Museum, Groton, Connecticut, USA:** The *Nautilus* was the first nuclear submarine, and the first vessel to make a submerged transit of the North Pole.

🛳 **USS *Olympia* (1892) Independence Seaport Museum, Philadelphia, Pennsylvania, USA:** This protected cruiser was Commodore Dewey's flagship at the battle of Manila Bay (1898).

🛳 **PT-617 (1943) Battleship Cove, Fall River, Massachusetts, USA:** PT-617 is the last surviving example of an 80ft (24m) Elco PT-Boat.

🛳 **HNLMS *Schorpioen* (1868) Dutch Navy Museum, Den Helder, Netherlands:** A rare survivor of the era of the ironclad.

🛳 **USS *Texas* (1911) San Jacinto State Park, Texas, USA:** One of several Second World War battleships to be preserved in the United States, this venerable old lady operated in both the Atlantic and the Pacific Theatres during the war.

🛳 ***Vasa* (1628) Vasa Ship Museum, Stockholm, Sweden:** The ill-fated *Vasa* was raised and restored, and now forms the centrepiece of a dedicated museum.

🛳 **HMS *Victory* (1765) Portsmouth Historic Dockyard, UK:** The *Victory* is the only surviving First Rate ship-of-the-line; she was Nelson's flagship at Trafalgar (1805) and is arguably the world's most famous historic ship.

🛳 **HMS *Warrior* (1860) Portsmouth Historic Dockyard, UK:** The first British ironclad, this magnificent and revolutionary warship has now been fully restored.

# FIGHTING ADMIRAL: CHESTER NIMITZ

The American naval commander who led the US Pacific Fleet to victory against the Japanese during the Second World War almost did not make it beyond the rank of lieutenant. The Texan-born Chester W. Nimitz (1885–1966) entered the US Naval Academy at Annapolis in 1901 and as a junior lieutenant his first command was a destroyer. He ran it aground in 1905, which meant he faced a court martial. If it had found him guilty of negligence he would have been dismissed from the service. In the end he escaped with nothing more than a reprimand, and a blotted record.

He decided to make up for things by volunteering for the US Navy's fledgling submarine fleet, which before the First World War was little more than an experimental force. Nimitz was determined to prove that submarines had an important role to play in naval warfare, and he soon displayed a talent for submarine command. He also earned acclaim when in 1912, as the commander of the submarine *E-1*, he rescued a drowning sailor, and was proclaimed a hero. He remained a submarine commander throughout the First World War, and demonstrated his ability both as a naval commander and as a leader of men.

In 1929 Captain Nimitz was given command of the US Navy's Submarine Division 20, the Navy's main Pacific submarine force, based at San Diego, California. This was his big chance – a vital rung on the ladder to flag rank. He was finally made a rear admiral in 1938, at which point he left his beloved submarines behind, and took up a desk-bound post as Chief of the Bureau of Navigation. History might then have passed him by, but on 7 December 1941 the Japanese attacked Pearl Harbor, and the US Navy was plunged into a war for which it was ill prepared. New ships were being built or fitted out, but in late 1941 the bulk of the Pacific fleet consisted of antiquated battleships and other surface warships, a handful of modern submarines and just two aircraft carriers.

Not having been in active command before the Pearl Harbor disaster, Nimitz was seen as a fresh man, unsullied by pre-war inertia. He was therefore picked out of obscurity and promoted over the heads of his fellow admirals. On 31 December, just over three weeks after Pearl Harbor, Nimitz was appointed the new Commander-in-Chief of the Pacific Fleet. He also became Commander-in-Chief, Pacific Ocean Areas, which effectively gave him control over air force and army units in the Pacific. In effect, the future of America's war in the Pacific now rested with him.

The responsibility would have weighed heavily on other shoulders, but Nimitz appeared to welcome the challenge.

The US Navy was badly demoralized after Pearl Harbor, and its battlefleet was badly damaged. Despite the devastation caused to his principal naval base, Nimitz reorganized the fleet, sending the worst damaged ships back to America's west coast to be repaired, and arranging those that remained around the aircraft carriers, rather than forming them into squadrons designed to fight a conventional surface action. Most admirals of his age would have been reluctant to acknowledge that the days of the big gun were over, and that the future lay with airpower. However, as a former submariner, Nimitz was able to look at the problem afresh, and to ignore the weight of tradition.

As a result, when the Japanese attacked again, Nimitz's fleet was able to meet them. He was also helped by an intelligence breakthrough – the cracking of the Japanese naval codes meant that Nimitz knew where to place his ships. During the battle of Midway he left his carrier commanders to fight the battle they wanted, without unnecessary interference. The result was a crushing American victory – one that turned the tide of war in the Pacific. Nimitz' next move was to direct the counter-attack – an operation on a hitherto unimaginable scale. This saw the Americans drive back the perimeter of the Japanese sphere of control, first around Guadalcanal, and then in the central Pacific. It culminated in an island-hopping campaign that saw American troops storm and capture Tarawa, the Marshall Islands, Saipan, Iwo Jima and Okinawa.

In 1944, Nimitz was promoted to the rank of fleet admiral, and it was in that position that he oversaw the final defeat and surrender of Japan. After the war he spent three years as the Chief of Naval Operations, before becoming a goodwill ambassador to the United Nations. His critics claimed that he lacked the strategic vision to make the most of the Pacific Fleet during the war. Many of these critics, of course, were the very admirals who resented

Nimitz when he was promoted over their heads in December 1941. In fact, at that time nobody was trained to fight a war on a global scale. Nimitz achieved miracles, largely through good leadership, choosing the right subordinates, making the most of his resources, and following through his plan, despite the critics. Without him, there might have been no victory in the Pacific.

# NO FLOWERS ON A SAILOR'S GRAVE

While most naval histories tell the story of dramatic sea battles, few bother to deal with the aftermath – what happened after a warship sank, leaving those who remained of her crew swimming in the oil-slicked ocean, or clinging for their lives to floating scraps of wreckage. During a sea battle there was often little chance to stop and pick up survivors, or else the sinking left these survivors alone in the darkness, floating on what must have seemed a cold, lonely ocean.

If the ship sank in the warm waters of the Pacific Ocean, the chances of avoiding hypothermia were much better than in the Atlantic or in the freezing waters of the Arctic, but there was another danger lurking beneath the surface – sharks. The fate of the survivors of the heavy cruiser USS *Indianapolis* showed just how deadly these predators could be. Just after midnight on 20 July 1945 the cruiser was struck by two torpedoes, fired by the Japanese submarine *I-58*. One blew off the bow, the other struck amidships, and the cruiser sank within 12 minutes, going down by the bow.

About 900 of her 1,200-man crew made it into the water, but very few rafts were launched before the ship went down. Most of the survivors wore lifejackets. The sharks began to attack at dawn, and continued to pick off the survivors until the sailors were rescued, almost five days later. Late on the fourth day a seaplane spotted them, and dropped rafts before landing to pick up some of the floating men. The following morning a destroyer arrived, to rescue the men remaining. By then, only 317 men were left, their shipmates having succumbed to exhaustion, dehydration, injury or the sharks. A Court of Enquiry was held, blaming fingers were pointed, but nothing could bring back the hundreds of sailors who died a horrific death during the closing weeks of the Second World War.

Of course, one problem these men didn't have to contend with was hypothermia. At 1945hrs on 26 December 1943, the crew of the German battlecruiser SMS *Scharnhorst* had to abandon ship in the dark, freezing waters off North Cape, off the northern tip of Norway. A survivor, Gunner Sträter, recalled what happened:

> The ship heeled over onto her side and sank by the bow. The propellers were still turning as they came out of the water. Indeed, they were all turning rather fast – there was way on the ship right until the end [i.e. her engines were still driving her forward]. In the water the crew were trying to find rafts. Those who found places in them sang both stanzas of the song 'No roses bloom on a sailor's grave'. I hear no cries for help from the water – everything happened smoothly, without the slightest panic.

Possibly as many as 1,000 German crewmen managed to abandon ship before she sank. Of these, some would have been sucked under as they were unable to swim clear in time. It was pitch-dark, a gale was blowing, and the seas were extremely rough. The chances of survival would have been slim. Cold water removes heat from the body 25 times faster than cold air of the same temperature. Physical activity such as swimming away from a sinking ship or towards a raft greatly increases the rate of heat loss. Statistics show that, in those temperatures, a swimmer would lapse into unconsciousness through hypothermia within 20 minutes, and survival time is estimated at around 40 minutes, depending on various factors, such as age, physical condition, whether the swimmer is wearing a life jacket or warm clothing, or has managed to find wreckage to cling to.

These figures are for so-called 'ideal conditions' – the well-monitored water of a diving tank or swimming pool. But the *Scharnhorst*'s sailors were pitched into a freezing, oil-covered sea at night, in the midst of a gale. Many would have been injured and many would have been in a state of shock. Exposure to freezing water can also lead to increased heart rate and blood pressure, which could easily result in cardiac arrest. Even those who reached the relative safety of a raft would have slipped into unconsciousness fairly rapidly. After all, 50 per cent of body heat is lost through the head. These men were lying in pitching rafts, which were half-filled with sloshing, freezing water, and it was snowing heavily.

The British did what they could. Destroyers moved in to pick up survivors, but many of the men simply drifted out of reach in the darkness. Others were too weak to hang onto the ropes which hauled them to safety, or to scramble up the boarding netting rigged by the British warships. HMS *Scorpion* used her searchlight to sweep the water, which revealed hundreds of floating and inert bodies. In the end, only 36 German sailors survived the sinking. The *Scharnhorst*'s complement was over 2,000 men.

On board another British destroyer, HMS *Onslaught*, Sub-Lieutenant Carey summed up the mood of the victors: 'After a brief cheer at the final sinking, our sailors fell silent, reflecting with real pity on the fate of so many of that green ship's company, consigned, in the Arctic twilight, and with little hope of rescue, to the wintry and unwelcome sea. There was almost tangible compassion ...' These British seamen were probably well aware of the anonymous sailor's poem, sung by those German survivors:

> There are no flowers on a sailor's grave,
> No lilies on an ocean wave.
> The only tribute is the seagull's sweep
> And the tear on a loved one's cheek.

# MERRIMACK, MERRIMAC
# OR *VIRGINIA*?

On 20 April 1861, following the secession of Virginia from the Union, the US Navy set fire to the Norfolk Navy Yard, before its facilities could fall into the hands of the Confederates. However, two key features were only partially damaged. The first of these was the dry dock, and the second was the wooden steam frigate USS *Merrimack*; she was set on fire and scuttled, but her hull and engines remained largely intact.

She was raised, and two months later Confederate Secretary of the Navy Stephen Mallory approved a plan to convert her into an ironclad. It was an ambitious idea, but then Mallory knew the odds facing his fledgling country. With no navy to speak of and a long exposed coastline, the Confederates were unable to match the power of the Union Navy. Mallory's solution was to close the gap by relying on technical innovation. By employing armoured warships and rifled guns, a handful of ships might be able to challenge the Union's naval blockade of the Confederacy.

Confederate engineers converted the hull into a casemate ironclad by adding an iron-plated casemate over the existing hull. The vessel itself was 275ft (84m) long. Approximately 160ft (49m) of this was covered by an iron casemate, sloped at a 36° angle to better deflect enemy shot. This casemate was built from oak and pine, 2ft (0.6m) thick, built up in layers. This roof-like structure was then covered in 4in (10cm) of rolled steel plate, produced at Richmond's Tredegar Iron Works. These plates were 8in (20cm) wide, and were held in place by countersunk bolts.

Her armament consisted of ten guns, a mixture of six 6in Dahlgren smoothbore pieces, and more modern Brooke rifled guns, 7in ones in the bow and the stern, and two 6.4in pieces on each broadside, alongside the smoothbores. Her weak point was her engines. The Confederates lacked the facilities needed to make new steam engines for her, so they re-used the engines which had already been fitted to the *Merrimack*. They had already been considered defective by the US Navy, and were due to be replaced. The Confederate engineers did what they could, but her propulsion system was far from ideal. Worse, because of her length, the *Merrimack* had a large turning radius, which made her difficult to manoeuvre in a sea battle.

The *Merrimack* was also given a new name. She had been named after the Merrimack River, which runs through New Hampshire and Massachusetts. In many official documents, though, she was referred to as the *Merrimac*, without the 'k', which is the name of a town in northern Massachusetts. Even her officers referred to her as both the *Merrimac* and the *Merrimack*, although the latter spelling was the correct one, adopted by the US Navy.

The Confederates were unwilling to use this old 'Yankee' name, so while the vessel was still being rebuilt in Norfolk, she was renamed the CSS *Virginia*. This meant that on 9 March 1862, when the Confederate ironclad sailed out to do battle with the Union ironclad warship USS *Monitor*, she was officially called the *Virginia*. The problem was, many Union newspapers refused to call her by her new name, and kept referring to her as the *Merrimack* (or even the *Merrimac*). For instance, the magazine *Harper's Weekly* consistently used *Merrimac* in their news articles. As for the US Navy, they still regarded the vessel as rightfully theirs. Therefore they continued to call her by her old name. That meant that during the first duel between two ironclad warships, which took place off Hampton Roads, Virginia on 9 March 1862, the two combatants were officially called the USS *Monitor* and the CSS *Virginia*. True to form, the Union newspapers reported the battle as having been fought between the *Monitor* and the *Merrimac*.

After the war, the victors got to write the history. Therefore, in the 'Official Records', the *Virginia* is consistently called the *Merrimack*. Also, in many post-war accounts, she was named the *Merrimac*, and by the end of the 19th century the vessel was usually referred to as the *Merrimac*, not the *Merrimack*. Even today, most people call her the *Merrimac* rather than the *Merrimack* or the *Virginia*. In fact, many historians regard this as a *fait accompli*, and prefer to use the term *Merrimac*, because that's the version most people are familiar with. Even to Southerners who should know better, the ironclad is the *Merrimac*.

While the alliteration of *Monitor* versus *Merrimac* sounds good, this isn't a sufficient enough reason to continue propagating the use of the wrong name for this important and revolutionary warship. The old USS *Merrimack* died in April 1861, when she was burned, then scuttled by the Federal authorities. In February 1862, she was reborn as the CSS *Virginia*, a new and powerful ironclad, ready to make her mark on history. After one and a half centuries, the least we can do is call the ironclad by her proper name – the *Virginia*.

# JACK SPEAK

Over the years, sailors of all nationalities have developed a range of expressions and a slang which is widely used, but which remains largely unintelligible to those outside the Navy. In Britain, this form of naval language has been unofficially labelled 'Jackspeak', after 'Jack' or 'Jack Tar', the archetypal British sailor. While much of it is technical, and most is decidedly lewd, some naval expressions have worked their way into everyday language. Here are a few examples of naval expressions which have entered our vocabulary.

The expression 'piping hot' had its origins in the days when food was collected from a ship's galley, after a 'pipe' was sounded. The sooner it was collected after the 'pipe', the hotter it would be. 'Swinging the lead' is used to describe the act of wasting time, or rather of avoiding work. The job of dropping a sounding weight and line over the bows to determine the depth of the water was seen as an easy job, and meant avoiding the more arduous tasks involved in coming into a harbour. 'Above board' meant things in plain view on the deck if a ship, and therefore visible to all. 'Copper bottomed' means something secure and reliable – and derives from the copper used to sheath the lower hull of a ship, to protect its timbers from the *toredo* worm.

Showing your 'true colours' means showing who you really are – as opposed to sailing under false colours by flying an enemy flag. This was a legitimate *ruse de guerre* used to entice an enemy within range. Before firing, a warship would run up its true colours. 'Toeing the line' comes from the procedure involved on pay day, or when being mustered on board a ship. A sailor would stand on parade on a particular line on the deck.

Others exist, but much naval slang remains a unique, humorous and distinctly non-politically correct assemblage of expressions, much of which can't be repeated here. However, here are a few of the less suggestive examples used by the Royal Navy.

| | |
|---|---|
| **Booties** | Royal Marines |
| **Burma Road** | The main passageway on a ship |
| **Crabs** | Air Force personnel (the RAF is often called 'Crab Air') |
| **Float Test** | Throwing something overboard |
| **Gloom Room** | The operations room (Command Information Center in the US Navy) |
| **Ickies** | Any form of foreign currency, be it a dollar, a rouble or a yen |
| **Jimmy** | The first lieutenant (executive officer in the US Navy) |
| **Mucker** | A good friend or drinking buddy |
| **Nooners** | The first drink of the day, after the sun has crossed the yardarm |
| **Pongo** | A soldier (after the idea that soldiers rarely wash – where the army goes, the pong goes too ...) |

| | |
|---|---|
| **Run ashore** | Time spent ashore, usually involving extensive drinking with your shipmates |
| **Shitehawk** | A seagull |
| **Slops** | Uniform, issued from store . |
| **Tannoy** | The internal loudspeaker system on a ship (originally made by a firm called Tannoy) |
| **Toybox** | The engine room |
| **Vasco** | The navigating officer |
| **Wafu** | Fleet Air Arm Personnel (standing for 'wet and ******* useless') |
| **Yonks** | A long time (as in it happened yonks ago) |